酒店英语

陈慧丽　崔秀红 主编 / 应丽娜　金凯　副主编

清華大学出版社
北京

内容简介

本书根据现代酒店业的快速发展对酒店服务人员提出的新要求，结合高校在实用型人才培养方面的实际需要，以岗位需求和工作情境为导向，再现工作中的实际情境，使相关工作人员或专业学生可以系统地使用本书学习业务知识，并提高用英语完成工作任务的语言素养，掌握相关英语词汇和常用句子，完善表达技巧和沟通方法，具备专业的酒店英语交际技能。本书设计了岗位知识导入，围绕听、说、读、译四个交际技能需求设置教学任务和练习模块，并补充不同岗位的相关词汇和句型知识，供学生自学使用。

本书听力原文可扫描二维码查看。

本书适合酒店管理和旅游服务相关专业教学使用，也可以作为酒店员工的培训教材，或供相关从业人员自学使用。

图书在版编目（CIP）数据

酒店英语/陈慧丽，崔秀红主编. —北京：清华大学出版社，2019（2024.8重印）
ISBN 978-7-302-53503-4

Ⅰ. ①酒… Ⅱ. ①陈… ②崔… Ⅲ. ①饭店－英语－教材 Ⅳ. ①F719.3

中国版本图书馆 CIP 数据核字(2019)第 180106 号

责任编辑：吴梦佳
封面设计：常雪影
责任校对：刘　静
责任印制：杨　艳

出版发行：清华大学出版社
网　　址：https://www.tup.com.cn，https://www.wqxuetang.com
地　　址：北京清华大学学研大厦 A 座　　**邮　　编**：100084
社 总 机：010-83470000　　**邮　　购**：010-62786544
投稿与读者服务：010-62776969，c-service@tup.tsinghua.edu.cn
质量反馈：010-62772015，zhiliang@tup.tsinghua.edu.cn
课件下载：https://www.tup.com.cn，010-83470410
印 装 者：三河市科茂嘉荣印务有限公司
经　　销：全国新华书店
开　　本：185mm×260mm　　**印　　张**：16.75　　**字　　数**：402 千字
版　　次：2019 年 10 月第 1 版　　**印　　次**：2024 年 8 月第 5 次印刷
定　　价：48.00 元

产品编号：072126-01

前　言

本书的编写目的是培养旅游管理、酒店管理专业学生及相关行业从业人员的英语交际能力和英语语言知识，可供高等院校旅游管理、酒店管理专业学生作为专业英语教材使用，也可供相关行业从业人员培训使用。

本书在内容上涵盖了大型酒店经营管理中所涉及的预订、接待、礼宾、商务中心、收银、宴会、餐饮、购物等各项服务和工作情境；涵盖了酒店从业者用英语进行交流的各项内容。本书主要有以下几个方面的练习：听力、对话、相关业务知识的阅读、翻译，以及相关文化拓展知识，并对英语交际中所需的常用词汇、常用句子等语言知识进行补充。练习立足于角色互动、情境交际及专业知识的补充。

本书的特色体现在以下几个方面。

(1) 专业性。本书专门针对高等院校旅游管理、酒店管理专业学生编写，在内容上与高校学生的英语基础知识相衔接。

(2) 行业性。本书紧密联系旅游、酒店业的实际运作情况、规范的服务流程和先进的服务观念，力求体现行业英语的特点。

(3) 实用性。本书以实用易学为原则，注重培养学生的实际应用能力，尤其是听说能力、专业阅读能力和翻译能力。

(4) 全面性。本书选材全面，基本涵盖了大型酒店各部门的服务领域，所提供的词汇知识和句型知识可以给相关学习者提供足够的便利。

本书主编为浙江师范大学陈慧丽(第 1～4 章)、浙江工业大学崔秀红(第 13～16 章)；副主编为浙江师范大学应丽娜(第 9～12 章)、金凯(第 5～8 章)。本书的编者长期从事相关英语教学工作，具有比较丰富的教材编写经验。

由于编者水平有限，书中难免有疏漏和不足之处，希望使用者不吝赐教，批评指正。

编　者

2018 年 6 月 30 日

目　录

目录

Chapter 1 Reservation

Study Objectives

1. To have a basic knowledge of reservation.
2. To grasp the words and expressions used in reservation.
3. To handle the guests' reservations and offer the information needed.

Lead in

For most hotels, Reservation is a department separated from the Front Desk. The reservationists are responsible for receiving and processing reservations for accommodation. It may be the first contact that the hotel could make with the guests which will leave an important impression on the customers. Think carefully and try to answer the following questions.

1. What are the reservationists responsible for?
2. How many ways are there for us to book a room in a hotel and what are they?

Part 1 Listening

Task 1 Dialogues. Listen to the dialogues and fill in the blanks with what you hear.

Dialogue 1

A: The Seashore Hotel. Reservations. What can I do for you?

B: ____.

Dialogue 2

A: Good afternoon. Reservations. May I help you?

B: ____.

Dialogue 3

A: Good morning. Reservations. Can I help you?

B: ____.

Dialogue 4

A: Is there a special rate for a group reservation?

B: ____.

Dialogue 5

A: How and in whose name has the reservation been made?

B: ____.

Task 2 Conversations.

Conversation 1 Mr. Charles Green is calling City Holiday Hotel to reserve a room. Listen and fill in the blanks with the words or phrases provided in the box.

reservations	settled	single room	confirm	expect
what time	front view	look forward to	how long	per night

(Reservationist-R Guest-G)

R: City Holiday Hotel. Room ________. Good morning.

G: I'd like to reserve a ________ for Tuesday next week.

R: That's fine, sir. A single room for Tuesday, July 8th, with a ________ or rear view?

G: What's the price difference?

R: A single room with a front view is 480 yuan ________, one with a rear view is 420RMB per night.

G: I think I'll take the one with a front view then.

R: ________ will you be staying?

G: I'll be leaving on Friday morning.

R: That will be three nights, sir. And your name please?

G: It's Charles Green. C-h-a-r-l-e-s, Charles, G-r-e-e-n, Green.

R: Thank you very much. ________ do you ________ to arrive, sir?

G: Oh, around 5 p.m. I suppose.

R: I'd like to ________ your reservation. A single room with a front view at 480 yuan per night for three nights from Tuesday, July 8th to Friday, July 11th. We ________ seeing you next Tuesday.

G: Good. That has been ________ then. Goodbye.

R: Goodbye.

Conversation 2 Jane Wood is a tour guide. She is calling to make a reservation for her tour group. Listen to the conversation and fill in the blanks with the information you hear.

480 yuan per night per room, with breakfast

Sorry to have kept you waiting, madam What kind of rooms would you like How much is the room rate, then May I know how many people there will be in the party May I book the rooms under your name

(**Reservationist-R Guest-G**)

R: Good morning. Room Reservations. How can I help you?

G: I am calling from the International Youth Travel Agency. I'd like to know if you have any rooms available for the nights from December 2nd to 6th.

R: ______________________________?

G: 28.

R: ______________________________?

G: Twin-bed rooms with bath.

R: Just a moment, please. Let me check... ______________________________. I can book 14 TWBs for you for those days.

G: ______________________________.

R: ______________________________.

G: That's good.

R: ______________________________.

G: Yes. My name is Jane Wood, J-a-n-e, Jane, W-o-o-d, Wood.

Conversation 3 A guest is calling the hotel to cancel a reservation. Listen to the conversation and fill in the blanks with the information you hear.

(**Reservationist-R Guest-G**)

R: ______________________________. May I help you?

G: Yes. ______________, because the travel schedule has been changed.

R: That's OK. Could you tell me ______________________________?

G: Tom Black.

R: ______________________________?

G: T-o-m Tom and B-l-a-c-k Black.

R: ______________________________?

G: From April 5th to 8th for three nights.

R: Excuse me. Is the reservation for yourself or for someone else?

G: It's for my boss.

R: Well, ______________________________?

G: Yes, it's Charles Green, and my cell phone number is 13934567890.

R: Thank you, Mr. Green. ______________________________, and his deposit will be refunded back to his account in a week. ______________________________.

G: Thank you.

R: It's my pleasure. Goodbye.

Part 2 Speaking

Task 1 Work in pairs. Read and complete the following dialogue by translating the Chinese sentences in the parentheses into English.

(**Reservationist-R Guest-G**)

R: Good morning. City Holiday Hotel. Reservations.

G: Good morning. ____________________ (我想预订一间下周二的房间). That's the 11th of March.

R: Certainly, sir. ____________________ (您需要预订几晚的房间)?

G: Three nights. ____________________ (我是替一个客户预订房间) who is arriving in Hangzhou on Tuesday.

R: I see. ____________________ (您的客户需要什么类型的房间)?

G: ____________________ (双人对床房).

R: Is that a superior twin or a deluxe twin?

G: ____________________ (这两种的价格有什么区别)?

R: The superior twin is 280 yuan per night and the deluxe twin is 360 yuan per night. ____________________ (两种都包括自助早餐).

G: I think I'll take the deluxe twin, please.

R: ____________________ (可以告诉我您的名字吗)?

G: Sure. My name's Black, Tom Black.

R: ____________________ (请您拼一下好吗)?

G: B-l-a-c-k, Black.

R: And may I have the name of the guest, please?

G: Mm. It's Elizabeth Williams. That's W-i-l-l-i-a-m-s, Williams.

R: Thank you, sir. ____________________ (可以告诉我您的电话号码吗)?

G: Sure. It's 88772399.

Vocabulary

reserve	*vt.* 储备;保留;预约;预订
book	*vt.* & *vi.* 预订 *vt.* 登记;(向旅馆、饭店、戏院等)预约
behalf	*n.* 利益;维护;代表;方面
client	*n.* 顾客;当事人
twin	*n.* 双胞胎之一;双人床
superior	*adj.* (级别、地位)较高的;上等的 *n.* 上级;优胜者

Notes

1. on behalf of 代表……

2. ... who is arriving in Hangzhou on Tuesday. 他将在周二到杭州。be arriving 在此处表示将来时，类似的用法还包括 be coming/going/leaving 等。
3. May I have your name, please? 此句型在询问客人名字时更为委婉礼貌，而 What's your name? 这样的句型显得突兀且不礼貌，应尽量避免使用。

Task 2 Work in pairs. Discuss and complete the conversation between a guest and a reservationist by filling in the blanks with appropriate sentences given below.

A. Could you tell me your name and telephone number, please
B. You can cancel up to five days in advance and we will refund your deposit
C. I will check the computer for room availability
D. And what is your address, please
E. What's the rate, please
F. I'd like a room with a lake view if that is possible

(**Reservationist-R Guest-G**)

R: Room Reservations. May I help you?

G: Yes. Do you have a double room available from April 21st to 26th?

R: Just a moment, please. ________1________. Sorry to have kept you waiting. Since it's the peak season now, all our double rooms are booked up on April 21st. Would you mind having a junior suite instead? And from April 22nd on, we do have a double room available for you.

G: ________2________?

R: For junior suite, the current rate is 650 yuan per night including breakfast, and for double room, it's 480 yuan.

G: That sounds reasonable. I'll take it.

R: Very good. ________3________?

G: Yes, it is Alice Green. (315) 8673-3589.

R: Thank you, Ms. Green. ________4________?

G: It is 168, 5th Avenue, New York City, the USA.

R: Yes, so it is 168, 5th Avenue, New York City, the USA.

G: That's right. By the way, ________5________.

R: A lake view room is preferred, OK.

G: Can I pay when I arrive?

R: Yes. We can keep the room for you until 6:00 p. m. on April 21st. If you want to hold the room, we require a 500 yuan credit card deposit. ________6________.

G: All right.

Task 3 Role-play. Work in pairs and make up a dialogue respectively according to the situations provided.

Situation 1 Michael Ford calls the Reservation Department. He wants to reserve a double room. You may use the following expressions for reference.

—Reservationist

Room Reservations. How can I help you?

For which dates?

How many guests will there be?

What kind of room would you like?

Wait a moment, please. Let me check.

Sorry to have kept you waiting.

Could I know if you have any special requests?

—Guest

Want to reserve a double room.

Tell the reservationist that you need the room from March 3rd to 5th and there will be 2 guests.

Prefer to have a room with a street view Express thanks.

Situation 2 Mr. Smith comes to the hotel to revise his reservation. Please role-play the situation with the help of the useful expressions provided below.

Reservationist	Guest
How would you like to change it? So that's a family suite for... nights from... to... Could you pay 200 yuan more to guarantee your revised reservation?	My name is... I made a reservation... Now I'd like to modify it. I'd like to change... into... and extend my reservation for two more nights till...

Part 3 Reading

Reservation

Since a **majority** of hotel guests **make reservations** in advance of their stay, the **Reservation Department** usually becomes their first contact with the hotel. To **achieve** its **objectives** of **profitability efficiency**, and guest satisfaction, the hotel must have effective **procedures** and systems **in place** to handle guest reservations.

On average, as to room reservation, there are five steps involved in the booking **process**. First, requests for reservations are received at the hotel through different **means**—by telephone, **fax**, letter, and telegram—or made by the guest **in person**, which belongs to Reservation Department. Hotels generally accept two types of reservations: **non-guaranteed** and guaranteed. Non-guaranteed reservations are held by the hotel until a certain cut-off hour which is set by hotel policy. Rooms reserved in this manner are returned to the room inventory after the cut-off hour has passed and can be sold to **walk-in guest.** A guaranteed reservation assures guests that a room will be held until the check-out time on the day following the date of arrival. This type of reservation also guarantees that the hotel will receive payment if the guest does not arrive and does not properly cancel the reservation.

Second, when a **reservationist** receives a reservation **request**, he may first check the hotel's booking situation, **forecast** occupancy levels and room **revenue**, see if the hotel has any **vacancy** during the specified period and finally maintain **availability** to ensure that no **over-booking** occurs.

Third, throughout the reservation process, information gathered about the guest and his stay should be recorded if a room is available. This reservation record must contain such information like guest name, address, telephone number, arrival date and time, and length of stay, type and number of rooms, number in the party, rate **quoted**, guarantee method, method of payment, guests' special requests and the purposes of their visits. Once the information is gathered and recorded, the Reservation Department will **issue** a reservation confirmation to the guest. This can be done by issuing a confirmation number over the telephone or by sending a letter of confirmation. Both methods verify the information on the reservation record and the guest's needs.

Fourth, the reservationist maintains the reservation record by making any changes or cancellations as needed. **In the event of** cancellation of travel arrangements due to any reasons, cancellation of the room reservation must be made to the hotel **in the first instance** by telephone and then in writing. **Deposits** may be returned **at the discretion of** the management, but **refund** would be restricted to a limited amount. **Cancellation charges** will be effective from the time or date the hotel receives the guests' **notification** in writing.

Finally, the reservationist produces **management reports** that **summarize** daily reservations activities. These management reports can also provide the other departments with a forecast of expected occupancy. The forecast is **extremely** important, since it provides the **Housekeeping**, **Food and Beverage**, and other departments with **continuous** information on anticipated occupancies, thus permitting the heads of these departments to plan their staff requirements and control their payroll casts.

Vocabulary

majority	*n.* 多数
achieve	*vt.* 取得;获得;实现;成功
objective	*adj.* 客观的;实体的;目标的 *n.* 目标
profitability	*n.* 赢利能力;收益
efficiency	*n.* 效率
procedure	*n.* 程序;手续;步骤
process	*n.* 过程;工序;做事方法;工艺流程
means	*n.* 方法;手段

fax	*n.* 传真
non-guaranteed	*adj.* 没有保证的；没有人担保的
reservationist	*n.* 预订处工作人员
request	*n.* 要求；需要
forecast	*vt.* 预报；预测 *n.* 预报；预言
revenue	*n.* （国家的）税收；（土地、财产等的）收益
vacancy	*n.* 空缺；空虚；空白；空位
availability	*n.* 有效；有益；可利用性
over-booking	*n.* 超额预订
quote	*vt.* 报价；引述 *vi.* 引用；引述 *n.* 引用；报价
issue	*n.* 问题；发行物 *vt.* 发行；流出
deposit	*n.* 储蓄；存款；保证金
refund	*n.* 退款；偿还数额 *vt.* 退还；偿还
notification	*n.* 通知；通知单；布告；公布
summarize	*vt.* 总结；概述
extremely	*adv.* 极端地；非常；很
continuous	*adj.* 连续的；延伸的

Phrases and Expressions

make reservations	预订
in place	适当的；相称的；在合适的位置
on average	总的来说
as to	关于
in person	亲自；本人
walk-in guest	非预约住客
in the event of	如果……发生；万一
in the first instance	在第一步；首先
at the discretion of	由……斟酌决定
cancellation charges	注销手续费
management report	管理报告

Proper Names

Reservation Department	预订部
Housekeeping Department	客房部
Food and Beverage Department	餐饮部

Task 1 True or false statements. Decide whether the following statements are True (T) or False (F) according to the text.

1. The Reservation Department usually becomes guests' first contact with the hotel. ( )
2. Hotels only accept guaranteed reservation. ( )

3. Rooms with guaranteed reservations are returned to the room inventory after the cut-off hour has passed and can be sold to walk-in guest. ( )
4. When a reservationist receives a reservation request, he may first check the hotel's booking situation. ( )
5. Deposits may be returned at the discretion of the reservationist. ( )
6. Reservationists produce management reports that summarize daily reservation activities. ( )

Task 2 Questions. Read the text again and answer the following questions.

1. Why does the Reservation Department usually become hotel guests' first contact with the hotel?
2. As a rule, how many steps are involved in the booking process to make room reservation?
3. What is the first step involved in the booking process?
4. What are the two types of reservations the hotels usually accept?
5. When will cancellation charges be effective?

Task 3 Blank filling. Fill in the blanks with the words given. Change the form when necessary.

confirm	in person	in the event of	at the discretion of	on average
achieve	procedure	vacancy	instantaneous	additionally

1. The vicar was given power to distribute money ________.
2. I had seen her before on TV, but she looked very different when I met her ________.
3. You can't just do it however you like—you must follow ________.
4. Death is ________ in a fatal accident.
5. ________ rain, the party will be held indoors.
6. We wanted to book a hotel room in July but there were no ________.
7. ________, we request a deposit of $200 in advance.
8. Though highly respected for her writing, she never ________ much commercial success.
9. The news ________ my resolution.
10. During exercise, you should drink ________ a half a cup every 15 minutes.

Part 4 Translation

Task 1 Translate the following passage into Chinese.

Couplets (*duilian*) are a literary form native to China and a combined product of Chinese national culture and Chinese folk culture. Unique to the Chinese characters both in form and sense, they cannot be closely reproduced by any other phonetic letters. Each couplet consisting of two lines, they usually do not contain many Chinese characters, but cover varied subjects, such as politics, economy, military affairs, history, religion, personages, mountain and water, and scenic and historic attractions. Dating from the Tang Dynasty (618—907), they are a component part of China's cultural treasure-house. Lots of well-known couplets are excellent literary works.

Task 2 Translate the following passage into English.

房内最中间摆放着一个古式屏风,四周陈列着文房四宝(笔、墨、纸、砚)及老式家具,左边则是一间茶室,果真是读书或喝茶赏景的好去处。您一定会喜欢。

Part 5 Cultural Norms

常用词汇

房间类型

single	单人房	suite	套房
double	双人房	twin	双人对床房
standard single	标准单人房	standard double	标准双人房
standard twin	标准双人对床房	superior single	高档单人房
superior double	高档双人房	superior twin	高档双人对床房
deluxe single	豪华单人房	deluxe double	豪华双人房
deluxe twin	豪华双人对床房	sea-view room	海景房
family suite	家庭套房	single bed	单人床
double-size bed	双人床	queen-size bed	大号双人床
king-size bed	特大号双人床		

酒店星级

one-star (economy) hotel	一星宾馆
two-star (some comfort) hotel	二星宾馆
three-star (average) hotel	三星宾馆
four-star (high comfort) hotel	四星宾馆
five-star (deluxe) hotel	五星宾馆

接待有保证的预订

接待有保证的预订(Receiving a Guaranteed Reservation)是通过以下方式完成的。

1. 预收款(Prepayment)保证预订:客人提前支付足额房费。
2. 信用卡(Credit Card)保证预订:记下客人的信用卡号码,如果客人没有按预订要求来酒店使用客房,酒店可以向持卡人收取费用。这是一种最常见的预订方式。
3. 押金(Advanced Deposit)保证预订:客人提前支付一天的房费。
4. 合同/协议(Contract or Agreement)保证预订:酒店与公司有协议在先,无论公司预订的客房是否被使用,房费由公司承担。

常用句子

接待预订或接听预订电话

1. Good morning. Reservation's Jane speaking. Can I help you? 早上好。我是订房部的Jane。有什么可以帮到您的吗？
2. Good afternoon. Welcome to City Holiday Hotel! May I help you? 下午好。欢迎光临城市假日酒店！有什么可以帮到您的吗？
3. I'd like to book a single room for Wednesday next week. 我想要订一间单人房，下周三入住。
4. I'd like to book a double room for my friend. 我想为朋友预订一间双人房。

从客户处获取信息

1. How long will you plan to stay? 您打算住多久？
2. How long will you be staying? 您打算住多久？
3. May I know who I'm talking with? (Making a phone) 请问您是哪位？
4. What type of room do you require? 请问您要哪种房型？
5. How many rooms will you require? 请问您要订多少间房？
6. May I have your name/telephone number, please? 请问您的名字/电话号码？
7. May I have the way to contact you? 如何与您联系呢？

提供和获知房价

1. How much does a double room cost? 一间双人房要多少钱？
2. How much a day do you charge? 每天收费多少钱？
3. Can I get a discount? 有优惠/折扣吗？
4. 380 yuan per night, with breakfast. 每天380元，含早餐。
5. We can do a standard/deluxe double room for 350 yuan per night. 我们有标准/豪华双人房，每天每间350元。
6. We charge 600 yuan for a deluxe twin per night. 豪华双人对床房，每间每天600元。
7. The price/rate for a minimum of 5 rooms is 20 percent off. 如果起订5间房，房价可以享受20%的优惠。
8. I'm sorry, there is no discount. 对不起，我们没有折扣。
9. There's a reduction for children. 儿童有优惠。
10. We have already cut the price very fine. 我们已经将价格降至最低限度了。

确认和登记

1. May I see your passport, please? 我可以看看您的护照吗？
2. Have you got any identification? 您有身份证吗？
3. Would you please complete this registration form? 请您填写这张登记表好吗？
4. I'm afraid our hotel is fully booked on that date. 对不起，我们酒店那一天的客房全部订满了。
5. Your room is confirmed for that day. We look forward to serving you. 您要的那一日房间已经确认了。我们期待为您服务。

房已订满

1. I'm sorry, but we're booked up. 很抱歉,我们没有空房。
2. I'm sorry, but we have no vacancies at the moment. 对不起,我们现在没有空房。
3. I'm sorry, but all rooms are taken. 很抱歉,所有的客房都已经订满了。

Part 6 Supplementary Reading

The Front Office

"Front Office" is a term used in hotels to cover various sections which deal with reservations, room allocations, receptions, billing and payments. Front Office is only one of the departments within a hotel.

The first contact most would-be guests have is with the telephone switchboard, which is a part of Front Office. The telephonist puts the guest through to someone in reservation department, who takes his booking and deals with any subsequent correspondence, such as confirmations, amendments and cancellations.

When a guest arrives, he may be assisted by a uniformed porter. He will have to go to the reception desk to register and obtain his room key. During his stay, he may well have an occasion to go back to reception several times, sometimes for information or to pick up a message, sometimes for help with the tickets for further travel. He will probably have to call there at the end of his stay in order to hand in his room key and deal with his bill.

All these contacts are the job of "Front Office", an American term used in place of an old word "reception". Strictly speaking, it only covers those staff who come to direct, face-to-face contacts with the guests, the other associated sections being known as "Back Office". However, the term "Front Office" is generally used to describe the whole range of "Front House" sections, namely:

- uniformed staff;
- reservations;
- reception;
- enquiries;
- switchboard;
- bill office;
- cashier;
- guest relations.

Chapter 2

Reception

Study Objectives

1. To have a basic knowledge of reception.
2. To grasp the words and expressions used in reception.
3. To handle the guests' reception and offer the information needed.

Lead in

The Reception Desk is not only a window but also a center of a hotel. A guest will get his first and deepest impression of a hotel in the place of the Reception Desk. Think carefully and try to answer the following questions.

1. Why is the Front Office so important to the hotel?
2. What service do you expect from receptionists?

Part 1 Listening

Task 1 Dialogues. Listen to the dialogues and fill in the blanks with what you hear.

Dialogue 1

A: How would you like to ________?

B: ________.

Dialogue 2

A: Mr. and Mrs. Simpson, could I see your ________?

B: Here you are.

Dialogue 3

A: A room with a ________ bed is better equipped and the ________ is only 120 yuan higher.

B: OK, ________.

Dialogue 4

A: Will you please fill out this ________?

B: Sure! Thank you.

Dialogue 5

A: Mr. Wood, you ________ from May 15th to 17th, 580 yuan per night. Is that correct?

B: Yes. That's correct.

Task 2 Conversations.

Conversation 1 Mr. Charles Ford arrives at a hotel to check in without a reservation. Listen and fill in the blanks with the words or expressions provided in the box.

separate	executive	registration	check in	junior
available	balcony	deluxe	high-speed	fully booked

(Reservationist-R Guest-G)

G: I'd like to ________, please.

R: Have you made a reservation, sir?

G: No.

R: What kind of room would you like, sir?

G: An ________ suite, please.

R: One moment, please... I'm sorry. Our executive suites are ________ tonight.

G: What a pity!

R: But we still have a few ________ suites and ________ suites ________.

G: How much is a junior suite?

R: 900 yuan per night. It has a king-size bed, a ________ seating area, a ________ and the ________ Internet access.

G: Fine. I'll take that.

R: May I have your name, please?

G: Charles Ford.

R: May I know for how many nights you are going to stay in our hotel?

G: Just one night.

R: Thank you, Mr. Ford. Could you please fill out this ________ form?

G: OK.

Conversation 2 Mr. Kevin Smith wants to stay in the hotel for three more days. Listen and fill in the blanks with the words or expressions provided in the box.

Please change your departure date and sign your name here.
How long would you like to extend your stay, Mr. Smith?
May I have your name and room number, please?
Good morning, sir. How may I help you?

I hope you are enjoying your stay with us. Would you mind changing to another room on the ninth floor tomorrow?

(**Reservationist-R Guest-G**)

R: ____?

G: I planned to check out this morning, but now I need to stay here for another three days. Could you arrange it for me?

R: Yes, sir. _______________________________________?

G: Kevin Smith. K-e-v-i-n, Kevin. S-m-i-t-h, Smith. Room 810.

R: ____? For three more nights?

G: Yes, for three more nights.

R: One moment, please. Let me have a check. Sorry, Mr. Smith. I'm afraid you may keep your room for only one more night. The eighth floor has been reserved for a conference. ________? We have several rooms on the ninth floor of the same standard.

G: I see. OK.

R: Please check back with us tomorrow. Here is your registration form. ____?

G: OK. Here you are.

R: Thank you, Mr. Smith. If you need any help, do let us know. ____.

Conversation 3 Charles Green, a tour guide of China International Travel Agency, is checking in for his group members at the Front Desk. Listen and fill in the blanks with the words or expressions you hear.

(**Reservationist-R Guest-G**)

R: Good morning. What can I do for you?

G: I'm Charles Green, tour guide of China International Travel Agency. ____________________________.

R: One moment, Mr. Green. I will check the list... Yes, we have your reservation. Your agency has booked 12 TWBs for five days. ____________________________?

G: No.

R: ____________________________?

G: Here you are.

R: Thank you... ____________________________. Here you are. Now would you please fill in the registration form with your personal information?

G: OK... Here you are.

R: Thank you very much. We'll give you 12 TWBs from Room 1501 to 1512. Here are the keys and room cards. ____________________________.

G: Thanks. ____________________________.

Part 2 Speaking

Task 1 Work in pairs. Read and complete the following dialogue by translating the Chinese sentences in the parentheses into English.

(**Reservationist-R Guest-G**)

R: Good afternoon! Welcome to our hotel.

G: Good afternoon! I'd like to have a single room, please.

R: ________________________ (您有预订吗)?

G: Yes. I have booked it from the United States. I'm Sam Green.

R: Oh, I'm sorry. ________________________ (您的名下没有预订).

G: I'm sure I have made a reservation. Could you check again the reservation from the United States?

R: All right. Let me check again. Ah, yes, a single room from Sam Green.

G: Is there a bath in the room? ________________________ (我想马上洗个澡).

R: Yes, ________________________ (每个房间都有浴室、电话和空调).

G: That's good!

R: ________________________ (我可以看下您的护照吗)?

G: Yes, this is my passport.

R: Thank you. Here is your passport. ________________________ (请填写这张表格).

G: The registration form is finished. ________________________ (可以给我钥匙吗)?

R: Of course. Here is the key to your room. Your room is on the third floor. ________________________ (行李员会带您去房间).

G: Thanks!

R: I guess you must be tired after a long trip. ________________________ (还有别的需要吗)?

G: I don't think there is anything else. ________________________ (您真是太周到了). Thank you very much.

R: You are welcome. Enjoy your stay. See you tomorrow.

G: See you tomorrow.

Vocabulary

reservation *n.* (旅馆房间、剧院座位等的)预订
receptionist *n.* 接待员
suite *n.* (房间、器具等的)一套;一组
passport *n.* 护照;通行证
bellboy *n.* (旅馆、俱乐部等的)行李服务员;侍者
registration *n.* 登记;登记证;登记人员的数目;注册
lobby *n.* (剧院、旅馆等的)门廊;门厅

Notes

1. I'd like to...相似的句型有"I want...""I prefer..."。

   I want a double room. 我想要一个双人间。

   I prefer a quiet room. 我想要一间安静的客房。

2. be equipped with 意思是"装备、配备"。

   The hotel is equipped with the Chinese traditional furniture. 饭店配有中国传统式样的家具。

3. fill in 填写

   He was filling in the application form. 他正在填写登记表。

4. I don't think there is anything else. 意思是"我想没有什么事情了"。

   不能说"I think there is not anything else"。

Task 2 Work in pairs. Discuss and complete the conversation between a guest and a receptionist by filling in the blanks with appropriate sentences given below.

A. Could I see your passport, please
B. How would you like to settle your bill
C. The bellman will show you up to your room
D. I have made a reservation with you
E. We hope you'll enjoy your stay with us
F. I'll check the reservation record

(Reservationist-R Guest-G)

R: Good afternoon, sir. How may I help you?

G: I'm Victor Smith. ______1______. Here's the confirmation notice.

R: Thank you, Mr. Smith. ______2______. Wait a moment, please... Sorry to have kept you waiting. According to our record, your reservation is for a double room from March 20th to 24th. The rate will be 90 dollars per night. Is that right?

G: Yes.

R: Could you fill out the registration form, please?

G: OK.

R: Thanks. ______3______?

G: Yes, here you are.

R: Thank you, Mr. Smith. Here is your passport. ______4______?

G: By credit card.

R: May I take a print of your card, please?

G: Sure.

R: Thank you, Mr. Smith. Your room number is 1012 on the tenth floor. Here is your receipt, and this is your key card. Please keep them. ______5______. Anything else I can do for you?

G: No more. Thank you.

R: You're welcome. ______6______.

Task 3 Role-play. Work in pairs and make up a dialogue respectively according to the situations provided.

Situation 1 Peter Anderson reserved a deluxe single room yesterday. Now he comes to the Front Desk to check in. Make up a conversation with the expressions given in the box.

Reservationist	Guest
Have you made a reservation, sir? So you've reserved... for the nights from...to... The room rate is 500 yuan per night. Is that correct? How would you like to pay? In cash, by credit card or with traveler's check? Your room number is... on the... floor. The bellman will carry your baggage and show you up to your room.	Yes, I have reserved a deluxe single room yesterday. Peter Anderson. Yes, here you are. By credit card, please. No more. Thank you.

Situation 2 The following is group check-in situation. Please act out according to the steps provided in the boxes.

Receptionist	Miss Brown
Greet and welcome the guest. Confirm reservation details with the guest. Ask the guest to show the group visas. Ask the guest to fill in the registration form. Tell the guest the room allotment and room numbers. Give the guest room cards and keys. Tell the guest that the bellmen will help them with their baggage. Wish the guests a nice stay.	Greet. Tell the receptionist the reservation information. Give the receptionist the group visas. Fill out the registration form. Tell the receptionist that you hope the tour group can be arranged on the same floor. Get the room cards and keys. Express thanks.

Part 3 Reading

The Receptionist's Work

When a guest arrives at the Front Desk, the **receptionist** greets him/her and asks if he/she has made a reservation or not. For the guest with a reservation, the receptionist should confirm with him/her the reservation **details**, such as the room type, room rate, length of stay, etc., and then give out a **registration** form to the guest to **fill out**.

For the **walk-in** guest, the **check-in procedures** may take a little longer time. The same questions by a reservationist in the reservation process must be asked, for example, how many nights, how many people in the party, what kind of room, etc. The receptionist should also check the guest's **requirement** against the room **availability** in the hotel's reservation system. After the guest decides to take a room in the hotel, the receptionist then **gives out** the registration form and continues the check-in procedure.

When the guest completes the form, the receptionist must **have a check** and make sure that such information items as the guest's full name, address, **nationality**, purpose of his/her visit and **signature** are entered correctly. If the visitor is a foreigner, information about his/her **passport** number, place of issue and date of issue also need to be recorded.

After registration, the receptionist tells the guest his/her room number and the floor it is on, and then gives the guest his/her room card and key card which were prepared while the guest was completing the registration form. The room card has the effect of being the **identity** card for the guest during his/her stay. Finally, the receptionist should wish the guest an **enjoyable** stay at the hotel.

With the **formalities** concluded, the receptionist will **inform** the bellman to carry the baggage and show the guest to his/her room. And the receptionist will check all the paperwork **undertaken** on the guest's arrival once again and make sure that the computer details are all correct.

Besides checking in guests, the receptionist **is also responsible for** answering any questions from the guests, helping them with any problems that they may have, answering telephones, taking messages for the guests, and **handling complaints** from unsatisfied guests.

Vocabulary

receptionist	*n.* 接待员
detail	*n.* 详述;细节　*vt.* 详述;清晰地说明
registration	*n.* 登记;注册;挂号
walk-in	*adj.* (服务)不必预约的;未经预约而来的
check-in	*n.* 签到;投宿登记手续;登记入住
procedure	*n.* 程序;手续;步骤
requirement	*n.* 要求
availability	*n.* 有效;有益;可利用性
nationality	*n.* 国籍;国家;民族性
signature	*n.* 签名;署名
passport	*n.* 护照;通行证
identity	*n.* 身份
enjoyable	*adj.* 愉快的;快乐的
formality	*n.* 礼节;拘谨;正式手续
inform	*vt.* 通知;告知
undertake	*vt.* 承担;从事;保证; 同意
complaint	*n.* 投诉;抱怨;控诉

Phrases and Expressions

fill out	填写(表格等)

give out	分发;公布
have a check	检查一下
be responsible for	为……负责;对……负责
handle complaint	处理投诉

Task 1 True or false statements. Decide whether the following statements are True (T) or False (F) according to the text.

1. It takes a longer time for the receptionist to check in walk-in guests than the guests with reservations. ( )
2. The walk-in guests should first fill out a registration form when checking in. ( )
3. The key card serves as the identity card for the guest during his stay. ( )
4. The receptionist should check the information on guests' registration forms and in the computer as well. ( )
5. The reservationist should wish the guest an enjoyable stay at the hotel. ( )
6. The receptionist is also responsible for handling complaints from unsatisfied guests. ( )

Task 2 Questions. Read the text again and answer the following questions.

1. What duties does a receptionist perform?
2. What should the receptionist do when a guest arrives at the Front Desk?
3. After registration, what should the receptionist do?
4. What should the receptionist do with the formalities concluded?
5. If the visitor is a foreigner, what information should be recorded?

Task 3 Blank filling. Fill in the blanks with the words given. Change the form when necessary.

reserve	complete	responsible to	give up	answer
wait	give in	honor	give out	responsible for

1. Your ________ is for a TWB from tonight to August 20th. Is that right?
2. We are greatly ________ for your presence, sir.
3. Jenny keeps begging me for a new bicycle, and I finally ________.
4. I'm afraid that your room is not quite ready yet. Would you mind ________ for a while, please?
5. Can you ________ the drinks, please?
6. When check-in procedures ________, the receptionist calls a bellman to carry the guest's baggage and show the guest the way to his/her room.
7. In addition to the check-in procedures, the receptionist is also responsible for ________ questions.

8. Cabinet (内阁) members are directly ________ the President.
9. He decided to ________ his job so that he could look after his wife.
10. Mr. Williams says that the hospital was ________ her husband's death.

Part 4 Translation

Task 1 Translate the following passage into Chinese.

The kite is one of the Chinese traditional folk arts. The Chinese kite came into being in the Spring and Autumn Period and since then it has had a history of over two thousand years. Kites were used for military purpose initially, like measuring distances, testing wind directions, and communications. Later, it is integrated with fairy tales, luck characters such as flowers, birds and beasts and auspicious meanings and thus a unique kite culture with characteristics has been formed. In sunny spring days, people usually go for company outings to fly kites. The Chinese kite has also been loved by people from all over the world, for it was introduced into the globe a long time ago.

Task 2 Translate the following passage into English.

当茶叶第一次从中国引进时，沏茶和饮茶的器皿也随之一并进口到英国。但是后来，许多英国公司开始自己设计和生产茶壶、茶杯和茶碟。这也为英国的陶瓷业注入了巨大的推动力。

Part 5 Cultural Norms

常用词汇

lobby	大堂	passport	护照
emergency exit	紧急出口	tariff	房价表
safety boxes	保险箱	baggage/luggage	行李
presidential suite	总统套房	face south	朝南
single room	单人间	trolley cart	行李车
standard room	标准间	special rate	优惠价
check-in	登记入住	arrival time	到达时间
check-out	退房	department time	离开时间
registration form	登记卡	flight number	航班号
room charge	房价	message	留言
service charge	服务费	envelope	信封
discount	折扣	receipt	收据
identification	身份证明	cheque	支票
operator	电话接线员	breakfast voucher	早餐券
elevator	电梯	credit card	信用卡
deposit	订金	morning call	叫醒服务

常用句子

1. I reserved a standard suite three weeks ago. I'm ...我是……,我在三周前预订了一间标准套房。
2. I've just arrived from Hong Kong. Could you let me have a room for tonight? 我刚从香港来,想知道今晚有没有空房?
3. I'll take care of the registration form. 我来填写入住登记表。
4. I should say I prefer to stay here. 我想说我更喜欢住在这家酒店。
5. A friend of mine highly recommended your hotel to me. 一位朋友向我极力推荐你们酒店。
6. Could I pay with traveler's checks? 我能用旅行支票付款吗?
7. Is this where I can pay my hotel bills? 是在这结账吗?
8. My room number is ... and I'd like to check out now. 我的房间号码是……,我想现在结账。
9. Is there a special rate for a group reservation? 团体预订有优惠吗?
10. What if there isn't any room then? 如果到时候没有空房怎么办?
11. Have you made a reservation? 请问您有预订吗?
12. We have no record of a reservation in your name. 您的名下没有预订记录。
13. Would you please complete this registration form? 麻烦您填下登记表,好吗?
14. Could you sign your name here, please? 请您在这里签名,好吗?
15. Leave it to me. I'll take care of your baggage. 交给我好了,我会照看您的行李的。
16. Your taxi will arrive shortly. 您的出租车很快就到。
17. You can use the house phone. It's on the other side of the lobby. 您可以使用内部电话,就在大堂的另一边。
18. Car rental service is available in our hotel. 我们酒店可以提供租车服务。
19. There are safety deposit boxes at the Front Desk. 前台有保险箱。
20. The newsstand has a wide selection of foreign newspapers and magazines. 阅报处有很多国外报纸和杂志可供选择。

常用委婉语

1. 自己要做什么事时,就使用 May I...?

May I have your name, please? 请问尊姓大名?

May I have your check-out time, please? 请问您什么时候结账退房?

May I see your passport, please? 请让我看一下您的护照,好吗?

2. 麻烦客人时,可使用 Could you...?

Could you fill out the form, please? 请您填写这张表格,好吗?

Could you write that down, please? 请您写下来,好吗?

Could you hold the line, please? 请不要挂电话,好吗?

3. 询问客人的喜好或是做什么时,可使用 Would you...?

Would you like tea or coffee? 请问您要喝茶，还是咖啡？

Would you like to take a taxi? 请问您要搭出租车吗？

Would you mind sitting here? 请问您介意坐在这里吗？

4. 在提供建议、协助和征求意见时，可使用 Shall I...? 或 Would you like me to do...?

Shall I draw the curtains? 请问需要我把窗帘拉上吗？

Shall I draw you a map? 请问需要我为您画一张地图吗？

Shall I make the reservation for you? 请问需要我为您安排预约吗？

5. 招呼语。

Good morning.（用于中午以前。）

Good afternoon.（用于中午至下午六点以前。）

Good evening.（用于下午六点以后。）

6. 招呼语后面接句子，例如：

Good morning, sir. Are you checking-out? 早上好，先生，请问您要退房吗？

Good afternoon, sir. Welcome to Li Jia Hotel. 下午好，先生，欢迎光临丽嘉酒店。

Good evening, Ms. May I help you? 晚上好，女士，请问我有什么能帮您的吗？

7. 后面也可以接上自己酒店名称、部门名称，例如：

Good morning, sir. This is the Front Desk. May I help you?

早上好，先生。这里是服务台，请问有什么能帮您的？

8. 交给客人某些东西时，可以说：

Here you are. 您要的东西在这里。

Here is your room key. 这是您的房间钥匙。

Here it is. 这是您的东西。

9. 当客人准备离开时，可以说：

Have a nice day. 祝您过得愉快。

Please enjoy your stay. 祝您住宿愉快。

We hope to see you again soon. 希望不久能再次见到您。

Thank you for staying with us. 谢谢光临。

10. 回答。

(1) 一般性的回答：

I see, sir. 我明白了，先生。

Certainly, sir. 好的，先生。

(2) 客人对自己说"Thank you"时回答：

You are welcome. 不客气。

Thank you, sir. 谢谢您，先生。

Thank you very much. 非常感谢您。

11. 道歉。

(1) 要麻烦客人或是拒绝客人的要求时：

拒绝客人时，不要一口回绝说"No"，要委婉一些。

I am afraid I can't do that. 不好意思，我恐怕没办法那样做。

Excuse me, sir. Please let me pass. 不好意思，先生，麻烦让我过一下。

(2) 如果是自己的错，就说"I'm sorry"；如果是公司的错，就说"We are sorry"。

I'm very sorry for the delay. 很抱歉延误了时间。

I'm very sorry for the inconvenience. 很抱歉给您造成不便。

I would like to apologize for the mistake. 对于这个错误，我深表歉意。

12. 请对方再等一会儿：

Just a moment, please. 请稍等。

Thank you for waiting. 让您久等了，先生。

I'm very sorry to have kept you waiting. 很抱歉让您久等了。

Could you wait a little longer, please? 请您稍候，好吗？

Part 6 Supplementary Reading

Etiquette of Compliment

Apparently the commendation is to praise a person's superior quality, the outstanding ability, the splendid work, the appearance, the clothing and personal adornments as well as good personal qualities. In fact, it is an important meaning to preserve and promote the interpersonal relationships. The people have a kind of mental disposition to listen to the praise words more or less. Appropriate praise will win the good will of the other side, carry on the human relations activity smoothly, and make the interpersonal relationships harmonious.

There are many big differences in terms of functions, ways, objects and restriction factors and so on. Compared with Chinese, the western people pay more attention to the praising, and are willing to listen to other people's compliments, but also glad to praise others.

The following expressions can do the job while presenting compliments to the others.

- You look great today.
- You did a good job.
- We're so proud of you.
- I'm very pleased with your work.
- This is really a nice place.
- You're looking sharp!
- You always know the right thing to say.
- You're very eloquent.
- Nice going!
- Everything tastes great.
- Your son/daughter is so cute.
- You're very professional.
- You've got a great personality.

- You're so smart.
- You have a good sense of humor.
- You have a good taste.
- Your Chinese is really surprising.
- You have a very successful business.

Chapter 3

Concierge

Study Objectives

1. To have a basic knowledge of concierge service.
2. To grasp the words and expressions used in concierge service.
3. To offer concierge service and meet the guests' needs.

Lead in

As many guest services have become computerized and standardized, concierge service often provides special attention that a guest would not otherwise receive. Thus most star-rated hotels are stressing great importance on concierge service. Think carefully and try to answer the following questions.

1. What duties does the concierge perform?
2. Do you know any special service that the concierge may provide?

Part 1 Listening

Task 1 Dialogues. Listen to the dialogues and fill in the blanks with what you hear.

Dialogue 1

A: Good evening, sir and madam. What can I do for you?

B: My wife and I would like to go on a tour of the city. ______________?

Dialogue 2

A: I'm picking up my parents at the airport this morning. ______________________________?

B: Sure. Your name and room number, please?

Dialogue 3

A: This is our last day here. My group of tourists would like to have a look at the beautiful coastline. Could you help me find a bus?

B: Sure. ____. Please fill out this form first.

Dialogue 4

A: ________________________________?

B: You can go to our beauty parlor on the 5th floor.

Dialogue 5

A: ________________________________. Is that right?

B: Yes. They are all here.

Task 2 Conversations.

Conversation 1 A guest calls the Concierge Desk asking for help to pick up his luggage. Listen and fill in the blanks with the words or sentences provided in the box.

packed	check out	valuable	handbag	Bell Captain's Desk
pick up	suitcases	fragile	come for	luggage

(Captain-C Bellman-B Guest-G)

C: This is the ________. May I help you?

G: Yes. I'm going to ________ soon. Could you ________ my ________?

C: Certainly, sir. May I have your name and room number, please?

G: It's David Green in Room 801.

C: Room 801. Mr. Green, what time are you checking out?

G: At around 11:30.

C: At 11:30. Let me see. It's almost 11 o'clock. Could you make sure your bags are all ________?

G: Sure.

C: I'll send a bellman to your room at once. Please wait for a while.

(*The bellman comes for the luggage.*)

B: Good morning, Mr. Green. I've ________ your luggage.

G: Thank you. Could you take these two ________, please? I'll take the ________ with me.

B: OK. So just these two suitcases?

G: Yes.

B: Is there anything ________ or ________ in them?

G: No.

(*They get to the lobby.*)

B: This is your claim tag, Mr. Green. We'll keep your bags at the Bell Captain's Desk. You can pick them up there.

G: OK. Thank you very much.

B: You're welcome. I hope you have enjoyed your stay with us.

Conversation 2 A car stops in front of the hotel and a bellman steps forward and opens the door of the car for the guest and helps the guest to check in.

we offer Chinese and Western cuisine in the two restaurants on the second floor
a beauty salon, a souvenir shop and a business center
That's very considerate of you
I hope you enjoy your stay
Let me take care of your suitcases.
where could I get a brochure about the hotel?

(**Bellman-B Guest-G**)

B: Good morning, sir. Welcome to our hotel.

G: Good morning.

B: ______________________________.

G: Thank you.

B: Please mind your hands in the revolving door.

G: ______________________________.

B: The Reception Desk is straight ahead.

(*After check-in, they walk to the elevator.*)

B: This way please, your room is on the 8th floor.

G: Thank you and could you tell me something about the hotel service?

B: Sure, our hotel is one of the first-class 5-star hotels in Beijing. There are all kinds of guest rooms here and ______________________________.

G: That sounds perfect.

B: There is also ______________________________ on the first floor which will provide all the necessary services for you.

G: Oh, I see. By the way, ______________________________?

B: You can get it from the Information Desk for free. And here we are. This is your room. Where should I put the luggage?

G: Just leave it in the corner and thank you so much for your help.

B: You are welcome and ______________________________. Is there anything else that you need?

G: No, thank you. See you around.

B: See you.

Conversation 3 Mr. Williams is asking the bellman about some hotel services after he has finished checking in. Listen to the conversation and fill in the blanks with the information you hear.

(**Bellman-B Guest-G**)

B: Mr. Williams, your room is on the 10th floor. Here's the lift. After you, sir.

G: Thank you. Can I ask you some questions?

B: Please feel ________ to ask.

G: I hear Chinese food is delicious. Can you ________ some nice restaurants?

B: Sure. Actually there's a very nice Chinese restaurant in our hotel on the second floor. There you can ________ different Chinese food.

G: Sounds great. I'll go there. And have you got a ________? I'll have a lot of paperwork to do, you see.

B: Yes. It's on the first floor. It provides all necessary services, such as ________, printing, translating and ________.

G: Great. I guess I'll have a relatively easy time here with the help of the staff in the business center. By the way, where can I get a brochure of your hotel?

B: You can get it from the ________ in the lobby. Oh, here we are. This is your room, Mr. Williams. Where should I put your luggage?

G: Just leave it on the ________. Thank you very much for your help. And this is for you.

B: Thank you, Mr. Williams. Hope you'll enjoy your stay.

Part 2 Speaking

Task 1 Work in pairs. Read and complete the following dialogue by translating the Chinese sentences in the parentheses into English.

(Bellman-B Guest-G)

B: ____________________ (这是您第一次来杭州吗), Mr. Black?

G: Yes.

B: Here we are, sir. Room 809. This is your room, sir. ____________________ (需要打开百叶窗吗), sir?

G: Yes, please.

B: ____________________ (把您的行李放在这儿的行李架上), sir.

G: Thank you.

B: ____________________ (桌子上有个文件夹)containing a room service menu and information about other hotel services. There's also some hotel stationery inside, and a "what's on?" guide to Hangzhou.

G: Mm. Thank you.

B: ____________________ (那边有床头控制台). It has three buttons. ____________________ (左边的是控制电视的), the one in the middle is for the radio, and the one on the right is for the lights.

G: I see. Is there a fridge?

B: Yes, there's a small fridge ____________________ (在电视旁边的迷你吧下面).

G: Thanks.

B: In the bathroom over the sink, ____________________ (有个剃须刀插座), and on the side of the door there's a bottle opener.

G: Thank you. That's most helpful.

B: You're welcome, sir. Goodbye.

G: Goodbye.

Vocabulary

blinds	*n.* 窗帘(blind 的名词复数);百叶窗帘
stand	*n.* 架子;台;看台
documentation	*n.* 证据;记录;参考资料;文件记录
folder	*n.* 文件夹;折叠机;折叠式印刷品
contain	*vt.* 包含;容纳;包括或由……构成
stationery	*n.* 文具;办公用品
console	*n.* 控制台;操纵台
button	*n.* 按钮;电钮;扣子
fridge	*n.* 电冰箱;冷冻机
minibar	*n.* 小酒吧;迷你酒吧
sink	*n.* 水池;洗涤槽

Notes

1. Here we are, sir. 我们到了(行李员带客人到房间时的招呼语)。
2. I'll put your suitcase here on the suitcase stand. 我把您的行李放在这儿的行李架上。
3. containing a room service menu 里面有客房送餐服务的菜单
4. a "what's on?" guide to Hangzhou 杭州城市信息手册
5. on the left 在左边(表示物体的方位)
6. a shaver point 剃须刀插座
7. bottle opener 开瓶器

Task 2　Work in pairs. Discuss and complete the conversation between a guest and a bellman by filling in the blanks with appropriate sentences given below.

A. the Beauty Salon's on your immediate right
B. it's at the end of the corridor
C. The Health Center is on the first floor
D. You're welcome, madam
E. Take the lift to the second floor
F. Can I help you

(Bellman-B　Guest-G)

G: Excuse me.

B: Yes, madam. ______1______?

G: Yes, can you tell me how to get to the Beauty Salon, please?

B: Of course, madam. _____2_____. Go straight ahead out of the lift and _____3_____.

G: Thank you. Is it on the same floor as the Health Center?

B: No, madam. _____4_____. Turn right out of the lift and _____5_____.

G: Thank you.

B: _____6_____.

Task 3 Role-play.

Situation 1 Mr. Lee arrives at City Holiday Hotel. The bellman comes over to help him with his luggage. Make up a conversation with the expressions given in the following boxes.

Bellman	Mr. Lee
Welcome to City Holiday Hotel. So you've got four pieces of luggage altogether? Your room is on the 10th floor. Every room is equipped with broadband Internet. Anything else I can do for you?	It's all in the trunk. Do you have Internet access in the guest room? Is the Internet service free of charge? No more. Thank you very much.

Situation 2 Mr. Green arrives at Shangri-La Hotel and asks about some services in the hotel. Please role-play the following situation according to the information provided in the following boxes.

Bellman	Mr. Green
Greet and welcome the guest. Confirm and carry the luggage. Show the guest to the Front Desk. Get to the guest room. Introduce the swimming pool and the Chinese restaurant. Say goodbye to the guest.	Greet. Thank the bellman for carrying the luggage. Finish registration. Ask about some services in the hotel, such as swimming pool and Chinese restaurant. Get to the guest room. Express thanks.

Part 3 Reading

Concierge

Concierge service is a common practice **throughout** the hotel. As many guest services have become **computerized** and **standardized**, concierge service often provides special attention a guest would not **otherwise** receive. Thus most star-rated hotels are **stressing** great importance on concierge service.

The basic duties of the concierge staff are to do bell service and to **attend to** guests' special needs which are not provided by the hotel.

In doing bell service, the concierge attends the guests from their first step into the hotel to the final room destination. On the guests' arrival, the bellman carries their luggage from the car. He leaves the luggage on the lobby floor until the guests finish registering. Then the bellman **accompanies** the guests with the luggage to the guest room. Once inside the room, the bellman checks the facilities and cleanliness in the room. He will also explain some special features of the hotel, and show how to use certain facilities. Normally the bellman points out some self-service items especially, for example, the minibar or the in-room safe, **in case** unnecessary **dispute arises** when the guests check out.

Besides the bell service, the concierge also provides information service. They should know the **surrounding** community as well as the hotel very well. Usually the concierge provides directions and information about local attractions and facilities. Actually the concierge assists guests with a lot more tasks like making restaurant reservations, arranging for car rentals, booking tickets for special events and assisting with various sightseeing arrangements.

As can be seen above, the concierge's job is **playing a more and more important role** in providing quality service for guests. A concierge needs to be able to do a number of tasks with great efficiency and perhaps at the same time. Thus it is a **challenging** job to be a **qualified** concierge.

Vocabulary

throughout	*prep.* 在……期间;遍及……场所 *adv.* 处处;始终
computerize	*vt.* 使计算机化
standardize	*vt.* 使……标准化
otherwise	*adv.* 否则;另外 *adj.* 别的 *conj.* 否则;不然
stress	*vt.* 强调
accompany	*vt.* 陪伴;陪同
dispute	*vt.* & *vi.* 辩论;争论 *n.* 辩论;争端
arise	*vi.* & *vt.* 产生;出现
surrounding	*adj.* 周围的;附近的
challenging	*adj.* 挑战性的;困难而有趣的
qualified	*adj.* 有资格的;胜任的;适当的

Phrases and Expressions

attend to	处理;注意;听取;照顾
in case	以免;万一
play a role	起着……作用

Task 1 True or false statements. Decide whether the following statements are True (T) or False (F) according to the text.

1. Most star-rated hotels are paying little attention on concierge service. ( )

2. The basic duties of the concierge staff are to do bell service and to meet guests' special needs. ( )
3. The bellman doesn't attend the guests until the guests finish their registering. ( )
4. The bellman's job is just to accompany the guests with the luggage to the guest room. ( )
5. Usually the concierge provides directions and information about local attractions and facilities. ( )
6. The concierge's job is playing a more and more important role in providing quality service for guests. ( )

Task 2 Read the passage again and put the steps in the job procedure of the bellman in the correct order.

A. Showing the guest into his/her room.
B. Waiting for the guest until he/she finishes checking in.
C. Carrying luggage for the guest.
D. Checking room cleanliness.
E. Introducing room facilities and hotel services.

Correct order: ________________

Task 3 **Blank filling.** Fill in the blanks with the words given. Change the form when necessary.

arrive	attraction	rent	accompany	efficiency
surround	arrange	register	qualify	assist

1. Sir, may I have your ________ date, please?
2. The police had searched the station and the ________ area, but still couldn't find the missing boy.
3. It's said that our boss lives in a big house with an ________ garden.
4. I'll tell the chief concierge to make travel ________ for your group as soon as possible.
5. I'd like to ________ this letter.
6. Personally, I consider the CEO a ________ leader.
7. He is an ________ manager.
8. Many personnel managers started as secretaries or personnel ________ and worked their way up.
9. I'll get in contact with a ________ car company.
10. Could you tell me what you want to buy when you ask me to ________ you shopping?

Part 4 Translation

Task 1 Translate the following passage into Chinese.

The Chinese Zodiac is the Chinese way of numbering the years. It attributes an animal to each year, according to a 12-year cycle. Since ancient times, the Chinese people began to use the Heavenly Stems and Earthly Branches to record the passing of years. At this same time, Chinese nomadic people who lived in northwest China instead used animals to number the years. The two ways of numbering the years were smoothly integrated, and the Chinese Zodiac took shape. The 12 animals in the Chinese Zodiac are: rat, ox, tiger, rabbit, dragon, snake, horse, ram, monkey, rooster, dog, and pig. The meaning of the symbolic animal of the birth year is that it can make people magnanimous and be of one mind in times of difficulty.

Task 2 Translate the following passage into English.

中秋节是我国的传统节日,一般在九月或十月。我们通常在户外吃着大餐就着月饼来庆祝中秋节。中秋节最重要的活动就是赏月。这一天的月亮似乎更亮更圆。我们把这样的月亮叫作满月。这一天,家人团聚,我们也把这一天叫作团圆节。这就是中秋节。

Part 5 Cultural Norms

常用词汇

concierge	礼宾部	shopping center	商场
doorman	门童	pick-up service	接机服务
bellman	行李员	morning call	叫早服务
tip	小费	wake-up service	叫醒服务
tour guide	导游	fragile object	易碎物品
luggage	行李	straight on	往前直走
luggage tag	行李牌	service center	服务中心
trolley	行李车	ticket service	票务服务
store room	行李房	Western restaurant	西餐厅
luggage rack	行李架	Chinese restaurant	中餐厅
keep luggage	行李寄存	lobby bar	大堂吧
valuables	贵重物品	clinic room	医务室
buffet breakfast	自助早餐	sauna	桑拿
limousine service	贵宾车服务	massage	按摩
five-star hotel	五星级酒店	meeting room	会议室
elevator/lift	电梯	parking lot	停车场

常用句子

1. Is this everything, sir? 先生，这是您的全部东西吗？
2. Here's the light switch. 这是电灯开关。
3. Here's the closet and there's the bathroom. 这儿是壁柜，这儿是洗澡间。
4. How do you like this room? 您觉得这个房间怎么样？
5. It's also quite spacious. 房间也很宽敞。
6. By the way, I'd like to tell you that the check-out time is 12:00 at noon, sir. 先生，顺便告诉您，退房时间是中午 12 点。
7. Have you used any hotel services this morning or had breakfast at the hotel dining room, Mr. Green? 格林先生，今天早晨您是否用过旅馆服务设施，或在旅馆餐厅用过早餐？
8. At what time would you like us to call you tomorrow morning? 您想让我们明天早上什么时候叫醒您？
9. That means that I'll have to be on the road by 7 o'clock at the latest. 这就是说我明天早晨最迟也要 7 点钟上路。
10. Will you pay by cash? 您能用现金支付吗？
11. No, if there is, I'll take it to you in time. 没有，如果有的话，我会及时给您送来的。
12. Here is a fax for you. 这儿有您一封传真。
13. I want to borrow *China Daily* of these days. 我要看这几天的《中国日报》。
14. Please get some copies of *China Daily* for me. 请拿几份《中国日报》给我。
15. All right, I'll get it for you right away. 好的，我就去拿。
16. Pardon me for interrupting. 对不起，打扰你们了。
17. Please excuse me for coming so late. 请原谅我来迟了。
18. Yes, certainly, just leave it to us, sir. 当然，您就将这件事留给我们去做吧。
19. Glad to be of service. Please feel free to contact us anytime. 很高兴为您服务。有需要请随时通知我们。
20. Would you like me to call a taxi for you? /Would you want a taxi? 需要我为您叫一辆出租车吗？/需要出租车吗？
21. Sorry, I have to go. Nice talking with you. 对不起，我不得不走了。和您谈话很开心。

Part 6 Supplementary Reading

Etiquette of Sending Flowers

When sending flowers, people should take the species and colors into consideration, i. e. what flowers are suitable for what occasions and what color of them is appropriate. Generally, red roses are the most precious gift for love. Yellow roses are the peace roses according to their designation during the World War Ⅱ. Roses of other shades such as pink and purple may be used for as diverse purposes as congratulations or compliments and so on.

Here is the spectrum of color tips.

Let's start with white. In early history, white signified purity or virginity. Yet today for the Japanese and other orientals, white is a symbolic representative of hope at funerals.

In Brazil and Mexico, purple is the color of death. Brown, as seen in withered leaves, is the funeral color in Persia.

In England, red is regarded as an "old" color, but in Japan the combination of red and white is widely regarded as appropriate for happy and pleasant occasions.

Americans see red when they are angry, green jealousy, blue coolness, black morbid.

Chapter 4

Business Center

Study Objectives

1. To have a basic knowledge of Business Center.
2. To grasp the words and expressions used in Business Center.
3. To offer services and meet the guests' various needs in Business Center.

Lead in

These days, the business centers are likely to be an essential section in a hotel. The services in the Business Center are very important to the guests who are on business trips. Think carefully and try to answer the following questions.

1. What services do you expect from Business Center?
2. How many kinds of airline tickets can be booked for the guests?

Part 1 Listening

Task 1 Dialogues. Listen to the dialogues and fill in the blanks with what you hear.

Dialogue 1

A: Excuse me, ____________________? I need 20 copies of them this afternoon.

B: No problem, sir. ____________________.

Dialogue 2

A: ____________________? Here is a convention schedule which should be sent to our headquarters right now.

B: Of course, madam. We have two fax machines here.

Dialogue 3

A: ____________________.

B: At what time, madam?

Dialogue 4

A: I have two manuscripts here. ____________________?

B: Certainly, sir.

Dialogue 5

A: We need an English-Chinese translator. Can you help us to find one?

B: No problem, sir. ________________________________.

Task 2　Conversations.

Conversation 1　Mr. Green comes to Business Center to photocopy his report. Listen and fill in the blanks with the words or sentences provided in the box.

how much	what time	urgent	binding them up	30 minutes left
sign the bill	pay in cash	how many	have this report copied	tariff list

(**Business Center Clerk-C　Guest-G**)

C: Good afternoon, Mr. Green. How may I help you?

G: Good afternoon. I would like to ________.

C: No problem. ________ copies would you like?

G: 10 copies with covers.

C: I see. ________ do you expect it?

G: It's ________. I have a meeting at 4:00 p. m.. Can you send them to my room before 3:30 p. m. ?

C: There are only ________ for us, but I will try my best. As soon as I finish ________, I will send them to your room.

G: Thank you very much. By the way, ________ shall I pay for the copies?

C: Here is our ________________. Your report has 4 pages, and 10 copies make 40 pages. Each page costs 1 yuan. Mr. Green, you should pay 40 yuan. Since you are our guest, you can also ________.

G: Sure, I will ________. Here you are.

C: Thank you.

Conversation 2　Mr. Black wants to book tickets at the Business Center. Listen to the conversation and fill in the blanks with the information you hear.

Please sign your name here Could you send the tickets to my room as soon as possible Are you going there by train or by air Could you book two tickets for me It's my pleasure to be at your service It is a non-stop flight

(**Business Center Clerk-C Guest-G**)

C: Good morning, welcome to Business Center. What can I do for you, Mr. Black?

G: I'm leaving for Shanghai the day after tomorrow. ________________________.

C: That's October 16th, isn't it?

G: That's right.

C: ________________________?

G: By air, of course. Planes are much faster and more comfortable. How many flights are there to Shanghai in the morning?

C: There are more than ten flights from 7:30 to 12:00. I suggest the 9:00 a. m. flight which arrives in Shanghai at 11:00 a. m.. ________________________, and you needn't transfer to another flight.

G: Fine, I'll take it then. I prefer the business class.

C: OK, Mr. Black. Would you please fill in this form? ________________________.

G: All right. Shall I pay cash now?

C: Yes, please pay 3000 yuan in advance.

G: Here you are. When can I get the tickets?

C: You can get them in the morning of October 15th.

G: Thank you. ________________________?

C: No problem, Mr. Black.

G: It's very nice of you.

C: ________________________.

Conversation 3 Mr. Smith comes to the Business Center to print his business card. Listen to the conversation and fill in the blanks with the information you hear.

(**Business Center Clerk-C Guest-G**)

C: Good morning, welcome to Business center. How may I help you, Mr. Smith?

G: Yes, ________________________.

C: No problem, sir. What design would you prefer?

G: Here is the original one. ________________________ "General Secretary of American Trade Committee."

C: OK. ________________________?

G: Please capitalize my name and use Arial Black font style in the size of 16.

C: No Problem, sir. When will you need it?

G: ________________________. Please send them to my room before this evening.

C: All right. I will.

G: How much is it?

C: 180 yuan.

G: That's too much! I am the VIP guest in your hotel. ________________________.

C: Oh, if you are the VIP guest, ____________________________. That is 126 yuan.

G: You are very helpful. Thank you.

C: It's my pleasure.

Part 2 Speaking

Task 1 Work in pairs. Read and complete the following dialogue by translating the Chinese sentences in the parentheses into English.

(Mr. Green comes to the Business Center in a hurry. The manager helps him to resolve his problems.)

(Manager-M Mr. Green-G)

M: What is the hurry, Mr. Green?

G: ______________________________(我们急需你的帮助).

M: What may I do for you?

G: ______________________________(我们的航班晚点了). We have to send some urgent emails back to our New York headquarters. ______________________________(但我的笔记本电脑现在不能正常工作). I wonder if you can help me to fix it.

M: No problem, sir. __________________________(我派一个技术员给您维修笔记本电脑). Take it easy. We have computers over there with speed Internet access, and ________________________(您可以给公司发邮件).

G: That's great! ______________________________(怎么收费)?

M: 10 yuan per hour. ______________________________(因为您是我们的贵宾,费用全免).

G: Wonderful! You are very helpful. By the way, do you have an IDD telephone? ___________________________(我必须打个国际电话).

M: Of course we have. In fact, ______________________________(您在自己房间就可以打电话). Every guest room in our hotel ______________________________(装有国际直拨电话).

G: I see. Thank you.

Vocabulary

urgent	*adj.* 急迫的;催促的;强求的
flight	*n.* (物体的)飞行;航班;飞翔
delay	*n.* 延迟;拖延 *vt.* 延期;推迟;耽搁 *vi.* 延缓
headquarters	*n.* 总公司;公司总部
laptop	*n.* 便携式电脑;笔记本电脑
technician	*n.* 技术人员;技师
access	*n.* 入口;出口;进入

Notes

1. in urgent need of... 急需……

2. Our flight has been delayed. 注意被动语态的用法："我们的航班晚点了。"
3. We have computers over there with speed Internet access. 那边的计算机有快速网络接口。
4. VIP: very important person 的缩写，贵宾。
5. IDD: international direct dial 的缩写，国际直拨电话。

Task 2 Work in pairs. Mr. Black has a meeting in Seoul next week. He comes to the Business Center to book two air tickets. Discuss and complete the conversation between Mr. Black and a Business Center Clerk by filling in the blanks with appropriate sentences given below.

A. One for me and one for my colleague
B. Is there any flight to Seoul on October, 25th
C. And do you prefer window seat or aisle seat
D. we will send the tickets to your room on October, 24th
E. How many tickets do you want
F. First class or economy class

(Business Center Clerk-C Guest-G)

C: Good afternoon, Mr. Black. How may I help you?
G: Good afternoon. ______1______? I will attend a meeting there.
C: Let me see. Yes, there are two flights: KA 819 is at 8 o'clock in the morning; KA 815 is at 5 o'clock in the afternoon.
G: I'd like to book the 8:00 a. m. flight.
C: No problem. ______2______?
G: Two. ______3______.
C: May I have your passports?
G: Here you are.
C: All right. ______4______?
G: Economy class.
C: ______5______?
G: Two aisle seats. How much will it take?
C: 4250 yuan. Mr. Black, ______6______.
G: That's great. Thank you.
C: It's my pleasure.

Task 3 Role-play. Work in pairs and make up a dialogue respectively according to the situations provided.

Situation 1 Mr. Black is a secretary of Shanghai Commercial Committee. He comes to the Business Center to print the address list for his committee members. Make a conversation according to the following instructions.

Clerk	Guest
Greet and welcome the guest. Ask the guest if he needs the list double-sided printed. Show the tariff to the guest and ask him to sign the bill. Promise to send the lists to each committee member's room by 4:00 p.m.. Say goodbye to the guest.	Greet the clerk. Ask the clerk to type the manuscript of the address list. Tell the clerk to photocopy the list for 20 copies, and staple each copy on the left side. Ask about the price. Make sure the lists will be sent to the committee members' rooms this afternoon, that is, from Room 2001 to Room 2020. Express thanks.

Situation 2 Mr. Green and his two children are going to Xiamen by train. He asks the Business Center clerk to book three tickets for him. Please act out using the useful expressions given in the boxes.

Clerk	Guest
Welcome to Business Center. Are you going there by train or by air? There are more than 5 trains in the morning. I suggest that you take the train D58. Would you please fill in the form? Please pay 700 yuan in advance. We will send the tickets to your room.	I need three tickets for my two children and myself. How many trains are there to Xiamen in the morning? I prefer the soft seat. When can I get the tickets? Could you send the tickets to my room as soon as possible?

Part 3 Reading

The Business Center

In the early 1990s, when Business Centers only existed in the upper-class hotels, they usually meant office machines, with staff to serve users. These days, however, the Business Center is likely to be an **essential section** in a hotel. The services in the Business Center are very important to the guests who are on business trips.

On a daily basis, the secretarial services, **convention** services and tickets services are the main jobs of the Business Center staff. In general, the secretarial services include **photocopying**, sending faxes, typing documents, printing business cards, etc. A **self-contained** Business Center **features** computers, Internet access and machines combining printer, scanner and photocopier. The Business Center staff must know how to **operate** the photocopier, fax machine, and printer. Besides, they must be **equipped** with some basic skills of computer.

Convention services **are always related to** all-sized meeting room rental, convention equipment rental (such as laptop computers, projectors, screens, white-boards with mark pens, roving microphones, etc.), and sometimes catering service. Meeting rooms are usually equipped with 24 hours Internet access and direct-dial multi-line telephones with voice mail to meet the requirements of efficiency-oriented customers. Translation and **interpretation** services are also provided by the Business Center. Some five-star Business Centers are equipped with the **simultaneous interpretation** booth in their meeting rooms.

Business Center staff will help the guest s to book airline tickets, train tickets, concert tickets, and show tickets, etc. They are well-connected with the ticket agency and are well-informed with the tickets information. They provide train timetable, suggest flights, explain time difference, and provide show information as well.

With the development of high technology, Business Center is playing an increasingly important role in the hotel. The electronic Business Center has become a worldwide tendency. Customers will **utilize** the Business Center more **conveniently** and efficiently.

Vocabulary

essential	*adj*. 基本的;必要的
section	*n*. 部分;部门
convention	*n*. 会议
photocopy	*n*. 影印本;复印件 *v*. 影印;复印
self-contained	*adj*. 独立的;设备齐全的;自给自足的
feature	*n*. 特征;特点 *vt*. 以……为特色 *vi*. 起主要作用
operation	*n*. 操作;经营;手术
equip	*vt*. 装备;配备;使……具备;使……有准备
interpretation	*n*. 口译;解释;说明
simultaneous	*adj*. 同时发生的;同时存在的
utilize	*vt*. 利用;使用
conveniently	*adv*. 方便地;便利地

Phrases and Expressions

be related to	与……有关
simultaneous interpretation	同声传译

Task 1 True or false statements. Decide whether the following statements are True (T) or False (F) according to the text.

1. The Business Center staff must know how to operate the photocopier, fax machine, and printer. ( )
2. Business Center staff may send the tickets to the guests' room without the guests' permission. ( )
3. If the Internet access service is not free of charge, the Business Center staff should inform the guest. ( )
4. The Business Center staff need to be well-connected with the tickets agency. ( )

5. Business Center staff will help the guests to know show information. ( )
6. With the development of high technology, Business Center is playing a little role in the hotel. ( )

Task 2 Questions. Read the text again and answer the following questions.

1. What are the main jobs of the Business Center staff?
2. What should a self-contained Business Center be equipped with?
3. What abilities or skills should the Business Center staff be asked to learn?
4. What are convention services related to?
5. Why should Business Center staff be well-informed with the tickets information?

Task 3 Blank filling. Fill in the blanks with the words given. Change the form when necessary.

non-stop	put forward	validity	take away	rent
catch up with	suggest	look after	arrange	look for

1. The police is still ________ the little girl missing in the forest.
2. It is a ________ flight, and you needn't transfer to another flight.
3. The ________ of the simultaneous interpretation system is 4500 yuan per day.
4. He decided to work hard to ________ his classmates in the new term.
5. Lily's open return ticket is ________ before October, 25th.
6. The Business Center clerk will give you some ________ if you ask them about the ticket information.
7. Why don't you ________ your opinion at the meeting?
8. The former CEO of the bank was ________ by the police.
9. As a secretary, you must know how to ________ the boss's schedule.
10. Jenny has been ill for several weeks and her husband is ________ her.

Part 4 Translation

Task 1 Translate the following passage into Chinese.

Osmanthus flowers represent friendship and good luck. During the Warring States (475-221 B. C.) some kingdoms exchanged osmanthus flowers as friendly gestures. In ethnic minority areas known for their sweet osmanthus, young people often exchange osmanthus flowers for mutual love. As the sound "gui" in "guihua" may stand for "honored" or "distinguished", the blooming of osmanthus flowers signifies the arrival of honored guests, especially those coming from afar. They will customarily be treated to osmanthus tea or osmanthus wine that dates back as early as the Spring and Autumn Period (770-476 B. C.). In feudal China, when someone became a successful candidate in the highest imperial examinations, he was described as having plucked the osmanthus (or laurel) branch from the moon, on which a folktale told of osmanthus tree is growing.

Task 2 Translate the following passage into English.

瓷器是中国最重要的手工艺品之一。中国瓷器有 3500 多年的历史,明清时期尤其繁荣。瓷器不仅可以用作日常餐具(dinnerware)、花瓶等,精美的瓷器更是常常被人们用来装饰家居。作为高档艺术品的象征,真品瓷器常常具有极高的艺术价值和经济价值,因此,常被很多人视为珍藏品。中国瓷器受到各国人民的欢迎,经常被用作表达中外友谊的礼物。

Part 5 Cultural Norms

常用词汇

photocopier	复印机
projector	投影仪
scanner	扫描仪
first class cabin	头等舱
open return ticket	不定期往返机票
soft berth	软卧
hard berth	硬卧
lower berth	下铺
single ticket/one-way ticket	单程票
economy class	经济舱
soft seat	软座
international postage	国际邮资
domestic postage	国内邮资
postage stamp	邮票
postal service	邮政服务
postal charge	邮费
postal money order	邮政汇票

常用句子

介绍服务项目

1. We can meet the needs of guests. 我们能满足客人的需要。
2. We can send a fax for you. 我们能为您发传真。
3. We can type a document for you. 我们能为您打印文件。
4. We can photocopy the document for you. 我们能为您复印文件。
5. We can send letters for you. 我们能为您寄信。
6. May I have your name/telephone number, please? 可以提供您的名字/电话号码吗?
7. May I have the way to contact you? 如何与您联系呢?

主动提供服务

1. Would you like me to try again? 要不要我再试一次?
2. Would you like me to try it a little darker? 要不要我再稍微调深一点?
3. Would you like me to try it a little lighter? 要不要我再稍微调浅一点?
4. Would you like me to reduce it smaller? 要不要我缩得更小一点?
5. Would you like me to photocopy on both sides of the paper? 要不要我用双面复印?
6. Would you like me to staple these for you? 要不要我把这些装订起来?

询问客人信息

1. May I have the fax number? 能告诉我传真号吗?
2. May I have your room number? 能告诉我您的房间号码吗?
3. May I have your telephone number? 能告诉我您的电话号码吗?
4. May I have the address of the party? 能告诉我对方的地址吗?

询问客人的具体要求

1. How many copies would you like? 您要复印多少份?
2. How small would you like it? 您要缩小多少?
3. How large would you like it? 您要放大多少?
4. What size would you like? 您喜欢哪种尺寸?
5. How big would you like it? 您希望它多大?

询问客人的寄件方式

1. Would you like it to go by ordinary or registered mail? 您要寄普通信还是挂号信?
2. Would you like to send it by airmail or surface mail? 您想寄航空邮件还是平寄邮件?

Part 6 Supplementary Reading

Etiquette of Gift Giving

Giving the appropriate gift in a timely fashion not only strengthens personal relationships in some cultures but also can enhance a company or personal image. The right gift conveys respect to the individual and by the same token can convey a company or a personal image of global sophistication. The main purpose of any gift should be to please and honor the recipient. If you keep this in mind, you will never produce a gift that can be inappropriate or, worse, insulting.

One basic rule of thumb in international gift giving: ideally, any present you give should be made in your home country. Take special care to make sure that the gift is not made in a country or region that may cause insult to the recipient.

Another point that should be remembered: gifts with company logos should be used as small tokens only, not as a major sign of appreciation. Even when logos are used they should only be placed on gifts of the highest quality and of the best taste. Remember, even the smallest gift reflects your company's image and personality. Keep the logo small so that it doesn't look as though the gift is nothing more than a company advertisement.

Chapter 5

Chamber Service

Study Objectives

1. To have a basic knowledge of chamber service.
2. To grasp the words and expressions frequently used in chamber service.
3. To get related information on chamber service and improve comprehension skills through listening and reading.
4. To be able to respond professionally to guests' questions and requests on chamber service and offer the information or services needed.

Lead in

Housekeeping Department is the heart of the hotel industry. The entire hotel depends on the smooth, efficient management of the Housekeeping Department. The major responsibility of this department is cleaning guest rooms and public areas. Chamber service is one of the services provided by the Housekeeping Department. Work in pairs and discuss with your partner and answer the following questions.

1. What is chamber service?
2. What are the steps in good customer service?

Part 1 Listening

Task 1 Dialogues. Listen to the following short dialogues and fill in the blanks according to what you hear.

(**Housekeeper-H Guest-G**)

Dialogue 1

H: (*Knock*) Housekeeping. ______________________________?

G: Come in, please.

Dialogue 2

H: ______________________________, sir?

G: You can do it now if you like.

Dialogue 3

H: Good morning, ________________________________?

G: Yes, I need more towels.

Dialogue 4

G: I would like ________________________________ left in the room.

H: ________________________________.

Dialogue 5

G: There seems to be something wrong with the ________________________________.

H: Don't worry, sir. I'll ________________________________ and ____________________ ____________________ repair it immediately.

Task 2 Conversations. Listen to the following conversations and fill in the blanks according to what you hear. The missing words and phrases in Conversation 1 and the missing sentences in Conversations 2 and 3 have been provided in the boxes, and you can choose them from the boxes to fill in the blanks.

Conversation 1 The guest meets the housekeeper in the hall.

missing	lamp	shower	check	enjoy
replace	hair dryer	report	light bulb	shower

(Housekeeper-H Guest-G)

H: Good afternoon, sir. May I help you with anything?

G: Yes, please. There is a problem in my bathroom. The ________ doesn't work. Also, you need to __________ the ____________ in the lamp next to the bed.

H: The ________ and the __________ don't work? May I have your room number?

G: 415.

H: Did you say 415? (*Writing on the paper*) I will __________ it and get someone to help you.

G: Thank you. Besides, I need a ____________.

H: It should be on the wall in the bathroom. Can I ________ it for you?

G: It's OK. I'll go and check it and tell you if it is __________.

H: OK. Let me know if it is not there. Is there anything else I can do for you?

G: No, that's all.

H: OK. Goodbye and ________ your stay.

G: Thanks. Goodbye.

Conversation 2 The housekeeper is in a guest room, cleaning, and the cart is across the door. The guest is in the hall.

Don't worry, Front Desk can get you a new one
I will call Front Desk and tell them that you are coming down
Just a minute. I need to move the cart first

(**Housekeeper-H Guest-G**)

G: Hi. I need to get in to pick up my briefcase and computer.

H: ____. For security reasons, I need to close the door and let you use your card key to get into the room.

G: (*Checking pockets*) I'm afraid I don't seem to have my card key.

H: ____.

G: Oh dear! I have to go back to Front Desk! I am in a hurry, too!

H: ____.

G: OK. Thanks.

H: You are welcome. I'm always at your service.

Conversation 3 The housekeeper knocks at the guest's door.

I'm sorry. I didn't mean to disturb you
Enjoy your stay here
Housekeeping
When is a good time to come back
I am just dressing

(**Housekeeper-H Guest-G**)

H: (*Knocks*) ____________________. May I come in?

G: Wait a minute. ________________________________.

H: ________________________________. I can come back later. ____________________ __________?

G: Can you come back after 12:00?

H: Certainly, sir.

G: Thank you.

H: You are welcome. ________________________.

Part 2 Speaking

Task 1 Work in pairs. Read and complete the following dialogue by translating the Chinese sentences in the parentheses into English.

(**Hotel Housekeeper-H Guest-G**)

H: (*Knocks*) Housekeeping. ________________________________ (我可以进来吗)?

G: Hi, ________________________________ (请进).

H：Good evening，madam. ________________（现在为您提供夜床服务可以吗）？

G：Thank you，but could you come back later? You see，________________（我有几个朋友一小时后会过来）.

H：Of course，madam. ________________（您什么时候方便）？

G：You can come back in four hours.

H：Sure，madam. ________________（我会转告夜班服务员，他们到时候会过来）.

G：Great. Well，would you tidy up a bit in the bathroom now? I've just taken a bath and it is quite a mess there.

H：Yes，madam.

G：Oh，wait，could you help me? ________________（电视遥控器在哪里）？

H：________________（应该在床头柜上）. Yes，it is on the night table，under your newspaper.

G：Thank you. By the way，I need more coat hangers in my room. When you have a minute，can you get me some?

H：Coat hangers? ________________（您想要几个）？

G：Half a dozen would be fine.

H：Yes，madam. ________________（我马上处理）.

H：(*Having done all as requested*) It's growing dark. ________________（需要我为您拉上窗帘吗）？

G：Why not? That would be so cozy.

H：May I turn on the lights for you?

G：Yes，please.

H：Yes，madam. ________________（您还有其他需要吗）？

G：No，that's great.

H：My name is Allen. ________________（有什么需要请告诉我）. Have a good evening.

Vocabulary

housekeeping	*n.* 客房部；内务处理；家务；家政；客房服务；家事
madam	*n.* 女士；小姐；太太
turndown	*adj.* 翻下的；翻折的（turndown service 夜床服务；开床服务）
convenient	*adj.* 方便的；便利的；便捷的
staff	*n.* 职员；员工；工作人员；全体职员（overnight staff 夜班员工）
tidy	*adj.* 整洁的 *vt.* & *vi.* 使整洁；收拾（tidy up 整理；收拾；归置）
mess	*n.* 混乱；肮脏；脏乱
remote	*n.* 遥控器
night table	*n.* 床头柜；床头桌

coat hanger　　*n.* 衣架

dozen　　*n.*（一）打；十二个

cozy　　*adj.* 舒适的；安逸的；惬意的

Notes

1. May I…？该句型表示委婉、有礼貌的请求，意思是"我可以……吗"。
2. have somebody over 邀请某人到家里来
3. Would you…？该句型表示有礼貌地请求别人做某事，意思是"你可以……吗"。
4. It should be on the night table. 它应该在床头柜上。should 在这里是情态动词，表示说话人猜想"应该会怎么样"的意思。
5. I will take care of that right away. Take care of somebody/something 意为"照顾；照料"，此句中的意思是"负责做某事"。
6. Would you like me to …？该句型表示有礼貌地主动提供帮助，意思是"要不要我来做某事；您愿意让我做这件事吗"。比如，Would you like me to set up the conference room? 需要我来布置会议室吗？
7. Please let me know if there is anything else you need. Please let me know if…意为"如果……请告诉我"。

Task 2　Work in pairs. Practice and perform the following dialogue with your partner. For scene 2，please put the sentences into the right order before you read it.

Scene 1　A guest makes a phone call to the Housekeeping Department.

(Housekeeping-H　Guest-G)

H: Housekeeping. How may I help you?

G: Hello, I'd like to have more towels and shampoo sent to my room.

H: Certainly, what room are you calling from?

G: Room 332.

H: And your name, please?

G: White. David White.

H: Thank you, Mr. White, I will have towels and shampoo sent up right away. How many towels would you like?

G: I'd like two extra bath towels and why don't you throw in two extra blankets? I'd appreciate that. I'm surprised it gets that cold here.

H: All right. So, that's two bath towels, one shampoo and two blankets for Room 332, is that correct?

G: Yes, thank you. Oh, could you make that two shampoos, instead?

H: Got it, two shampoos. Thank you, Mr. White. They will be brought up to you within the hour.

G: Thanks, that's perfect.

H: You're welcome. Anything else you need today?

G: No. Oh, wait a minute, do you provide laundry service? Could you send someone up for my laundry, please?

H: Sure. If you have any laundry, please just leave it in the laundry bag behind the bathroom door. The hotel chamber maid will be there to collect it in half an hour. Is there anything else we can do for you?

G: No. That's all.

H: OK. Goodbye and enjoy your stay.

G: Thanks, I am. Goodbye.

Scene 2 The chamber maid is knocking at the door of Room 332 to collect laundry for Mr. White.

(Chamber Maid-M Guest-G)

1. **M**: My pleasure. May I collect your laundry now?
2. **G**: Well, I'll take the quick service.
3. **M**: Housekeeping. May I come in?
4. **G**: Yes, please.
5. **G**: No, thank you.
6. **G**: Thank you.
7. **M**: Goodbye, Mr. White. Have a nice day.
8. **M**: OK. Is there anything else I can do for you?
9. **M**: Good morning, Mr. White. Here are two bath towels, two shampoos and two blankets as you requested.
10. **G**: Yes, it's in the laundry bag. By the way, when can I get my laundry back?
11. **M**: If you are in a hurry, we have a two-hour quick service with an extra charge of 50%.
12. **M**: It usually takes ten hours.
13. **G**: Oh, dear. Can I get it back this afternoon?

Task 3 Role-play. Work in pairs and make up a dialogue respectively according to the situations provided.

1. **If you act as the chamber maid:** You come to the room and find out if the guest would like to have the room cleaned.

   If you act as the guest: You are going to take a nap, so you don't want the room cleaned. You just want some fresh towels and tell the chamber maid to leave them at the door.

   Chamber maid: You promise to bring them right away.

2. **If you act as the chamber maid:** You come to the room and find out if the guest would like to have the room cleaned.

   If you act as the guest: You want the room cleaned. But you tell the chamber maid some instructions on cleaning the room.

Chamber maid: You respond to instructions for servicing the room and you take every step on the guest's request.

(The following is a list of instructions given by the guest on cleaning the room. You can refer to it when do the role-play.)

- Don't worry about vacuuming or the bed. Just clean the bathroom.
- Vacuum the floor but leave the bed.
- Make the bed. Empty the garbage and dispose of recycling.
- Disinfect the sink please.
- Vacuum up the crumbs under the table but don't bother with the rest of the room.
- Leave the window open but keep the curtains closed.
- You can throw out the newspapers but don't touch the papers on the desk.
- Straighten up the bedroom but don't clean it.
- Replace any missing bottles in the bathroom.
- The toilet isn't flushing properly.
- Don't move anything in the room when you clean it.
- Can we have more coffee and coffee mugs?
- There's a stain on the carpet.
- Please refill the tissue box and leave extra bathroom tissue
- The curtain is falling off.
- The sink overflowed, and the floor is wet.
- Please sort the problem with the TV remote.
- The mirror is dusty.
- The room is stuffy.

Task 4 Dialogue completion. Choose the correct sentences provided to complete the following dialogue, and then practice it with your partner.

A. Don't worry, madam
B. May I ask if you have put your key card in the electricity slot by the door?
C. Which room are you in, madam?
D. I'll send an engineer straight up to see to it. Please wait a moment
E. What seems to be the problem, madam?
F. I'm very sorry to have caused you so much trouble

(Clerk-C Guest-G)

C: Good morning. Guest Service Center. Can I help you?

G: I certainly hope so. I am very annoyed.

C: ______1______

G: The air-conditioner in my room isn't working and there's a lot of water under it.

C: I see. ______2______

G: Room 1103. What's more, it's very dark in my room. The lights don't work. And also the television doesn't seem to work, either. There's nothing on the screen.

C: Mm, madam. ____________3____________

G: Excuse me?

C: The electricity slot. Well, madam, those facilities that you just mentioned won't work unless you put the card in the slot.

G: Oh, I see. But why doesn't it say so on the card? And why didn't anybody tell me this?

C: ____________4____________, madam. You'll use the facilities in your room if you put the key in the slot.

G: OK. I got it. But what about the water under the air-conditioner?

C: ____________5____________. ____________6____________.

G: OK. I'll just wait. Thanks.

Part 3 Reading

Housekeeping Service Procedures (Guest Service Centre)

Guest Service Centre provides extra items available **on loan** to **in house** guest on request to ensure guest enjoys **maximum** comfort for the **duration** of their stay and ensure "small items" requests are under express service.

1. All GSC staff have to know the list of items and the time when they are served:

—Pillows and **duvets**

—Towels and **bathrobes**

—Iron and board, **adapters**, **transformers**

—**Kettles**

—Hangers

—**Mineral** water and etc.

—**Extension cords** and boards

—**Vases**

2. When guest needs extra items on loan, GSC staff have to:

—**Obtain** room number, and items required correctly.

—Ensure Housekeeping sends the items without delay.

3. Make a record on the Internal Logbook.

4. When guest leaves something behind, GSC staff have to make sure the following things.

Any item that is left behind by the guest must be handed to the shift leader. He or she records the item in the **Lost and Found Book**, and hands it immediately to the Housekeeping Office for **safe keeping**.

Normally, the guests would come back to the hotel, if they think that they left their

belongings here. When they do so, check the Lost and Found Book for the record and direct them to the Housekeeping Office.

All items that are returned to the guests must be signed by them on the Housekeeping's Lost and Found Book. Also ask the guests for the **description** of the items which they **claim** to be theirs, to be certain that they are given the right ones.

If there's no record of an item which the guests claim to have left in the restaurant, bars or in the room, check with Housekeeping as it could have been left elsewhere or found by the cleaners who handed it directly to the Housekeeping Office.

Vocabulary

maximum	*adj.* 最大值的;最大量的
duration	*n.* 持续;持续的时间;期间
duvet	*n.* 床罩;羽绒被
bathrobe	*n.* 浴衣;浴袍
adapter	*n.* 适配器;转接器
transformer	*n.* 变压器
kettle	*n.*(烧水用的)壶;小汽锅
mineral	*n.* 矿物;矿石;矿物质;汽水 *adj.* 矿物的;似矿物的
extension	*n.* 伸展;扩大;延长;延期
cord	*n.*(细)绳;线
vase	*n.* 装饰瓶;花瓶
obtain	*vt.* 获得;得到;达到(目的)
normally	*adv.* 正常地;通常地;正常情况下;一般情况下
belongings	*n.* 财产;所有物;行李;财物
description	*n.* 描述;形容;种类;类型
claim	*vt.* 声称;断言;索取 *vi.* 提出要求 *n.* 声称;索赔

Phrases and Expressions

on loan	暂借的;出借
in house	内部的;室内的
safe keeping	妥善保管

Proper Names

Guest Service Centre	宾客服务中心
Lost and Found Book	失物招领记录本

Task 1 True or false statements. Decide whether the following statements are True (T) or False (F) according to the text.

1. Extra items can be lent to the guests who are staying in the hotel. ( )
2. When a guest needs more coat hangers, GSC staff should ask him for his room number and send them immediately. ( )

3. When a cleaner finds a wallet left behind by a guest, he or she should hand it only to the shift leader. ( )
4. If the shift leader finds an item left behind by a guest, he or she can take it home to keep it safe. ( )
5. If a guest claims to have left his item in the hotel and the staff finds the record in the Lost and Found Book, the staff should give the item back to the guest immediately. ( )

Task 2 Questions. Read the text again and answer the following questions.

1. What should we do with the belongings left behind by a guest?
2. What should we do when a guest comes to claim the items?

Task 3 Blank filling. Fill in the blanks with the words given. Change the form when necessary.

maximum	in-house	on loan	normally	duration
belongings	claim	description	mineral	obtain

1. For the ________ of the strike, our shop will remain closed.
2. The police had come to my house and impounded all my ________.
3. Gregory's father had implanted in him an ambition to ________ an education.
4. The slim booklets ________ a range of services and facilities.
5. Dry curly hair naturally for ________ curl and shine.
6. A man ________ to be a journalist threatened to reveal details about her private life.
7. A lot of companies do ________ training.
8. The high quality ________ water has passed the state-level test.
9. This picture is ________ from the Louvre to the National Gallery.
10. ________, the transportation system in Paris carries 950000 passengers a day.

Part 4 Translation

Task 1 Translate the following passage into Chinese.

Help Us to Help Our Environment

Dear Guests,

Please help us to reduce the use of laundry chemicals and save precious energy. Placing towels on the bathroom floor will indicate that you wish to be provided with clean linen. Used towels placed on the rack will not be changed.

Your actions will make a world of difference.

Task 2 Sentence translation.

1. 我们的洗衣服务有两种。普通洗衣：8 小时；快洗：4 小时。请问您要哪一种？

2. 非常抱歉,您的药瓶被意外打碎了。我真诚地为此道歉。
3. 上午八点到下午六点的送洗的衣物将会在当天午夜前送回;而下午六点到次日八点的衣物将会在第二日下午两点之前送回。

Task 3 Translate the following passage into English.

中国结(The Chinese Knot)是一种古老的艺术形式。人们发现,绳结可以追溯到10万年前。中国人不仅用绳结来固定、包裹、狩猎、捕鱼,还用来记事,有些绳结纯粹起装饰作用。中国结具有文化内涵(culture connotation)。由于结在汉语中的发音与"吉"相近,吉的意思为"福、禄、寿、喜、财、安、康",这是中国人永恒的追求,因此有些中国结表达出人们的各种愿望。例如,新婚夫妇的房间通常用一个盘长结(Pan-chang Knot)来装饰,象征着永恒的爱情。

Part 5 Cultural Norms

常用词汇

Housekeeping	客房部	folding chair	叠椅
turndown service	夜床服务	fridge	冰箱
overnight staff	夜班员工	TV/television	电视
tidy up	整理	air conditioner	空调
extra	额外的	iron	熨斗;熨衣
laundry service	洗烫服务	lamp	灯
laundry form	洗衣单	bulb	灯泡
chamber maid	清理房间的女服务员	switch	开关
blanket	毯子	notepad	记事本
hotel directory	酒店指南	alarm clock	闹钟
TV remote	电视遥控器	wardrobe	衣柜
night table	床头柜	carpet	地毯
coat hanger	衣架	balcony	阳台
Venetian blind	百叶窗帘	ashtray	烟灰缸
French window	落地窗	ironing board	熨衣板
curtain	窗帘	coffee table	咖啡茶几
folding screen	屏风	luggage rack	行李架
plug	插头	bath tub	浴盆
socket	插座	shower bath	淋浴
wastebasket	废纸篓	shower head	花洒;淋浴喷头
chair	椅子	mirror	镜子
bench	条凳	washroom	卫生间
sofa	长沙发	water closet	厕所;抽水马桶
armchair	扶手椅	bath towel	浴巾

facecloth/face towel	洗脸毛巾	box spring	弹簧床垫
hand towel	擦手巾	fitted sheet	床垫套;床单
towel rack/towel rail	毛巾架	headboard	床头架
bathroom cabinet	卫生间镜箱	pillow	枕头
faucet/tap	水龙头	pillow case	枕头套
garbage bag	垃圾袋	top sheet	上层床单
toilet paper	卫生纸;手纸	bed spread	床罩
bath mat	浴室防滑垫	duvet cover	被套
laundry bag	洗衣袋	mug	马克杯
shampoo	洗发水	glass	玻璃杯
body wash	沐浴露	coffee maker	咖啡机
soap	肥皂	ice bucket	小冰桶
hair conditioner	护发素	coffee-mate	咖啡伴侣
body lotion	润肤乳液	white sugar	白糖
hot tub	热水浴盆	brown sugar	红糖
bed pad	床垫子;褥子	tea bag	茶包
mattress	床垫	straw	吸管

常用句子

1. Responses to requests：面对客人提出的要求，可以这样回应：
   Yes, sir. I'll take care of that right away. 好的，先生。我马上处理。
   I'll attend to that immediately. 我马上处理。
   I'm not sure. Let me talk to my supervisor. I'll be back in a moment. 我不确定。我先和我的主管谈谈。一会儿就回来。
   Of course, ma'am. I'll get right on that. 好的，女士。我马上处理。
   Certainly, sir. I'll be right back with that item. 好的，先生。我马上为您拿来。
   I'll see if I can find some. 我去看看能不能找到。
   I'll get some right away. 我马上拿一些过来。
2. Responses to problems or complaints：面对客人提出的问题或投诉，可以这样回应：
   I'll see to that right away Ma'am. 我立即来处理这件事，女士。
   I'll correct the situation immediately, sir. 我马上予以纠正，先生。
   I'm so sorry sir. That should never have happened. 非常抱歉，先生。这种情况不该发生。
   I'll take care of that right away sir. 我马上着手处理此事，先生。
   I'll see to it immediately. 我会立刻着手处理。
   I'll check about it and get back to you. 我去了解一下情况，稍后给您答复。
3. If you are not sure what a guest is asking for, you can say：如果没有听清楚客人的要求是什么，或者不确定是否正确理解了客人的话，那么你可以这样说：
   I'm sorry, would you please repeat? 抱歉，请您重复一遍您的话可以吗？

I beg your pardon? 您能再说一遍吗？

I'm sorry, sir. I'm not sure I understand. 抱歉，先生。我不确定是否听懂了您的意思。

I'm not sure I'm following you, sir. 我没听懂，先生。

或者你也可以重复一下所听到的话和你的理解，问问客人：Did you say...? 您是不是说……？

更多表达

1. Housekeeping. May I come in? 我是客房部的，可以进来吗？
2. Could you come back in three hours? 你能不能过 3 小时再来整理？
3. Excuse me. Can you clean my room now? 请问，你现在能为我打扫房间吗？
4. When would you like me to do your room, sir? 要我什么时间来给您打扫房间呢，先生？
5. You can do it now if you like. 如果您愿意，现在就可以打扫。
6. We will come and clean your room immediately. 我们马上过来为您打扫房间。
7. I'm sorry, sir, but could you wait another 30 minutes, please? 抱歉，先生，您能再等 30 分钟吗？
8. Your room will be ready before you come back from the restaurant, I promise. 我保证您的房间在您从餐厅回来之前就能整理好。
9. It's getting dark. Shall I draw the curtains for you? 天黑了，需要我拉上窗帘吗？
10. The hotel provides free shoe shining service for its guests. 本酒店免费为客人提供擦鞋服务。
11. I'll place some clean towels there. 我去换几条干净的毛巾。
12. Please tidy up a bit in the bathroom. I've just showered and it's quite a mess. 请打扫一下浴室。我刚刚洗过澡，浴室很乱。
13. I'd like you to replace the soiled tea cups. 我想让你把脏茶杯换掉。
14. Why don't you throw in two extra blankets? 再拿两条毯子过来，可以吗？
15. I would like you to get me a bath towel. 我想请你给我拿一条浴巾。
16. Certainly, sir. I'll be right back. 好的，先生。我马上就回来。
17. I'd appreciate it if... 如果……的话，我会很感激。
18. Got it. = I got it. 我明白了。
19. I'm always at your service. 乐意效劳。
20. I'm awfully sorry, sir. 非常对不起，先生。
21. I do apologize. 我向您道歉。
22. No problem, sir. 没问题，先生。
23. Could you wait till tomorrow? 您能等到明天吗？
24. When can I get my laundry back? /When can I have my laundry back? 我何时能取回送洗的衣服呢？
25. Excuse me. Have you any laundry? 打扰一下，请问有没有要洗的衣服？
26. The laundry man is here to collect it. 洗衣房服务员来这儿收要洗的衣服了。
27. If you have any, please just leave it in the laundry bag behind the bathroom door. 如果

您有衣服要洗，请放在浴室门后的洗衣袋里。

28. Please tell us or notify in the list whether you need your clothes ironed, washed, dry-cleaned or mended and also what time you want to get them back. 请告诉我们或在洗衣单上写明您的衣服是否需要熨烫、水洗、干洗或缝补，还要写明需要何时取。
29. Could you send someone up for my laundry, please? 请问，你们能派人来收要洗的衣服吗？
30. A valet will be up in a few minutes. 洗熨工马上就到。
31. Will the color run in the wash? 洗衣时会掉色吗？
32. We'll dry-clean the dress. 我们将干洗这条裙子。
33. We'll stitch it before washing. 我们会在洗之前把衣服缝好。
34. I'd like this sweater to be washed by hand in cold water. 这件毛衣要用冷水手洗。
35. The room is too cold for me. I feel rather cold when I sleep. 这个房间太冷了。我睡觉时感到很冷。
36. There seems to be something wrong with the toilet. 我房间里的抽水马桶好像出了点问题。
37. What's the trouble? 哪里出问题了？
38. The toilet doesn't flush. 抽水马桶不冲水了。
39. Let me see. Oh, it's clogged. 让我看看。噢，它堵住了。
40. The water tap has been dripping all night long. 水龙头一整夜都在滴水。
41. Hi, I'm in 408 and my TV doesn't seem to be working. 你好，我在408号房，这里的电视机好像有些问题。
42. The picture is wobbly. 图像不稳定。
43. Please wait just a few minutes. 请稍等几分钟。
44. We will send someone up to take a look at it in a few minutes. 我们马上派人上来看看。
45. We'll send someone to repair it immediately. 我们会马上派人来修的。
46. We can have it repaired. 我们能找人修理。
47. Anything else you need today? = Is there anything else that you need today? 您今天还有什么需要的吗？
48. If there is anything more you need, please let us know. 如果您还有其他什么需要，请告诉我们。

Part 6 Supplementary Reading

Directions: Have you ever come across some guests who would make all kinds of requests? Read the following dialogue between a guest (**A**) and a hotel housekeeper (**B**) and find out what the guest wants exactly. Also, think about whether there are other sentences to replace the underlined one, with its meaning unchanged.

A: I'd like to request some more amenities (酒店一次性用品).

B: I'm sorry, sir. I'm not sure I understand.

A: I'm talking about the free stuff, like soap, lotion and shampoo.

B: Oh, I see. So, you're saying that you've already run out of your amenities.

A: No, no. I've got plenty left, enough for the next few days.

B: Now I'm confused again! What is the problem?

A: What am I going to do about souvenirs (纪念品)? I need to take home some souvenirs.

B: Oh, I get it! You would like souvenirs!

A: Yes, souvenirs.

B: Sir, our souvenir shop carries all those items, and as a guest you get a discount.

A: Please! Free souvenirs are the only true souvenirs.

B: I understand completely, sir. Housekeeping will bring you souvenirs in just a moment.

Here are some sentences to replace the underlined one:

- What do you mean by amenities, sir?
- Could you be a little more specific, sir?
- I'm sorry, sir. I'm not sure I understand.
- By amenities, exactly what do you mean, please?
- I'm not sure I'm following you, sir.
- I'm losing you, sir. What's the problem?

So what the guest wants exactly are some soap, lotion and shampoo as souvenirs, which is bizarre and funny. Some guests would make all kinds of requests, which are sometimes quite demanding. How should you respond to them? The following example might give you some hints. At a hotel in North Carolina, a guest asked for a unicorn to be waiting in his room upon arrival. Concierge Katie Brown purchased a unicorn plush toy and drafted a cheeky but amiable note as a special surprise.

Beloved Guest,

We saw your request for a unicorn. Unfortunately this is the wrong season. Due to their migratory habits, unicorns currently inhabit the second star to the right of twilight. They are expected to return here sometime this June. In the meantime, we hope that you can accept this very accurate artist rendition of our native fauna. If this is unacceptable, we do profusely apologize. As you are not the first guest to express interest in our local wild-life, we have planned a meeting with the head unicorn, on perhaps adjusting mythical creatures' move to somewhere outside the universe to better align with our guest wishes.

Our sincerest apologies.

Katie Brown

Chapter 6

Information Desk

Study Objectives

1. To have a basic knowledge of Information Desk service.
2. To grasp the words and expressions frequently used at Information Desk.
3. To get related information and improve comprehension skills through listening and reading.
4. To be able to respond professionally to guests' questions and requests and offer the information or services needed, including giving directions and recommending activities or tourist attractions.

Lead in

Generally speaking, Information Desk offers information service. Work in pairs and discuss with your partner and answer the following question.

What does an Information Desk clerk in a hotel do to help guests?

Part 1 Listening

Task 1 Dialogues. Listen to the following short dialogues and fill in the blanks according to what you hear.

(**Guest-G Staff-S**)

Dialogue 1

G: Could you tell me how to get to ____________________?

S: Sure. Take this ____________________ and go down the steps on your right. At the ____________________ of the steps there is a ____________________. Go over the bridge and turn right. ____________________ until you get to the Spa. It's about 100 meters from the bridge.

Dialogue 2

G: Excuse me. Where can I buy some ____________________?

S: There is a ____________________ on the ground floor selling all kinds of __________.

Dialogue 3

S: Good afternoon, madam. ________________?

G: Yes, please. I need some information about ________________.

Dialogue 4

G: Would you please tell me ________________ of the dining room?

S: Certainly, sir. ________________, it nearly serves all day long.

Dialogue 5

G: Good morning. ________________ whose name is Henry Jackson.

S: ________________, please?

Task 2 Conversations. Listen to the following conversations and fill in the blanks according to what you hear. The missing words and phrases in Conversation 1 and the missing sentences in Conversations 2 and 3 have been provided in the boxes, and you can choose them from the boxes to fill in the blanks.

Conversation 1 A guest is asking questions at the Information Desk.

free	lobby	accommodate	elevator	trainer	hours
extra	present	patrons	fitness	satisfactory	gym

(Guest-G Staff-S)

G: Excuse me. Does this hotel have a gym?

S: Yes, sir. We try to ________ all needs of our ________, including ________. I think you'll find our ________ quite ________.

G: So, would you tell me where it is?

S: The gym is just below the ________. Take the ________ or the stairs. You can't miss it.

G: Am I going to be charged ________ for using the gym?

S: No, the gym is ________ to guests. Take your room key, however, so you can get in.

G: Great! What are the ________ of this gym?

S: Sir, the gym is open seven days a week, twenty-four hours a day.

G: One more question, do you offer trainer services along with the gym?

S: I'm sorry, sir, but we have no ________. We might be getting one in the near future. But at the ________ time, no.

G: All right. Thank you.

S: You're welcome. Have a nice day.

Conversation 2　A visitor looks for a guest.

Please wait a minute, let me phone him Mr. Miller said he's waiting for you in his room It's my pleasure May I have his full name, please Just a moment, please. I'll look over the register

(Guest-G　Staff-S)

S: Good afternoon. How may I help you?

G: Good afternoon. I'm looking for a friend, Mr. Miller. Could you tell me which room he is in?

S: Mr. Miller? ______________________.

G: OK. Thanks.

S: (*The staff looks over the register*) Miller, Mr. Miller? There are several Millers here today.

____?

G: Mr. Andrew Miller from the United States. Isn't he staying at this hotel?

S: Oh, yes, here's his name Mr. Andrew Miller and family. They are in Suite 603.

____.

S: (*After making a phone call to Mr. Miller*)

____.

G: Thank you. By the way, would you please show me where the lift is?

S: Sure, sir. This way, please. Here it is.

G: Thank you.

S: ______________________.

Conversation 3　A guest picks up his room key.

Could you please sign here for the receipt of your key Excuse me, sir, but may I see your Room Identification Slip Could you sign for that, too

(Guest-G　Staff-S)

G: Hi, my name is Daniel Bush and I am in Room 1225. May I have my key, please?

S: ____, please?

G: Sure. Here it is.

S: Thank you, sir. ________________________________?

G: OK.

S: Thank you. Your key, sir, and there is a registered mail for you. ______________?

G：Yes，of course.

S：Thank you，sir. Have a good night.

Part 2 Speaking

Task 1 Work in pairs. Read and complete the following dialogue by translating the Chinese sentences in the parentheses into English.

(Guest-A Information Desk Clerk-B)

A：Hi，is this where I can get information on tours?

B：Yes，I can help you with that. ________________________ (您想要什么类型的旅游)? There are some great city tours that are half-day or full-day.

A：You know，we've explored the city a lot since we've been here. I was actually thinking of a side trip.

B：Oh，sure. We have excursions to nearby attractions. ________________________ (有一日游或两天一晚之旅，就看您选择哪个了).

A：I think I'm interested in a hiking trip to the mountains. I'm big on nature. Are the overnight trips expensive?

B：No，not at all. They are very moderately priced，starting at ＄100 and up. Here's a brochure on the three hiking tours that are available. ________________________ (这三个行程都有导游陪同，且均包括餐饮和交通).

A：________________________ (需要提前预订吗)?

B：Yes，sir. ________________________ (该公司要求您提前24小时预订).

A：All right. I'll take a look at the brochure. Can you book that for me or do I call the company directly?

B：________________________ (我可以帮您预订). Just stop by when you've made a decision and I'll take care of it for you.

A：That's great. Thanks a lot for your help.

B：It's my pleasure. ________________________ (有什么问题请告诉我).

A：I will. Thanks.

Vocabulary

explore	*vt.* 探索；探测；探险
excursion	*n.* 远足；短途旅游
attraction	*n.* 吸引；观光胜地；景点
overnight	*adj.* 通宵的；晚上的；前夜的
moderately	*adv.* 适度地；(价格)适中地；公道地
reservation	*n.* 预订；保留意见
brochure	*n.* 小册子
available	*adj.* 可用的；可得到的；有用的；有效的

transportation　　n. 运输;运输系统;运输工具

decision　　n. 决定;决策

Notes

1. There are some great city tours that are half-day or full-day. 有几条很棒的半天或全天城市观光线路。

   给客人提供旅游信息或其他介绍说明时,可以用"There be..."句型,意思是"有",表示"人或事物的存在",也可以用"We have..."或者"We've got"等句型,后者更为口语化。

   这里的 half-day 是指"半天的",而 full-day 意思是"一整天的"。关于旅游的类型有很多,比如,本对话中出现的 city tour(城市观光)、side trip("便游",意思就是随意地走走看看)和 hiking trip(徒步旅行)。除此之外,还有 coach tour (乘大客车旅游)、luxury tour(豪华游)、budget tour(经济实惠游)、self-driving tour(自驾游)、cruise and water tour(邮轮和观光船游览)、private tour(私人游)、package tour/group tour(跟团游),以及 SIC(全称为 seat-in-coach tour,意思为"拼团游")等。

2. They are very moderately priced. 它们(这些旅游线路)的价格非常公道。

   这里的 price 是动词,而 be priced 用的是被动语态,意为"被定价",因此 be moderately priced 的意思就是"定价公道的",相当于 be reasonably priced,"价格合理的"。例如:

   Think about your sales and marketing strategy, include information on how the product or service will be priced, channels to market, advertising and marketing plans.

   想想你的销售和营销策略,包括产品和服务如何定价、市场渠道、广告和营销计划。

3. I'm big on nature. 我热爱大自然。

   词组 be big on 主要用在口语中,意为"喜爱,对……狂热的;偏爱,特别喜欢;热衷于"。

4. 词组 stop by 意为"顺便访问;顺便过来一下"。例如:

   No need to stop by the reception. Guests can go straight to their room and place their phone in front of the lock and the door opens.

   不需要在前台停留。客人可以直接走到他们的房间,把手机放在房门锁的前面,门就开了。

Task 2　Work in pairs. Choose the correct sentences provided to complete the following dialogue and then practice and perform it with your partner.

A. Of course, madam.

B. Our bellman can arrange for a taxi.

C. My pleasure.

D. Good afternoon, madam. Can I help you?

E. I will get him to take care of that immediately. What time would you like to be picked up?

F. A taxi will be here shortly, madam.

G. You may take a taxi, madam. It saves a lot of trouble.

H. Well, our hotel is in Xiaoshan District. It's a pretty long way to go to Lou Wai Lou Restaurant.

(**Hotel Staff-A Guest-B**)

A: ____________1____________

B: Could you tell me how to get to Lou Wai Lou Restaurant on Gushan Road? I have an appointment with a friend there, but I can't find the exact spot on the map.

A: ____________2____________ You can take the Bus No. 323 and get off at Xintang Road. Go across the road. There you can change to Bus No. 45, and there is a stop right by Lou Wai Lou Restaurant.

B: It seems too complicated. I'll get lost, I'm afraid.

A: ____________3____________

B: That's a good idea.

A: ____________4____________

____________5____________

B: The sooner the better.

A: ____________6____________

B: Fantastic. I'll just wait in the lounge area. Will you please let me know when the taxi arrives?

A: ____________7____________

B: Thank you very much.

A: ____________8____________

Task 3 Role-play.

1. Work in pairs and make up a dialogue according to the following situation: A guest is asking the hotel staff at Information Desk about facilities in the hotel. You can refer to the sample below and use the given words.

Sample:

Given words: cigarette, souvenir, Chinese restaurant, western-style restaurant, the second floor

(**Guest-G Staff-S**)

G: Excuse me, would you please tell me where I can buy some cigarettes?

S: Of course, sir. There is a shop on the ground floor which sells both Chinese and foreign cigarettes.

G: Can I also get some souvenirs there?

S: Yes. There is a counter selling all kinds of souvenirs.

G: OK. Another question: Where is the restaurant?

S: We have Chinese restaurant and a western-style restaurant. Which one do you prefer?

G: I'd like to try some Chinese food today.

S: Then you can go to the second floor. The Chinese restaurant is right beside the lift.

You can't miss it.

G: Thanks a lot.

S: It's my pleasure.

Now it's your turn to make up a dialogue!

Given words:
dining room service hours: 7:00 a. m. to 10:00 p. m.
bar and cafe service hours: 2:00 p. m. till midnight
hot water supply: 6:00 a. m. till midnight
other services: barber shop, laundry, store, post and telegram services, newspaper stand, table tennis

2. Work in pairs and practice the following dialogue, and then make up a new dialogue according to the following situation: A guest is asking the hotel staff at Information Desk for sightseeing advice, and the staff recommends some famous attractions in Hangzhou and ways to get there. You can use the given information for reference.

(Guest-G Staff-S)

G: Good morning. The Front Desk told me to ask you for sightseeing advice.

S: Of course. I'd be more than happy to help. I am, after all, the hotel's concierge.

G: Concierge? What exactly is that?

S: We advise you on where to visit, eat, or shop during your stay here in New York.

G: Great! So where should I start my sightseeing?

S: The Statue of Liberty is always a good place to begin.

G: I saw the Statue of Liberty on my last visit here. Can you recommend somewhere else?

S: Hmm. What type of interests do you have?

G: In my spare time, I really like to view art and go running.

S: Aha! Have you been to Central Park or the Museum of Modern Art?

G: No, but I've heard a lot about both.

S: Well, Central Park is wonderful for running. Afterwards, you should head to the Museum to enjoy the art.

G: That sounds like a plan. Thanks a lot. But can you tell me how to get there?

S: It's a little far away from here. Would you like me to call a taxi for you?

G: Yes. That would be great! Thank you!

S: My pleasure. I'm sure you'll have a good time there.

Now it's your turn to make up a dialogue!

Information for references:

West Lake (西湖): It is a unique national park, which was named a UNESCO World Heritage Site in 2011.

Broken Bridge (断桥): Located at the east end of the Bai Causeway, the bridge tells of the love between a secular boy and a snake-turned girl.

Zhejiang Provincial Museum (浙江省博物馆): It has a large collection of cultural relics exceeding 100000, and features archaeological finds unearthed within the province.

Lingyin Temple (灵隐寺): It is also known as Monastery of the Soul's Retreat.

The Xixi National Wetland Park (西溪国家湿地公园): By now it has remained China's first and the only national wetland park.

Song Dynasty Town (宋城): It is perhaps China's largest theme park of Song Culture at present.

Part 3 Reading

Information Desk Clerk Training, Qualifications, and Advancement

Hotel, **motel**, and **resort** desk clerks **deal** directly **with** the public, so a professional appearance and a pleasant **personality** are important. A clear speaking voice and fluency in English are also essential, because these employees talk directly with hotel guests and the public and frequently use the telephone. Good spelling and computer literacy are needed, because most of the work involves use of a computer. In addition, speaking a foreign language fluently is increasingly helpful, because of the growing international guests of many **properties**.

Most hotel, motel, and resort desk clerks receive **orientation** and training on the job. Orientation may include an explanation of the job duties and information about the establishment, such as the arrangement of sleeping rooms, availability of additional services, a business or fitness center, and location of guest facilities, restaurants and other nearby retail stores. New employees learn job tasks through **on-the-job** training **under the guidance of** a **supervisor** or an experienced desk clerk. They often receive **additional** training on **interpersonal** or customer service skills and on how to use the computerized reservation, room **assignment**, and **billing systems** and equipment. Desk clerks typically continue to receive instruction on new procedures and on company policies after their **initial** training ends.

Formal academic training generally is not required. Most employers look for people who are friendly and customer-service oriented, well **groomed**, and display the **maturity** and self-confidence to demonstrate good judgment. Desk clerks, especially in high-volume and **higher-end** properties should be **quick-thinking**, show **initiative**, and be able to work as a member of a team. Hotel managers **typically** look for these personal characteristics when hiring first-time desk clerks, because it is easier to teach company policy and computer skills.

Large hotel and motel chain may offer better opportunities for advancement than small, independently owned establishments. The large chains have more extensive career ladder programs and may offer desk clerks an opportunity to participate in a management training program. Employment of hotel, motel, and resort desk clerks is expected to grow about as fast as the average for all occupations through 2014, as more hotels, motels, and other lodging establishments are built and **occupancy rates** rise. Job opportunities for hotel and motel desk clerks also will **result from** a need to replace workers, because many of these clerks either transfer to other occupations that offer better pay and advancement opportunities or simply leave the workforce altogether. Opportunities for part-time work should continue to be plentiful, because these businesses typically are staffed 24 hours a day, 7 days a week. Employment of hotel and motel desk clerks should **benefit from** an increase in business and leisure travel. With the increased number of units requiring staff, employment opportunities for desk clerks should be good.

Vocabulary

motel	*n.* 汽车旅馆
resort	*vi.* 求助于或诉诸某事物　*n.* 求助；诉诸；度假胜地
personality	*n.* 人格；人品；个性
property	*n.* 特性；属性；财产；地产
orientation	*n.* 方向；定位；取向；任职培训
supervisor	*n.* 监督者；管理者；主管
additional	*adj.* 额外的；附加的；另外的
interpersonal	*adj.* 人与人之间的；人际的
assignment	*n.* 分给；分配；任务；工作
initial	*adj.* 最初的；开始的
groom	*vt.* 使整洁；使(动物)清洁；准备　*vi.* 打扮　*n.* 新郎
maturity	*n.* 成熟；完备
initiative	*n.* 主动性；主动精神；倡议　*adj.* 自发的；创始的
typically	*adv.* 典型地；代表性地；通常

Phrases and Expressions

deal with	处理；对待；处置
on-the-job	在职的
under the guidance of	在……指导下
billing system	付费系统
high-end	高端的；高档的
quick-thinking	思维敏捷的
occupancy rate	房屋占用率；居住率
result from	产生于……；由……引起
benefit from	通过……获益；受益于

Task 1　True or false statements. Decide whether the following statements are True (T) or False (F) according to the text.

1. Hotels, motels and resorts are receiving a growing number of international guests. (　　)

2. Typically, you need to receive formal academic training to be a qualified hotel Front Desk clerk. ( )
3. Hotel employers prefer employees who look neat and friendly and put customer service first. ( )
4. If you pursue better career advancement chances, small establishments provide a good choice for you to take part in a management training program. ( )
5. It is estimated that through 2014, employment of hotel, motel, and resort desk clerks will increase at the average growth rate for all occupations. ( )

Task 2 Questions. Read the text again and answer the following questions.

1. What are the qualifications for a hotel information desk clerk?
2. What trainings do hotel desk clerks receive?
3. What do you think of the employment of hotel desk clerks in the future?

Task 3 Blank filling. Fill in the blanks with the words given. Change the form when necessary.

resort	orientation	benefit from	result from	initiative
typically	assignment	supervisor	initial	additional

1. If you ________ an activity or a person, you make sure that the activity is done correctly or that the person is doing a task or behaving correctly.
2. If you ________ a piece of work to someone, you give them the work to do.
3. We should provide them with ________ background or with supplementary information.
4. ________ is basic information or training that is given to people starting a new job, school, of course.
5. She was disappointed by his lack of ________.
6. I feel that women in all types of employment can ________ joining a union.
7. For a beach ________ with a difference, try Key West.
8. Many hair problems ________ what you eat.
9. You use the word ________ to describe something that happens at the beginning of a process.
10. ________, the Norwegians were on the mountain two hours before anyone else.

Part 4 Translation

Task 1 Translate the following passage into Chinese.

Dear Guest, welcome to our hotel. I'd like to give you some information about our services in order to make your stay here pleasant and comfortable.

Our Central Service Desk is in the lobby on the first floor. It provides services such as check-in and check-out, plane and train ticket booking, taxi hiring, etc. Also, there are umbrellas, rain shoes and coats on loan. The restaurant is on the second floor and there is a coffee room on the first floor, where you may taste wines and spirits, drinks and snacks. The hotel also has a specialty restaurant to the east of the courtyard where famous local dishes are prepared by our top chefs. For banquet, reception, cocktail party, or birthday cake reservations, please contact the service desk of the dining hall.

Task 2 Sentence translation.

1. We have both group prices and FIT (Foreign Independent Tourist) prices.
2. 酒吧在这一层,请沿着走廊一直走,到尽头右转,酒吧就在左手边。
3. 酒店后面有很漂亮的花园和水塘,那里非常适合跑步和散步。

Task 3 Translate the following passage into English.

丝绸之路沿途的大批历史文物、引人入胜的自然风光及富有情趣的地方文化,使这一长途远游成了世界上最精彩的旅游项目之一。在丝绸之路的中国段,沿线散居着许多热情好客的中国少数民族,他们对来自世界各地的游客都以礼相待。这里的食物和工艺品不同于中国中部的食物和工艺品。这里的民间传说,如同《天方夜谭》中的一般神奇,听来别有一番情趣。

Part 5 Cultural Norms

常用词汇

concierge	礼宾员	roof garden	屋顶花园
lounge	休息室	cigarette	香烟;纸烟
amuse	给……娱乐	souvenir	纪念品;纪念物
amusement	消遣;娱乐;乐趣	corridor	走廊
lobby	大厅;休息室	baby-sitting service	托婴服务
supply	供应	on-call doctor	应召医生
bar	酒吧间	vending machine	自动售货机
cafe	咖啡厅	elevator/lift	电梯
afternoon tea	下午茶	Chinese restaurant	中餐厅
cafeteria	自助餐厅	Western-style restaurant	西餐厅
barber shop	理发店;美发厅	business center	商务中心
beauty salon	美容厅	conference hall	会议厅
souvenir	纪念品	entertainment center	娱乐中心
post and telegram services	邮政和电报服务	sauna room	桑拿房
newspaper stand	报亭	fitness center/gym	健身房
table tennis	乒乓球;桌球	dumbbell	哑铃
tennis court	网球场	stationary bicycle	锻炼用固定自行车

stair climber	阶梯踏步机	night life	夜生活
massage	按摩	bus route	公交车线路
spa	水疗	subway route	地铁线路
spa pool	矿泉疗养浴场	first aid kit	急救工具箱
indoor pool	室内游泳池	arrival/departure transfer	到店/离店接送
outdoor pool	露天游泳池	car rental	汽车出租
children's pool	儿童游泳池	yacht rental	游艇出租
movie theatre	影戏院	parking	泊车
acrobatic show	杂技表演	museum	博物馆
folk art	民间艺术	coach	旅游大巴
ball room	舞厅	shuttle bus	班车
playroom	游戏室;娱乐室	travel agent	旅行社;旅游代理
golf	高尔夫	tourist sites	旅游胜地;景点
scuba diving	器械潜水	airline	航空公司
horse riding	骑马	time table	时刻表
water sports	水上运动	departure time	出发时间;起飞时间
fashion boutique	时装精品店	arrival time	到达时间
shopping area	购物中心	flight	航班

问询处介绍

酒店、宾馆的问询处需要回答客人的各种提问,准确清楚地给予客人相应的信息。这些问询可大致分为以下三大类。

1. 有关酒店内部的问询。

   有关酒店内部的问询通常涉及:

   (1) 餐厅、酒吧、商场所在的位置及营业时间。

   (2) 宴会、会议、展览会举办的场所及时间。

   (3) 酒店提供的其他服务项目、营业时间及收费标准。

2. 有关住宿旅客的问询。

   有关住宿旅客的问询通常涉及:

   (1) 客人是否住在本酒店。

   (2) 客人的房间号。

3. 有关店外情况的问询。

   有关店外情况的问询通常涉及:

   (1) 酒店所在城市的旅游景点及其交通情况。

   (2) 主要娱乐场所、商业区、商业机构、政府部门、大专院校及有关企业的位置和交通情况。

   (3) 近期内大型文艺、体育活动的基本情况。

   (4) 市内交通情况。

   (5) 国际国内航班飞行情况。

相应地，问询处员工也需要熟练掌握相关表达方法来回应这些问询。

常用句子

1. 掌握酒店内所有设施、服务、活动、会展等的中英文表达及其准确的服务时间等。

   例如：

   Guest：Does the guest house offer any other service? 宾馆里还有哪些服务项目？

   Information desk clerk：We have a restaurant，a cafe，a barber shop，a laundry，a store，post and telegram services，a newspaper stand，a billiard room，table tennis，video games and so on. 我们有餐厅、咖啡厅、理发室、洗衣房、小卖部、邮电服务、报刊供应柜、台球厅、乒乓球和电子游戏等。

   若一时忘了某一设施的服务时间，可以说"Just a moment，please. Let me check it for you"，马上查证之后告知客人，切勿给出模糊或错误的信息。

   表达服务时间的时候，可以说"It's open from ... to ..."，例如：

   When will the bar and cafe be open? 酒吧和咖啡馆什么时间开放？

   From 3:00 p. m. till midnight. 从下午三点到晚上十二点。

   实际对话中可以参考以下例子：

   （Staff-S　Guest-G）

   S：Good morning. What can I do for you?

   G：Can you tell me when I can get a meal in the hotel restaurant this evening?

   S：Yes，certainly. The service of dinner starts at 7:30 and last orders are taken at 9:45.

   G：I see. Do I need to book a table?

   S：No，that's not really necessary.

2. Giving directions 导览。

   导览的基本用词：

   —A is next to B.

   　A 在 B 旁边。

   —B is between A and C.

   　B 在 A 与 C 之间。

   —A is on top of B.

   　A 在 B 上方。

   —A is under B.

   　A 在 B 下方。

   —A is along the hallway on the left.

   　A 在走廊的左侧。

   —A is along the hallway on the right.

   　A 在走廊的右侧。

   —A is to the left.

   　A 在左转的地方。

   —A is to the right.

A 在右转的地方。

—A is at the end of the hallway to the left.

A 在走廊尽头的左侧。

—A is at the end of the hallway to the right.

A 在走廊尽头的右侧。

—A is through B.

穿过 B 就是 A 了。

—Go straight.

请直走。

—This is the Lobby floor.

这是大厅。

—The garage is two floors down.

车库是在地下二楼。

—(*First*,)**go down** this street (for ________ blocks).

(首先,)沿着这条街走(________个街区)。

—(*Then*,)**turn left/right** at the traffic light.

(然后,)在红绿灯处向左转/向右转。

—(*After that*,)**go straight** on ________ Street **until you get to** the ________.

(之后,)沿着 ________街一直走到 ________。

—(*When you get to the* ________,)turn left/right again.

(到 ________之后,)再左转/右转。

—(*Then*,) **stay on** ________ Avenue for about ________ meters.

(然后,)沿着 ________大道走大约 ________米。

—It's on your right, next to the ________. You can't miss it.

就在你的右边, ________旁边。你一定能找到。

实际对话中可以参考以下例子:

(Guest-G Staff-S)

G: Excuse me, can you tell me where the nearest supermarket is?

S: There is a supermarket two blocks away from the hotel.

G: How can I get there?

S: After you go out of the hotel, turn right and walk along the street until you see a red building. The supermarket is in it.

G: Thanks. By the way, where can I find an ATM near here?

S: At the bank next door.

G: Which way?

S: Take a left turn after stepping out of the hotel. The bank is at the corner. You can't miss it.

G: Thank you very much.

S: You're welcome.

3. 有关店外情况的英文表达由于内容涉及面非常广，需要问询处员工平时对酒店所在城市的旅游点及大型活动和交通情况多多关注，而且在外宾来询问时需要清楚哪里可以查找到具体信息，平时还需积累这些信息的英文表达。比如，在提供火车出发时刻和到达时刻时可以说"The train leaves at ...（出发时刻）and arrives in...（目的地）at...（到达时刻）"。

实际对话中可以参考以下例子：

（**Staff-S　Guest-G**）

S：Information. How can I help you?

G：I'd like some information about trains from Guangzhou to Beijing，please.

S：Yes. There are two. One leaves Guangzhou at 8：00 and it arrives in Beijing at 11：35 the next morning.

G：Leaving at 8：00 and arriving at 11：35?

S：That's right. Alternatively，there's another at 15：00 which arrives in Beijing at 16：00 the next day.

G：Did you say 16：00?

S：Yes.

G：Oh，well，that one sounds better. Thank you so much.

S：You're welcome.

给客人提建议或者推荐逛街和旅游地点时可以说"I think it would be better to go to..." "I recommend..."或者"The best place is..."，例如：

S：Good morning，sir. May I help you?

G：I'd like to buy a watch. Where is the best place to go?

S：The best place is Xidan. There are many shops selling colorful watches there. The prices are expensive as well. It's about 20 minutes by taxi from here.

G：That sounds fine. Thanks a lot.

S：You're welcome，sir.

更多表达

1. Do you have a place where I can exercise? 这里有健身的地方吗？
2. Would you tell me where it is? 你能告诉我在哪里吗？
3. You're actually standing above it. Just take the elevator or stairs down one level. 您正站在健身房上方。乘电梯或走楼梯往下一层就是了。
4. Am I going to be charged extra for using the gym? 使用健身房需要额外付钱吗？
5. Sir，you can use the gym for free. All you need is your room key. 先生，您可以免费使用健身房。只需您的房门钥匙即可。
6. And the gym hours are? 健身房开放时间呢？
7. Sir，our gym is open around the clock，every day of the week. 先生，我们的健身房一周七天、每天 24 小时开放。
8. One more question：do you have a trainer? 再问一个问题：有健身教练吗？
9. I'm sorry，sir，but we have no trainer. 抱歉，先生，我们没有教练。

10. Good afternoon. May I help you? 早上好。我能为您效劳吗？
11. Yes. I need to go to the Board Room. How do I get there? 是的。我要去董事会会议室，我该怎么走呢？
12. Take the elevator to the 7th floor. Turn right. It's on the right, Room 737. 乘电梯到七楼，然后右拐，它就在右边，737 号房间。
13. I don't know if they will have refreshments in the meeting. Where can I get something to drink? 不知道会议期间是否提供茶点。哪里有饮料呢？
14. There is a vending machine for Coke and soft drinks on all guest floors near the elevator. You can also find a coffee shop on the main floor after you go past the Front Desk. 所有住客楼层的电梯旁均有自动售卖机出售可乐和软饮料。您经过一楼前台之后会看到主楼层有一个咖啡厅。
15. Thanks a lot. 多谢。
16. You're welcome. Have a nice day. 不客气。祝您愉快。
17. May I help you with anything? 有什么可以为您效劳的吗？
18. Yes, please. Is there a coffee shop in the hotel? 是的。宾馆里有咖啡厅吗？
19. Yes. It's on the ground floor, near the Front Desk. 有，就在一楼，前台附近。
20. Do they sell food or just coffee? 那里出售食物吗？还是只卖咖啡？
21. They usually have a few sandwiches and snacks. 他们通常会提供一些三明治和点心。
22. Also, I need a razor. Should I try the gift shop? 我还需要一把刮胡刀。我是不是该去礼品店看看？
23. Did you say you need a razor? 您是说您需要刮胡刀吗？
24. Front Desk can probably help you. They usually have supplies like that. 前台也许可以帮您。通常他们会提供这类物品。
25. Madam, what can I do for you? 夫人，我能为您做些什么？
26. I'm looking for a man whose name is John. 我在寻找一位男士，他的名字叫约翰。
27. I'm looking for a friend, Mr. Brown. Could you tell me if he is in the hotel? 我在找一位朋友，布朗先生。你能告诉我他是住在这个饭店吗？
28. Could you tell me his room number, please? 请问他的房间号是多少？
29. I suppose it is 735. 我想他的房间号是 735 号。
30. Just a minute, please. I'll see if he is registered. 请稍等片刻。我看看他是否登记了。
31. He is in suite 705. Let me phone him. 他住在 705 号套房。我给他打电话。
32. There are two trains going to Xiamen every morning, No. D2291 and No. D377. 每天早晨有两列火车开往厦门，D2291 和 D377 次列车。
33. What time does the train No. D377 leave? D377 次列车什么时间发车？
34. At 8:05 in the morning and arrives in Xiamen at about 14: 57 in the afternoon. 早晨 8:05 出发，大概 14:57 到达厦门。
35. Good, I'll take this one. Could you get me two tickets for tomorrow here? 好，我就坐这趟车。能否帮我买两张明天的车票？
36. Sorry, sir. Please go to the Travel Service Agency in our hotel. It's on the first floor.

抱歉,先生。请去我们宾馆的旅行社订购。旅行社位于一楼。

37. Is there any place in the hotel where we can amuse ourselves? 旅馆里有娱乐场所吗?
38. If you want to take a walk, you can go to the garden. 如果您想散步,可以去花园。
39. There is a recreation centre on the first floor. 在一楼有个娱乐中心。
40. You can play billiards, table tennis, bridge, and go bowling. 您可以打台球、乒乓球、桥牌和保龄球。
41. Is there a place where we can listen to some music? 有听音乐的地方吗?
42. There is a music teahouse where you can enjoy both classical music such as Beethoven, Mozart, Liszt, and modern music, while having some Chinese tea or other soft drinks. 有个音乐茶座,您可以一边欣赏古典音乐,如贝多芬、莫扎特、李斯特的乐曲和现代音乐,一边品尝中国茶或其他软饮料。
43. Would you please tell me the daily service hours of the dining room? 请告诉我餐厅每天的服务时间,好吗?
44. From 7:00 a. m. till 10:00 p. m., nearly serving all day long. 从早上七点一直到晚上十点,几乎全天供应。
45. The vending machine is on the first floor of the hotel. Take the hall way to the left and pass the Front Desk to the stairs. Go down the stairs and continue along to the next set of stairs. Go up these stairs and the vending machine is to the right. 自动售货机在宾馆的一楼。沿着这条走廊左转,通过前台到楼梯口。走下楼梯,再往前走,到另一个楼梯口,走上楼梯,自动售货机就在右边。

Part 6 Supplementary Reading

Qualities of a Concierge

A concierge usually works as part of the Front Office team within a hotel. His job is to create a positive first impression of the hotel on guests, making their stay or visit more comfortable. To be a qualified concierge, he needs to possess some essential qualities and skills. For example, a good concierge should be familiar with his surroundings. At least he has to know the basics—the restaurants, the clubs, and the theaters, and be able to recommend places to guests on request. Secondly, a concierge needs to be patient because he may carry out more than one task at the same time. He might be showing one guest to the Reception Desk while another guest comes up for theater ticket booking.

Good communication skills are another quality for a concierge. He should be interested in meeting people and have a desire to help them. Problem-solving is also a key quality for a concierge. He needs to be able to solve problems that a guest encounters in a professional and efficient manner.

In order to ensure the above qualities, and of course many other qualities, a professional organization for concierges was formed in France in October 1929 by Ferdinand Gillet, which was called Les Clefs d'Or, meaning the Golden Keys. The Golden Key refers to an experienced concierge who stands behind the service booth in suit or tailcoat every day, ready to settle all the questions put forward by the guests. You can recognize the Golden Keys by the keys on the lapels on their uniforms.

These crossed golden keys are more than just the symbol of the organization, and they are the symbol of qualified and standardized service. The Golden Keys, who have received professional training, find joy in giving guests pleasant surprise and thus find their own value of life in serving others.

Cashier

Study Objectives

1. To have a basic knowledge of working as a hotel cashier.
2. To grasp the words and expressions frequently used by a hotel cashier.
3. To get related information on checking out, cashing checks, exchanging foreign currencies, etc., and improve comprehension skills through listening and reading.
4. To be able to respond professionally to guests' questions and requests and offer the information or services needed.

Lead in

Work in pairs and discuss with your partner and answer the following questions.

1. What does a hotel cashier do to help guests?
2. What skills should a hotel cashier acquire?

Part 1 Listening

Task 1 Dialogues. Listen to the following short dialogues and fill in the blanks according to what you hear.

(Cashier-C Guest-G)

Dialogue 1

C: Sir, 250 dollars ______________. Are you paying ______________ or ______________?

G: Credit card.

Dialogue 2

G: Can I pay with ______________?

C: Certainly, sir. May I have your ______________, please?

Dialogue 3

G: What's the 15 yuan for?

C: ____________ the phone calls you made from your room.

Dialogue 4

C: ____________. Would you like to check and see if the ____________ is correct?

G: OK.

Dialogue 5

C: Here are your ____________ and your ____________, sir. Thank you.

G: Thank you. Goodbye.

Task 2 Conversations. Listen to the following conversations and fill in the blanks according to what you hear. The missing words and phrases in Conversation 1 and the missing sentences in Conversation 2 have been provided in the boxes, and you can choose them from the boxes to fill in the blanks.

Conversation 1

charge	Certainly	in cash	settle	check
total	receipt	hotel services	meals	change
amount	makes a total of	long-distance phone call	at 500 yuan each	

(**Cashier-C Guest-G**)

C: Good morning, sir. May I help you?

G: Yes, I'd like to ____________ my bill.

C: ____________, sir. May I have your name and room number, please?

G: John Swift. Room 501. Here's my key.

C: Yes, Mr. Swift. Just a moment, please. Have you used any ____________ this morning?

G: No. I didn't use any services this morning.

C: OK, three nights ____________, and here are the ____________ that you had at the hotel. That ____________ 2150 yuan. Here's your bill. Would you like to ____________ and see if the ____________ is correct?

G: OK. Oh, what's this ____________ for?

C: Oh, that's for the ____________ you made from your room.

G: Yes, I remember now. OK. This is the ____________, right?

C: Yes, 2150 yuan in all. How would you like to pay, ____________ or by credit card?

G: In cash. Here you are, 2200 yuan.

C: Here are your ____________ and your ____________. Thank you.

G: Thank you. Goodbye.

Conversation 2

You would like to use it until July 10th Your box number is 520 Could you fill out this form I'd like to use a safety deposit box

(**Cashier-C　Guest-G**)

C: Good morning. May I help you?

G: Yes. ________________________.

C: Certainly, sir. ________________________, please?

G: Here you are.

C: Thank you, sir. ________________________?

G: Yes.

C: All right. This way, please. ________________________.

G: Thank you.

C: You're welcome.

Part 2　Speaking

Task 1　Work in pairs. Read and complete the following dialogue by translating the Chinese sentences in the parentheses into English.

(**Cashier-C　Guest-G**)

C: Good afternoon, sir. How may I help you?

G: Good afternoon. I'd like to settle my bill, please.

C: Certainly, sir. May I have your room key, please?

G: Sure. Here you are.

C: Just a minute, please. So ________________________ (您的账单总共为1522元).

G: Wait a minute, that's too much! I thought it was 1400 yuan even. That's what they said yesterday when we checked in. ________________________ (你介意让我看一下吗)?

C: ________________________ (一点都不介意，先生). Here you are.

G: Thanks. Well, what's this item for?

C: ________________________ (那是额外的送餐服务费).

G: Oh, I forgot. My wife did order a plate of nachos. Sorry.

C: No problem.

G: But it says the extra service charge is 112 yuan, so the total charge would be 1512, not 1522 yuan, isn't it?

C：Let me see. Oh，I'm sorry，sir，______________（您的账单有一个错误）. It is 1512 yuan indeed. ______________（请稍等，我为您纠正）.

G：OK. By the way，can you tell me how much that is in dollars，please?

C：Just a moment，sir. I'll calculate that for you. ______________（按今天的汇率，总计是 249 美元 12 美分）.

G：I see. OK.

C：______________（您要用信用卡付款吗）？

G：Yes. Here's my Credit Card. I'd like a receipt，please.

C：______________（抱歉，您的信用卡已被停用）. According to the regulations of bank，it must be cancelled. Here is your credit card.

G：Oh really? Then I'll pay cash. Here you are.

C：Thank you，sir. 1600 yuan. ______________（这是您的账单、收据和找零 88 元）. Could you check it，please? ______________（感谢您选择我们酒店）.

C：Thanks. Goodbye.

G：______________（欢迎下次光临）. Goodbye.

Vocabulary

total	*vt.* 总数达
item	*n.* 条款；项目记录；事项
charge	*n.* 费用
nachos	*n.*（墨西哥人食用的）烤干酪辣味玉米片
error	*n.* 误差；错误；过失
correct	*vt.* 改正
calculate	*vt.* 计算
regulation	*n.* 管理；规则
change	*n.* 找回的零钱

Notes

1. What's this item for? 这一项是什么费用？
   “what...for”表示目的或用途，这里的“what”是“for”的宾语，例如：
   That's what we're here for. 这是我们来这儿的目的。
2. My wife did order a plate of nachos. 我妻子确实点过一盘烤干酪辣味玉米片。
   这里的“did”表示强调，可以翻译为“确实/的确……”。用于表示强调的 do 可以有时态的变化，但其后的动词要用原形，例如：
   He does speak well! 他的确讲得很精彩！
   He did come but soon went back. 他的确来过，但很快就回去了。
   用于强调的 do 通常只用于现在时或过去时（即只有 do、does、did 这样的形式），不能用于进行时、完成时等形式（如不用于 is doing、has done 等）。

另外，do 还经常用于祈使句中表示强调。例如：

(1) 表示强调的请求。例如：Do come with us. 请一定要和我们一起去。

(2) 表示委婉或客气。例如：Do try this fish. 请尝尝这道鱼。

Do have another cup of coffee. 请再喝杯咖啡吧。

(3) 表示不耐烦。例如：Do stop talking！别说啦！

(4) 希望说服对方。例如：Do help me with this math problem. 请帮我解答这道数学题。

3. Can you tell me how much that is in dollars，please? 你能告诉我那相当于多少美元吗？
“in＋货币名称”表示的是“用……货币；换算成……货币；以……货币”。例如：
So how much is that chair worth in dollars? 这把椅子值多少美元？

4. But it says the extra service charge is 112 yuan. 但是上面写着额外的服务费是 112 元。
“say”在这里是“写着”的意思，例如：
Look at that sign. It says “No Parking”. 看那个标志，上面写着“禁止停车。”

Task 2　Work in pairs. Choose the correct sentences from A to L which are provided below to complete the following dialogue and then practice and perform it with your partner.

A. Would you like to sign the hotel guestbook too while you wait?
B. That's good to hear. Thank you again for staying at the Grand Woodward Hotel.
C. According to today's exchange rate，100 U. S. dollars is equal to 625 yuan. How much would you like to change?
D. I'm sorry，we don't，but we do offer exchange service.
E. Oh，before you go，would you be able to settle the mini-bar bill?
F. We do have a free airport shuttle service.
G. And here is your receipt and the change 62.5 yuan.
H. Would you please show me your passport?
I. Did you enjoy your stay with us?
J. Let's see. The bill comes to 237.50 yuan.
K. Yes. Here is the change and your receipt. Keep this exchange memo.
L. Thank you. Please fill in this exchange memo and sign your name on it.

(Cashier-C　Guest-G)

C: ____________1____________

G: Yes，very much so. However，I now need to get to the airport. I have a flight that leaves in about two hours，so what is the quickest way to get there?

C: ____________2____________

G: That sounds great，but will i t get me to the airport on time?

C: Yes，it should. The next shuttle leaves in 15 minutes，and it takes approximately 25 minutes to get to the airport.

G: Fantastic. I'll just wait in the lounge area. Will you please let me know when it will be leaving?

C: Of course, sir. ______3______

G: Oh, yes, certainly. How much will that be?

C: ______4______ How would you like to pay for that?

G: I'll pay cash, thanks, but I'll need a receipt so I can charge it to my company. Do you accept dollars?

C: ______5______

G: Could you change some U. S. dollars for me?

C: No problem, sir.

G: What is today's exchange rate for U. S. dollars?

C: ______6______

G: One hundred dollars. Here you are.

C: ______7______

G: Yes, here it is.

C: ______8______

G: I'll take care of it. Is that all right?

C: ______9______

G: Thank you for your help. Here is the 300 yuan for the mini-bar bill.

C: Thank you. ______10______ And, if you like you can leave your bags with the porter and he can load them onto the shuttle for you when it arrives.

G: That would be great. Thank you.

C: ______11______

G: Sure, I had a really good stay here and I'll tell other people to come here.

C: ______12______

Task 3 Role-play.

1. Read the conversation at the Cashier's Office. The parts are not in the correct order.
   Which parts are spoken by the Guest? Mark the parts with a "G".
   Which parts are spoken by the Cashier? Mark the parts with a "C".
   Write numbers on the lines.
   Then act out the conversation with a partner.

   (1) ________: Ah, so service is included. Don't you go in for tipping in China?
   (2) ________: Certainly sir. It's Mr. Arkwright, isn't it?
   (3) ________: Certainly sir. May I have the card please?
   (4) ________: Good morning sir. Can I help you?
   (5) ________: Here you are.
   (6) ________: I'd like to settle my bill.

(7) ________: Just a moment sir... Here we are. Four nights at 93 dollars, and here are the meals that you had at the hotel. That makes a total of 665 dollars.

(8) ________: Not very much sir.

(9) ________: Right. Now can I pay by VISA Card?

(10) ________: That's right. I'm leaving today, so I'd like to have my bill.

(11) ________: That's the twelve and a half percent service charge.

(12) ________: Um...What is this amount here?

(13) ________: Would you sign here please?

2. Work in pairs and make up a dialogue according to the following situation: A guest is settling his bill in the hotel. In Sample 1, the guest is paying by cash, while in Sample 2, he/she is charging the fee to his/her room. Refer to the samples below and make up your own dialogue by using the given words.

Given words: cocktail, tequila, swimming pool, fitness centre

Sample 1

(**Cashier-C　Guest-G**)

C: How will you be settling your bill sir?

G: I'll be paying by cash.

C: Yes sir, here's the bill.

G: Excuse me, but what is this charge for?

C: Let me see, it's for an apple pie.

G: But we didn't order apple pie.

C: I'm terribly sorry for the error, sir. Let me refigure this. Here you go, sir.

G: That looks right. Thank you.

C: Sorry for the error sir, and please come again.

Sample 2

(**Cashier-C　Guest-G**)

C: Would you like to pay for the tennis court in cash or charge it to your room?

G: Just charge it to my room please.

C: Yes sir, if you could just sign here.

G: There you are.

C: Thank you sir, have a pleasant day.

Part 3　Reading

Job Description for Front Office Cashier in the Hotels

Front Office cashiers **assume** responsibility for any cash used in processing Front Desk **transactions**. He/She normally **entails** answering guest inquiries regarding **fees** and services. They may also perform a **variety** of banking services for guests, such as check cashing and foreign currency exchange. All guest accounts are **balanced** by the cashier at the close of each shift.

Duties and responsibilities:

Operates **Front Office posting software.**

Completes guest check-in procedures.

Clarifies customers' questions or concerns about the charges on their bills.

Maintains adequate supplies of **stationery** for cashiers.

Assists with distribution of month end reports as directed by accounts or Front Office manager.

Attends meetings as required.

Maintains a **track** of all **high balance guests.**

Checks and follows up all bills on hold.

Gives on-the-job training for new staff.

Follows up all deposits to be paid.

Posts charges to guest accounts.

Handles **paid-outs.**

Transfers guest balances to other accounts as required.

Cashes checks for guests following the **approval** policy.

Completes guest check-out procedures.

Settles guest accounts.

Handles cash, traveller's cheques, credit cards and direct billing requests properly.

Posts non-guest **ledger payments.**

Makes discount adjustments.

Balances department totals at the close of the shift.

Balances cash at the close of the shift.

Manages **safe deposit boxes.**

Assists Front Desk staff on check-in when required.

Pre-requisites:

Education: High school graduate or **equivalent.** Must speak, read, write, and understand the primary language used in the workplace. Good presentation and team worker.

Experience: Previous hotel-related experience desired. Experience in operating hotel Front Office software.

Working Conditions

The environment in which a hotel cashier works is normally comfortable. She usually sits or stands behind a counter to perform her job. **Manual dexterity** is needed to operate adding machines and **cash registers.** Professional business **attire** is typically required for this position. Some hotels provide uniforms to all staff members to present a **unified** team image to guests and make their employees easily recognizable.

Educational Requirements

A high school diploma or equivalent is generally required to be a hotel cashier. Completed coursework in hospitality management or customer service is considered a **plus** for hotel cashier **applicants**. Previous experience in cash handling, accounting, public relations or customer relations is **desirable**.

Vocabulary

assume	*vt.* 假定;认为;承担;呈现
transaction	*n.* 交易;业务;事务;办理
entail	*vt.* 牵涉;需要;使必要
fee	*n.* (加入组织或做某事付的)费;专业服务费;业务报酬
variety	*n.* 多样;种类;变化
balance	*n.* 平衡 *vt.* & *vi.* (使)平衡 *vt.* 结平(账目)
stationery	*n.* 文具;办公用品
track	*n.* 小路;踪迹;轨道;方针;路线;追踪 *vt.* 监测;追踪
approval	*n.* 同意;批准;赞成
prerequisite	*n.* 先决条件;前提;必要条件 *adj.* 必须先具备的;必要的
equivalent	*adj.* 相等的;相当的
manual	*adj.* 手的;手工的 *n.* 手册;指南
dexterity	*n.* 灵巧;熟练;敏捷
attire	*n.* 服装;衣服
unified	*adj.* (unify 的过去式和过去分词)统一的;统一标准的
plus	*prep.* (表示运算)加;[口语]和 *n.* 加号;好处;附加物 *adj.* 附加的
applicant	*n.* 申请人;求职人;请求者
desirable	*adj.* 令人满意的;值得拥有的 *n.* 称心如意的人/[东西]

Phrases and Expressions

Front Office posting software	前台过账软件
high balance guest	高额消费客人(如果客人的消费已超出其现金或信用卡授权的押金额,就属于 high balance 房客,必须即刻联系客人补交押金)
paid-out	支出
ledger payment	分类账收支
safe deposit box	保险箱
cash register	(美)收银机,现金出纳机

Task 1 True or false statements. Decide whether the following statements are True (T) or False (F) according to the text.

1. The Front Office cashier performs banking services for guests, and he or she should balance all guest accounts at the beginning of his or her shift. ( )

2. It is the Front Office cashier's responsibility to train new staff. ( )
3. The Front Office cashier should always cash checks for guests. ( )
4. Front Office cashiers are required to dress casually to work in order to present a friendly image to guests. ( )
5. It would be an advantage for hotel cashier applicants if they have completed related coursework in customer service. ( )

Task 2 Questions. Read the text again and answer the following questions.

1. Does a hotel cashier need to help Front Dest staff with check-in?
2. What are the requirements of being a hotel cashier?

Task 3 Blank filling. Fill in the blanks with the words given. Change the form when necessary.

assume	entail	fee	variety	approval
equivalent	manual	unified	plus	desirable

1. West Hampstead has a ________ of good shops and supermarkets.
2. The state is not a ________ and internally coherent entity.
3. I told my mother I wanted to leave school but she didn't ________.
4. Eight kilometers is roughly ________ to five miles.
5. His ________ dexterity and fine spatial skills were wasted on routine tasks.
6. If someone ________ power or responsibility, they take power or responsibility.
7. He responded positively and accepted the ________ of £1000 I had offered.
8. Rolls Royce produces around 1000 extremely ________ cars a year.
9. The job of a choreologist（舞谱学家）________ teaching dancers the technique and performance of dance movements.
10. Experience of any career in sales is a big ________.

Part 4 Translation

Task 1 Translate the following passage into Chinese.

The Chinese like to drink green tea. Longjing, or to be exact, West Lake Longjing, is the name of one of the best green teas in China. It is only grown in the West Lake producing area in Hangzhou proper. Longjing green tea falls into different grades and the best is the first picking of the year and processed by hand.

Task 2 Sentence translation.

1. 不好意思，酒店规定不可以用信用卡来套取现金。您可以去银行提取现金，离这里才400米。

2. 先生，很抱歉您的签名和我所得到的打开保险箱的签名不一致。为了安全起见，我能看一下您的护照吗？
3. 我们只能兑换外汇牌上的这些外币，其他外币您可以去银行兑换。

Task 3 Translate the following passage into English.

京剧被称为中国的国粹(national opera)，起源于18世纪晚期，是将音乐、舞蹈、艺术和杂技(acrobatics)综合于一体的戏曲。在中国，京剧是所有戏曲中最有影响力和代表性的。中国的京剧有着200多年的历史，是中国的民族瑰宝。京剧有着丰富的剧目(repertoire)、众多的表演艺术家和大批的观众，在中国有着其他戏曲无法匹及的深远影响。

Part 5 Cultural Norms

常用词汇

exchange memo	兑换清单；水单	currency	流通货币
extra charge	额外费用	folio	客户个人账目
full price	全价	traveler's check	旅行支票
discounted price	折扣价	dispute	争议；纠纷
rack rate	标准价	F&B (food and beverage)	餐饮
special price	优惠价	SERV (service charge)	服务费
complimentary rate	免费	L. DIST (long-distance call)	长途话费
price list	价目表	LNDRY (laundry)	洗衣费
check, cheque	支票	MISC (miscellaneous)	杂费
interest	利息	TR. CH. (transfer charge)	转出
tip	小费	TR. CR. (transfer credit)	转入
complimentary breakfast	免费早餐	ADJ. (adjustment)	调整
deposit	预付金	PD. OUT (paid out)	代付
late charge	滞纳金	PAID (paid)	付现

常见信用卡

VS	VISA(Bank American Card) (美国)维萨卡
AE	American Express (美国)运通卡
JCB	(日本)信贩卡
MC	Master Card (美国)万事达卡
MC	Million Card (日本)百万信用卡
DC	Diners Club (美国)大来信用卡
BC	Barclays (英国)巴克利卡
FC	Federal Card (中国香港)发达卡
CB	Cart Blanche (美国)国际万用卡

OTB （中国香港）海外信用卡

EC Euro card（英国）欧洲卡

CC Current Card（中国香港）行通卡

AC Access（英国）阿赛斯卡

常用句子

1. There are four methods of payment now. 目前有四种付款方式。

   They are paying the bill in cash（现金付款）, by debit card（借记卡付款）, by credit card（信用卡付款）, and with trave ler's check（旅游支票付款）. 有些宾馆还接受其他付款方式，比如，客人在账单上签字、用公司的账户付款(paying the bill on the company account by signing the bill)。因此，在询问客人要用何种方式付款时，可以说：

   How will you be paying for this? 您用何种方式付款呢？

   Will you be putting this on your card? 您用信用卡结账吗？

2. 询问客人结账当天是否使用收费的设施或服务时可用以下句型。

   Have you ______________ this morning?

   例如：

   Have you used the mini-bar this morning? 您今天早上使用过客房食品柜吗？

   Have you had your breakfast in the hotel restaurant this morning?

   您今天早上是在本酒店餐厅用早餐的吗？

3. 向客人出示并解释账单。

   (1) 向客人出示账单时，可以说：

   Here is your bill. Would you please check and see if there is any mistake?

   这是您的账单。请您核对一下看看是否有误。

   (2) 表达总共多少钱，可以说：

   That will be＋总金额.

   The total amount is＋总金额. 或者 That comes to＋总金额 altogether.

   例如：Your credit card will be charged a total of ＄256.78. Can you sign on the bottom?

   您的信用卡将扣除总计256.78美元的费用。您能在账单底部签字吗？

   (3) 解释账单的项目时，可以用以下句型：

   (Item number...) is (money) for ...

   例如：Item six is 15 yuan for the garage. 第六项的15元是车库使用费。

   可以用到的表达如下：

   The first number is your room number 222. 第一项是您的房间号222。

   The second entry here is the restaurant. 第二项是餐费。

   Item 9 is a mistake. 第九项算错了。

   (4) 结账时的其他表达：

For Cashier 收银员	For Guests 客人
Will that be cash or charge? 付现金还是挂账?	I'll be paying with cash. 我付现金。
How will you be paying? 您用何种方式付款?	Do you accept VISA or Master Card? 你们这里可以刷维萨卡或者万事达卡吗?
Could you sign here please? 请您在这里签字,好吗?	There you are. 好了,给。
Here's your change, sir. 这是找您的零钱,先生。	That's OK, keep the change. 没关系,不用找零了。
Would you like a receipt? 您要开发票吗?	Could I have a receipt please? 给我发票可以吗?
I'll check the bill again if you like. 您需要的话,我再核对一遍账单。	This seems a bit much. Can this be right? 费用好像太多了。算得都对吗?
Yes, a service charge is included in the bill. 是的,账单中包括了服务费。	Is a tip or gratuity included in the bill? 账单中包括小费吗?
Let me double check that for you madam. 我再为您仔细检查一遍,女士。	I think there's been a mistake on the bill. 我觉得账单中有错误。

4. 兑换外币。

(1) 向客人说明汇率时,可以这样表达:

According to today's exchange rate, every 100 U. S. dollars in cash comes to 650 yuan.

Today's exchange rate for 1 U. S. dollar is 6. 5 yuan.

Today's exchange rate is 6. 5 yuan for 1 dollar.

It's 6. 5 yuan for 1 U. S. dollar.

以上四句的意思都一样,为"今天的汇率是 1 美元兑换 6. 5 元人民币"。

你也可以让客人自己去看汇率公告牌,这时你可以这样表达:

The rates of exchange are on the board there. 今天的兑换牌价在那边的牌子上。

How much would you like to change? 您要换多少?

(2) 要求客人填写兑换水单时,可以这样表达:

Would you please write down your name, passport number, and room number or permanent address on the exchange memo? 请在水单上写一下您的姓名、护照号、房间号或常住地址。

(3) 让客人保存好兑换水单时最好向他说明理由:

Please check it, and keep this memo. You can change it back into U. S. dollars at the Bank of China or the Airport Exchange Office. And there you are required to show the memo. 请检查一下,保存好兑换水单。您可以把换好的人民币在中国银行或者机场外汇兑换处再兑换成美元,那时就需要您出示此单据。

5. 与客人道别时,可以说:

Enjoy the rest of your holiday. 祝您假期愉快。

Have a safe trip home. 祝您旅途平安。

Thank you for staying with us. We look forward to seeing you again. 感谢您入住本酒店。欢迎您下次光临。

实际应用如下。

(Guest-G　Staff-S)

G：I'd like to check out please.

S：Of course sir，could I have your room number and room key?

G：The room was 333. Here's the key.

S：Did you use the mini bar sir?

G：Yes，I had a couple of sodas.

S：The total comes to ＄577.99. Will you be charging this sir?

G：Yes，put it on my VISA card.

S：Sign here please. And thank you for staying with us.

G：There you go. Thanks.

更多表达

1. Could you tell me what the total bill is? 请告诉我总共是多少钱?
2. Have you used any hotel services this morning? 请问您今天早晨是否用过旅馆内的服务设施?
3. Do you have any charges for this morning? 您今天早上是否挂账使用过酒店的服务?
4. We'll have to charge you ＄10 extra. 我们要向您额外收取10美元。
5. Did you make any phone calls from room，sir? 先生，您从房间打过电话吗?
6. Four nights at 90 U.S. dollars each，and here are the meals that you had at the hotel. That makes a total of 665 U.S. dollars. 4个晚上，每晚90美元，加上膳食费，总共是665美元。
7. Let me figure it out. 让我把您的账算出来。
8. It's ＄827 including tax. 含税是827美元。
9. Here's your bill. Please check it. 这是您的账单。请您过目。
10. Excuse me，what's this charge? 对不起，这是什么费用?
11. That is wine and other potables charge. 那是葡萄酒及其他饮料费。
12. Are all the expenses included，please? 请问所有的费用都包括在内了吗?
13. Yes，the price is not exclusive of accommodation and the extra charge. 是的，价格包括住宿费和额外费用。
14. What is the extra charge? 额外费用是什么?
15. Have you ordered room service，laundry service，morning call service and such kind of things? 您订过客房用餐服务、洗衣服务、叫醒服务或其他的类似服务吗?
16. Do you want one bill or separate bills? 你们是一起结账还是分开结账呢?
17. How would you like to pay，sir，in cash or by credit card? 先生，请问您是用现金付款还是用信用卡付款?
18. Can I charge it on my VISA Card? 我可以用维萨卡付款吗?
19. Can I pay with a credit card? 我可以用信用卡付款吗?
20. I wonder if I can pay by credit card? 请问我是否可以用信用卡付款?
21. May I have your card，please? 请把信用卡给我，好吗?

22. I'd like a receipt, please. 请给我开发票。
23. Do you have the receipt? 有发票吗?
24. Here are your bill and invoice. 请收好您的账单和发票。
25. Please check it and sign here. 请核对一下,在这里签个字。
26. Excuse me, sir, but I don't think that will be enough. 先生,对不起,我认为钱数不够。
27. I'm sorry, sir, there has been an error in your bill. Please wait a minute while I correct it. 对不起,先生,您的账单算错了。请稍候,我马上把它改过来。
28. Due to the communication problem between banks, the left amount will be refunded to your account in a couple of days. 由于银行间的通信问题,余款可能会在几天后退回到您的账户中。
29. You could withdraw cash from ATM with your credit card. 您可以用信用卡从 ATM 机中提取现金。
30. I'm sorry, this bank note is damaged, so we couldn't help you to exchange it. This is the rule of our hotel. Thank you for your understanding. 对不起,这张纸币有破损,我们无法为您兑换。这是酒店的规定。谢谢您的理解。
31. We guarantee that the cash changed by our hotel is genuine. We have closely examined it before we change it to the customer. 我们保证从酒店兑换出的现金全部是真的。每张纸币在给客人前我们都会用验钞机检查。
32. The genuineness and amount of the cash should be checked as soon as you get it. I'm afraid we bear no responsibilities for that after you leave the Front Desk. 您应该当场检验核对现金的真伪与数量。现金一旦离开前台我们将不再担负任何责任。
33. Sorry, traveler's check is not allowed to be cashed in our hotel. You could have this service in the bank. 对不起,酒店不能为您兑现旅行支票。您可以去银行办理。
34. I'm sorry, we really want to help you exchange your money, but the machine says this paper money is fake. We can't help you to change it. 对不起,我们真的想为您兑换,但验钞机检查出您的这张纸币可能是假的。我们不能为您兑现。
35. I'm sorry, the staff is clearing the currency, please wait a moment. 对不起,工作人员正在进行外币结算,请您稍等一会儿。
36. I'm sorry, but the exchange service is only provided to the guests staying in our hotel. 对不起,外币兑换服务只提供给住店客人。

Part 6 Supplementary Reading

Guest Safe Deposit Box Signature Card

Guest Name: ________ Room NO. ________ Safe Deposit Box NO. ________
(*Please Print*)

ID NO. /Passport NO. ________________________________

Permanent Address: ____________________

Authorized Signature (s) ____________________

The use of the safe deposit box is subject to the following terms:

1. Safe deposit boxes are furnished to hotel guests only.
2. Since the exclusive combined key of the safe is kept by the guest, the hotel is not liable to any losses.
3. If the key is lost or not returned to the hotel, the guest will be charged 600 yuan.
4. If the key to the above numbered safe deposit box is not returned to the hotel within 7 days after check-out, the hotel reserves the right to open the safe deposit box without any liabilities.

Date: ______________ Key Delivered by ______________

I hereby certify that I have examined this safe deposit box immediately after using it and returning the key, and I found that I have taken out all my belongings placed in this safe deposit box.

Room NO. ____________ Authorized Signature(s) ____________________________

Staff Signature ____________ Date ____________ Time ________________

Chapter 8 Switchboard

Study Objectives

1. To have a basic knowledge of hotel telephone etiquette and effective communication through telephone.
2. To grasp the words and expressions frequently used by a hotel switchboard operator.
3. To get related information on effective telephone communication and improve comprehension skills through listening and reading.
4. To be able to respond professionally to guests' questions and requests through telephone and offer the information or services needed, including making wake-up calls, introducing hotel telephone service, transferring phone calls or leaving messages for the guests.

Lead in

Work in pairs and discuss with your partner and answer the following questions.

1. What telephone service does a hotel normally provide?
2. What does a hotel switchboard operator do to help guests?

Part 1 Listening

Task 1 Dialogues. Listen to the following short dialogues and fill in the blanks according to what you hear.

(Operator-O Guest-G)

Dialogue 1

O: Good morning. Thank you for calling Maple Hotel. ______________ ______________?

G: I need to speak to someone from Room Reservations.

O: Reservations. ____________________________.

Dialogue 2

O: Good afternoon, Maple Hotel, James speaking.

G: Hello, I would like to know what time the pool is open.

O: Let's see, ____________________________?

____________________________.

G: OK, I can wait a few minutes.

Dialogue 3

O: Good afternoon. ____________________________ My name is Wendy. ______________

______________?

G: I need to speak to the Travel Desk.

O: Certainly, sir. ____________________________.

Dialogue 4

O: ____________________________. How may I help you?

G: I need to make a reservation for dinner at your coffee shop.

O: ____________________________.

Dialogue 5

O: Good evening. Star Hotel. How may I help you?

G: I need to book a room at your hotel.

O: Sure, ____________________________.

Dialogue 6

O: Good morning, Mr. White. ____________________________. It's 6 a. m. now. Wish you a nice day!

G: Thank you.

Dialogue 7

G: My luggage hasn't been brought to my room yet. I have been waiting here for half an hour.

O: I ____________________________ for ____________________________, sir. May I have your name and room number, please?

Task 2 Conversations. Listen to the following conversations and fill in the blanks according to what you hear. The missing words and phrases in Conversation 1 and the missing sentences in Conversation 2 have been provided in the boxes, and you can choose them from the boxes to fill in the blanks.

Conversation 1

dial tone	outside line	try it	Operator	place a call

(Operator-O Guest-G)

O: __________. May I help you?

G: Yes. How do I get an ________, please?

O: Just dial "0", wait for the ________, and then dial the phone number you want to call. Or we can ____________ for you, if you want.

G: No, thanks a lot. I'll ____________ myself.

Conversation 2

You will receive a wake-up call at 5:30 a.m. tomorrow morning. I'll have to be on the road by half past six at the latest. And the time of your wake-up call? This is the hotel operator. May I have your name and room number, please? You wouldn't know how long it takes to drive to Shanghai from here, would you?

(**Operator-O Guest-G**)

O: ______________________________. May I help you?

G: Yes, I'd like to be awakened tomorrow morning.

O: Certainly, sir. ______________________________?

G: Jack Robinson, Room 612.

O: ______________________________?

G: Well, I'm not really sure. But I have to be at the conference room of Shanghai International Hotel by 9:30 tomorrow morning. ______________________________?

O: About three hours.

G: That means that ______________________________.

O: That's right.

G: Well, in that case, I would like you to call me at 5:30.

O: OK, Mr. Robinson, ______________________________. Is that correct?

G: Yes. Thanks.

O: You're always welcome, Mr. Robinson.

Part 2 Speaking

Task 1 Work in pairs. Read and complete the following dialogue by translating the Chinese sentences in the parentheses into English.

(**Operator-O Guest-G**)

O: Good afternoon. Continental Hotel. May I help you?

G: Yes. I'd like to speak to Peter Williams. He is staying in your hotel.

O: ______________________________(请问他的名字怎么拼呢)?

G: P-e-t-e-r, Peter. W-i-l-l-i-a-m-s, Williams.

O: What's his room number, please?

G: I think it's Room 8320, but I'm not sure. Can you check it for me?

O: I see. May I know your name, Madam?

G: Susan Smith.

O: ____________ (请稍候), Miss Smith. ______________________________ (我给您查一下,然后把您的电话转接到他的房间).

G: Thanks.

O: ________________ (让您久等了), Miss Smith. ______________________________ ____________________ (彼得·威廉姆斯先生住在 8202 号房间,但是没人接电话).

G: Could you try again, please?

O: Certainly, madam. Just a moment, please. ______________ (我为您转接).

G: Thanks.

O: Thank you for waiting. I'm afraid there is still no one answering the phone. ________ __________________________________ (您需要留言吗)?

G: Yes. I'll do that. Please tell him to call me back before 9 o'clock this evening.

O: Could you tell me your phone number, please?

G: Yes, my phone number is 13802037076.

O: Thank you, Miss Smith. ______________________________ (现在我跟您确认一下留言内容,您看对不对). "Miss. Smith asks Mr. Williams to call her back before 9 o'clock this evening. Miss Smith's phone number is 13802037076." Is that correct, madam?

G: Yes, exactly.

O: ____ (威廉姆斯先生一回来我们就向他转达留言).

G: Thanks a lot. Bye.

Vocabulary

continental	*adj*. 大陆的;大陆性的
transfer	*vt*. 使转移;转接
connect	*vt*. 给……接通电话
exactly	*adv*. 完全正确;恰好地;正是;精确地

Notes

1. "I see""I got it" 和"I know"三种表达的区别如下。

   "I see" 是一种比较普遍的用法,和 "I got it" 类似,强调之前不了解,通过沟通之后明白了,意思是"我明白了"。而 "I know" 强调说话者原本就很了解对方谈论的事情,语气稍微有些强硬,带有不谦虚的意味,隐含的意思是"这个不用你说我就知道"。所以,在了解客人情况后表达自己知道了,用前两种表达较为合适,即 "I see"和"I got it"。

2. Thank you for waiting. 意思是"让您久等了"。

   This is information desk. Thank you for waiting, sir. 这里是问询处,先生让您久等了。
   Sorry to have kept you waiting. I've got it. 对不起,让您久等了,我找到了。

还可以这么说：

We are extremely sorry for the delay. 非常抱歉，让您久等了。

3. Please tell him to call me back before 9 o'clock this evening. 请让他今晚九点钟以前给我回电话。

这里的"call sb. back"是一个词组，表示"给某人回电话"。如果要表达打某个具体号码来给某人回电话，则可以说"call sb. back at＋具体的电话号码"。例如：

Please have him call me back at 291-3986 when the meeting is over.

请告诉他开完会后回电到 291-3986 找我。

Task 2 Work in Pairs. Read the conversation below. The parts are not in the correct order. Which parts are spoken by the operator? Mark the parts with As. Which parts are spoken by the guest? Mark the parts with a Bs. Write numbers on the lines. Then act out the conversation with a partner.

(Operator-A Guest-B)

1. ________: Yes. I'd like to call my friend in his room. What should I do?
2. ________: Fine. Thanks a lot.
3. ________: Do you know the room number, sir?
4. ________: For domestic long-distance calls, please dial "0" and then the area code and the local telephone number. For international direct dials (IDD), please dial "0" first, then the international prefix "00", followed by the country code, area code and the expected telephone number.
5. ________: You're welcome, sir.
6. ________: This is the Hotel Operator. May I help you?
7. ________: For calls inside Hangzhou, please dial "0" first. Then dial the telephone number after the line-through tone is heard.
8. ________: What about outside Hangzhou? I'd like to call Beijing and Sydney.
9. ________: I see. Well, what if I want to make outside calls?
10. ________: Yes, it's 2114.
11. ________: For 4 digit rooms, please dial "1" and then the room number.
12. ________: Do I have to be charged for both local calls and direct dials?
13. ________: Local calls made from hotel rooms are free of charge. The hotel will collect 15% and 10% as service charge from IDD and DDD calls respectively. We will collect 5.00 yuan as service charge for a collect call or a call paid by credit card. Direct dials are charged on a per minute basis from the moment the call is answered. Calls are automatically charged to your account. For direct dialing calls, you are still requested to pay even if you dial the wrong number. Telephone bills with details will be given to you upon checking out.

Task 3 Short telephone scenario cards. The teacher prepares 6 cards marked A to F respectively and 10 cards marked 1 to 10 respectively. In groups of three or four, students draw a card from A to F and then draw another one from 1 to 10. Then make up a conversation according to the chosen scenario.

A—You know the answer and help the guest. (solve a problem)

B—You don't know the answer but know the person who does. (transfer)

C—You know the answer but need some time to look it up. (put on hold)

D—You know the answer, but there are two other phones ringing. (put on hold)

E—You don't know the answer but know the person who does. However, he's not here today. (take a message)

F—You know the answer, but you need to call the person back. (take information to follow up)

1) A guest wants to know what time the pool is open.

2) A guest has a broken air conditioner and needs someone to fix it.

3) A guest wants to leave a message for another guest in the hotel.

4) A guest wants to make a reservation at Russo's.

5) A guest wants to know what the weather will be tomorrow.

6) A co-worker needs to speak to the housekeeping manager.

7) A guest wants to speak to someone in accounting.

8) A caller wants to know how to apply for a job at the Sheraton Hotel.

9) A guest wants to know if there is wireless Internet access in the hotel.

10) A guest wants to know if the hotel offers kosher meals.

Part 3 Reading

Basic Telephone Etiquette for Switchboard Operators

Have you ever called a business and received poor customer service from the exact moment that the other person **picked up** the phone? I have and it seems like it is becoming more common nowadays. For me, such an experience is **particularly frustrating** because I spent a good deal of my career working in the **hospitality** industry. Part of that time was spent training Front Desk clerks on how to answer the hotel's switchboard properly. As such, every telephone etiquette **infraction** tends to make me **cringe.** With that said, I thought that I would share some of what I use to teach my staff in the hopes that it will help others in their training **endeavors.** Here are the basics.

Answering the Call

One of the first things that I trained my staff to do was to answer each call by the third ring. If the Front Desk clerk on duty was already on another phone call, it was the manager's responsibility to jump in and answer the other line. The staff was also trained to smile before picking up the phone. Once they hit the answer button on the switchboard they were told to clearly **enunciate** a specific greeting in an eager but **well-modulated** voice. The greeting included the name of the hotel and their first name. It went like this, "Good morning and thank you for calling the XYZ Hotel. This is Suzy speaking, how may I direct your call?"

Conducting the Call

Because my staff were responsible for taking hotel reservations, they were also instructed to obtain the proper spelling of the caller's name and refer to the caller by name throughout the call. They were also instructed to repeat back the information given by the caller in order to ensure that all the data entered into the computer was correct.

For example, let's pretend that Bob White called to make a reservation for one king size, non-smoking room for the night of June 4, 2014. The clerk would be trained to say, "I am now showing that I have a reservation for one king size, non-smoking room, under the name of Bob White, with an arrival date of June 4, 2014. Is that correct Mr. White?"

In my opinion, those techniques are also helpful when it comes to taking telephone messages. In addition, the hotel clerks were trained to avoid using **slang.** They were also asked not to answer the phone while chewing **gum** or doing anything else that may **impede** their ability to speak clearly.

Placing a Call on Hold

Specific instructions were also given to the clerks **regarding** the use of the **hold button.** They were trained to ask **permission** to **put** the caller **on hold.** For example, they would say something like, "Mr. White, would you mind if I **place** you **on hold** while I pull up your reservation?" Once they took the call off hold, the staff was told to say something like, "Thank you for waiting Mr. White, I have your reservation in front of me now."

Dealing with Angry Callers

There were occasions when a caller would get rude with my staff. On those occasions, they were instructed to put the **irate** customer in contact with me or another appropriate manager. For example, let's pretend that an irate caller wants the clerk to give him a free room. In such instances, the clerk would say something like, "I am sorry Mr. White, but I don't have the authority to **grant** such a request. Please allow me to connect you to Suzy Manager. She has the **authority** to handle your request."

Concluding the Call

The hotel clerks were also instructed to repeat the customer's name and the name of the hotel at the end of the call. An example would be, "Thank you for calling the XYZ Hotel, Mr. White. Have a nice day."

Vocabulary

particularly *adv.* 特别;尤其

frustrating	*adj.* 产生挫折的；使人沮丧的；令人泄气的
hospitality	*n.* 殷勤好客；招待；款待；(气候、环境等的)宜人；适宜
infraction	*n.* (对规则、法律等的)违背；违犯
cringe	*vi.* & *n.* 厌烦；畏缩；卑躬屈膝
endeavor	*v.* & *n.* 尝试；试图；尽力
enunciate	*vi.* & *vt.* (清晰地)发音；确切地说明
slang	*n.* 俚语；黑话
gum	*n.* 口香糖；树胶
impede	*vt.* 阻碍；妨碍；阻止
regarding	*prep.* 关于；就……而论；至于
permission	*n.* 允许；批准；正式认可；认可
irate	*adj.* 盛怒的
grant	*vt.* 承认；同意；准许；授予
authority	*n.* 权威；权力；当局

Phrases and Expressions

pick up	捡起；接载；学会；接起(电话)
well-modulated	声音或声调优美的
hold button	通话保持键
put...on hold	搁置；延期；暂停
place...on hold = put...on hold	搁置；延期；暂停

Task 1 True or false statements. Decide whether the following statements are True (T) or False (F) according to the text.

1. The author can tolerate any violation of telephone etiquette because he/she works in the hospitality industry. ( )
2. The manager is responsible for supervising the Front Desk clerk on duty and doesn't have to answer any phone line when the clerk is on another phone call. ( )
3. Repeating back the information given by the caller is very helpful when taking telephone messages. ( )
4. It's OK for the Front Desk clerk to polish nails while taking a phone call, because the caller cannot see what the clerk is doing. ( )
5. If the Front Desk clerk has to put the caller on hold, it's advisable to get the caller's approval first. ( )

Task 2 Questions. Read the text again and answer the following questions.

1. Why is it important to build telephone skills for telephone operators?
2. What will you do if an irate caller makes some requests that you cannot handle?

Task 3 Blank filling. Fill in the blanks with the words given. Change the form when necessary.

frustrating	hospitality	pick up	authority	endeavor
impede	regarding	permission	irate	particularly

1. We ________ to make our customers satisfied.
2. Fallen rock is ________ the progress of rescue workers.
3. The owner was so ________ he almost threw me out of the place.
4. She has said nothing ________ your request.
5. Employees are ________ to use the golf course during their free hours.
6. Every visitor to Georgia is overwhelmed by the kindness, charm and ________ of the people.
7. I'm pretty desk-bound, which is very ________.
8. They depend on the goodwill of visitors to ________ rubbish.
9. Not everyone thinks that the government is being ________ generous.
10. The ________ must make suitable accommodation available to the family.

Part 4 Translation

Task 1 Translate the following passage into Chinese.

Dragon dance is a form of traditional dance and performance in Chinese culture. It originated from the Han Dynasty and was started by the Chinese who had shown great belief and respect towards the dragon. It's believed to have begun as part of the farming and harvest culture, also with origins as a method of healing and preventing sickness. Dragon dance was already a popular event during the Song Dynasty. Dragon dance is an important part of the Chinese culture and tradition. It has spread throughout China and to the whole world and become a special performance of arts in Chinese physical activities, symbolizing good luck and prosperity in the year to come for all the human beings on earth.

Task 2 Sentence translation.

1. 这里是总机，您有一个外线电话，介意我接入您的房间吗？
2. 晚上好，先生，您的朋友怀特先生邀请您今晚7点到二楼中餐厅用晚餐。
3. 宾客服务中心通过向客人提供可靠、有效的服务和信息咨询，帮助客人解决问题，以建立宾客忠诚度。宾客服务中心的理念是更好地综合利用酒店的各种资源，来提高工作效率。

Task 3 Translate the following passage into English.

每年的农历八月十八，浙江省海宁市盐官县都会挤满来观看钱塘江大潮的八方宾客。

钱塘江大潮这一蔚为壮观的自然现象令中外游客叹为观止。每年八月十八日那天，月球、太阳的共同作用使得海水受到的引潮力最大，因此，那天的钱塘江涌潮最为壮观。

Part 5 Cultural Norms

常用词汇

switchboard	总机	long-distance call	长途电话
operator	接线员	domestic long-distance call	国内长途电话
put through	接通电话	collect call	对方付费电话
transfer	转接	Domestic Direct Dial (DDD)	国内直拨
wake-up call	叫醒电话	International Direct Dial (IDD)	国际直拨
urgent	紧急的	line-through tone	电话接通音
receiver	电话听筒	service charge	服务费
telephone hook	电话机座	service directory	服务指南
area code	区号	phone card	电话卡
house phone	内线电话	phone line	电话线
local call	市内电话	emergency call	紧急电话

常用句子

1. How long should you let the phone ring before you answer it? 接线员需要在电话铃响几声之内接起电话?

   三声之内。电话响过三声之后还没接起来就等于在告诉打电话的人你不想接电话。

2. What are some ways to make your voice sound more professional over the phone? 如何让你的声音在电话里听起来更专业?

   拿起话筒之前就应开始微笑。尽量坐直一些;说话时口齿清楚,礼貌周到;不能抢对方的话,不能大喊大叫。接电话过程中应一直保持微笑,在得知对方遇到问题时应显示出关心和同情。说话时的语调应具有权威感,灵活主动,时刻准备帮助对方,切勿表现出懒散、冷漠、吞吞吐吐、困惑、杂乱。

3. What is a professional way to answer the phone? 接电话的正式用语是什么?

   接起电话时,不可以简单地回应"Hello",正式的回应方式应是先问候对方(greeting),如"Good morning""Good evening"等,再自报家门说出你所在的单位、所属部门或姓名,然后再提出礼貌性问题(polite question),如"How may I help you?""How may I direct your call?"因此,接电话时可以这样说"Information Desk speaking. May I help you?"或者"Good morning and thank you for calling Lily Hotel. This is Jenny speaking, how may I direct your call?"

4. How do you help the guest? 如何帮助客人?

   (1) 别人打错电话时,如果是外线打错,可以回答"I'm afraid you have the wrong number."(不好意思,您打错电话了。)如果是总线转错内线时,可以回答"This is Room Reservations. I'll transfer your call to Restaurant Reservations."(这里是客房预约处,我帮

您转接到餐厅预约柜台。)若无法为客人转接,则可以说"I am afraid this is a direct line. We can't transfer your call to the Chinese Restaurant. Could you dial 3513-1156, please?"(抱歉,这是直拨电话,我们无法为您转接中式餐厅。请您改拨 3513-1156,好吗?)

为客人转接时可以说"I'll transfer you."或者"I'll put you through."。

(2) 回答客人提问时,若需要从文件、计算机或他人处查询信息后才能给出回答,应先询问客人是否能稍等一下,此时可以说"Hold on please."或者"Would you please hold on a minute?"。

若需要转接他人回答客人的提问,应先将该人的姓名和电话留给客人(以免客人电话被意外切断而得不到帮助),然后再为其转接。若你需要进行查询后再给客人答复,则应先确保记下客人的姓名和电话号码,查询完并回复客人之后还应联系客人进行跟进,这样做会给客人留下好印象。

(3) 若客人来电想找的某人刚好不在,去了洗手间或其他地方,可向客人解释清楚或者询问是否留言或者转接语音信箱。例如:"I'm sorry, but Miss Li has just stepped away from her desk. May I transfer you to her voice-mail?"(抱歉,李小姐刚好走开了。需要为您转接到她的语音信箱吗?),"I'm afraid Mr. Wang is on another line. Could you hold the line, please?"(抱歉,王先生正在讲电话。请您在线上稍候,好吗?),"I'll tell him to call you back when he returns. May I have your name and phone number, please?"(他回来时我会请他回电。请告诉我您的姓名和电话,好吗?)或者"I'm sorry, but the person has just stepped away from her desk. May I take a message?"(抱歉,您要找的人刚离开。您需要留言吗?)。

(4) 如何更礼貌地表达自己不清楚对方在说什么?可以说:"If you'll repeat it for me, I'll be happy to assist you.",或者"Could you explain the situation to me again? And I'll do my best to help you or I'll find someone who can."。

(5) 如何帮助正在气头上的来电客人?

电话中应对生气的客人所用的技巧与当面处理此类问题一样:首先,要道歉,显示同情;其次,提供帮助,做出回应并跟进。电话中碰到此类问题可遵循 ASAP 原则,即:

(A) Apologize & Acknowledge the caller's feelings (道歉并承认客人当时的心情确实糟糕)。应对整件事情过程中可能需要花 80%的时间来安抚客人,而另外 20%的时间用来解决实际问题。

(S) Sympathize & Empathize(体谅客人,显示同情)。可以这样说"I don't blame you for being upset. That's got to be very frustrating."。

(A) Accept responsibility(承担责任)。可以这样说"Let me see how to help. My name is Mary, Front Desk agent, and I am speaking with...?"。

(P) Prepare to help(准备帮助客人)。此时,可以开始询问客人,了解客人所遇到的麻烦和具体细节,以便更好地帮助客人解决问题。

5. How do you end a phone conversation? 如何结束电话谈话?

首先由衷地感谢客人来电,提出未来随时可以提供帮助,应让客人先挂电话。可以这样说"Thank you for calling. If you need anything further, please don't hesitate to call me. My name is Li Min. ",或者简单地说"Thank you for calling the Maple Hotel. Have a nice day. "。

更多表达

1. May I help you? 有什么能为您效劳的吗?
2. I'll call back. 我会给您回电。
3. I got your message. 我收到了您的留言。
4. I'm returning your call. 我正给您回电话。
5. Hello, Palace Hotel. This is David, how may I assist you?
   您好,皇宫酒店。我是戴维,有什么可以为您效劳的吗?
6. I need to speak to someone from the Reservations. 我想联系客房预订。
7. Certainly, I will connect you to the Reservations. 好的,为您转接客房预订。
8. Good morning. Thank you for calling Maple Hotel. How may I direct your call? 早上好。欢迎致电枫叶大酒店。您需要将电话转接到哪里?
9. I need to speak to someone from Room Reservations. 我需要联系客房预订。
10. Reservations. Connecting your call. 客房预订。正在为您转接。
11. I'd like to have a wake-up call. /I'd like to be awakened tomorrow morning. 我需要叫醒服务。
12. I wonder if your hotel has the morning call service. 不知道你们饭店是否有叫醒服务。
13. Would you like a morning call service? 您需要叫醒服务吗?
14. I want to go to the Bund to enjoy the morning scenery there. 我想到外滩去欣赏那儿的清晨景色。
15. At what time do you want me to call you up, sir? 先生,您需要我什么时候叫醒您?
16. At 6 sharp tomorrow morning, please. 请在明早6点钟。
17. What kind of call would you like, phone or by knocking at the door? 您需要哪种方式的叫醒服务,电话叫醒还是敲门叫醒?
18. By phone. I don't want to disturb my neighbors. 电话叫醒,我不想吵醒邻居。
19. Good morning, Mr. White. This is the morning call for you. It's 6 a. m. now. Wish you a nice day! 早上好,怀特先生。您的叫醒时间已到。现在是早上六点。祝您今天愉快!
20. I'm sorry we can't transfer calls from the house phones. 很抱歉,内线电话无法转接。
21. Wait a minute, and I'll put you through to Room Reservations. 请稍候,我帮您接通到客房预订部。
22. Should you have any questions, you may refer to the *Service Directory* in your room. 您有任何问题的话,可以查阅房间内的《服务指南》。
23. After completing your call, please see to it that the receiver is properly placed on the telephone hook. 打完电话之后,请确保您的话筒挂好在电话机座上。
24. Could you put me through to Room 2512, please? 麻烦你帮我接2512房间,好吗?
25. Can I speak to Mr. Nick Adams in Room 3322? 你好,麻烦帮我找3322号房的尼克·

亚当斯先生，好吗？

26. Thank you for waiting, sir. Mr. Frank Stephens is staying in Room 322. I'll connect you. 先生，让您久等了。弗兰克·斯蒂芬斯先生住在322房间，我为您转接。
27. Thank you for waiting. I'm afraid there 's no one answering in Room 8202. Would you like to leave a message? 让您久等了，8202号房没有人接听电话。请问您要留言吗？
28. I'll connect you with the Message Desk. Just a moment, please. 我来为您转接留言台，请稍候。
29. This is the hotel operator. May I help you? 这里是总机。能为您服务吗？
30. I'd like to call my friend in his room. What should I do? 我想打到朋友的房间。要怎么打呢？
31. For 4 digit rooms, please dial "1" first and then the room number. 四位数的房间号，请您先拨"1"，然后再拨房间号就可以了。
32. How do I get an outside line, please? 请问外线电话怎么打？
33. For calls inside Hangzhou, please dial "0" first and then the number you want to call. Or we can place a call for you, if you want. 如果是杭州市内电话，请先拨"0"，然后再拨电话号码。需要的话，我们可以替您拨打。
34. What about outside Hangzhou? I'd like to call Beijing. 那杭州市以外的电话怎么打？我想打到北京。
35. For calls outside Hangzhou, please dial "0" first and then the area code and number. 外市电话请先拨"0"，再拨区号，最后拨电话号码。
36. Whom would you like to speak to? 您找哪位？
37. Could you repeat that, please? 请再说一次，好吗？
38. Could you speak more slowly, please? 请您说慢一点，好吗？
39. Could you hold the line, please? 请别挂断，好吗？
40. I'll put you through to our Western restaurant. 我这就为您转接到我们的西餐厅。
41. Go ahead, you're through. 请讲，您的电话已接通。
42. I'm afraid the line is engaged. 恐怕电话正占线。
43. I'm afraid the line was cut off. 恐怕电话已挂断。
44. I'm afraid there is no reply from Room 515. 恐怕515房间没人接听。

Part 6 Supplementary Reading

Hotel Switchboard Policies and Procedures

Guidelines for the hotel employees while on duty

It is the policy of the hotel that there should be no personal incoming and outgoing calls while on duty except the senior managers and emergency call. Disciplinary action will be taken against the associates who violate the approved policy and procedures.

1. The telephone switchboard has to be manned 24 hours.
2. The telephone operator answers all calls within 3 rings.

3. The telephone operator answers the call promptly with a crystal clear voice in a well intonation manner.

4. Transfer the call to the requested extension immediately (If the call is for the in-house guest, double check the name before transfer the call to the room). Use "Certainly Sir/Madam, please hold on".

5. Attend to the next call as soon as possible.

6. If the caller has any inquiry, inform the caller that his call will be transferred to the relevant department. This is to ensure that the telephone switchboard is not jammed up and allows the operator to attend to the next call.

7. Rules and regulations at the Telephone Communication Room have to be set to minimize the traffic at the switchboard:

—No unauthorized personnel are allowed to enter the Telephone Switchboard Room to make phone calls from the switchboard.

—No food is allowed in the Telephone Switchboard Room.

—All hotel employees are not allowed to call the switchboard for service.

—The Telephone Room has to be well maintained and quiet at all time.

8. Telephone extension numbers for hotel offices must be made available at the switchboard console to facilitate the transfer of the calls efficiently.

Do Not Disturb

1. When receiving the instructions from the guest to place his call as Do Not Disturb, the telephone operator has to clarify with the guest to take down the following instructions:

—Guest name and room number;

—Duration;

—Any specific instruction.

2. The operator repeats the information to check accuracy with the guest.

3. Then proceed to enter the above information to the computer system.

4. The phone line of the guest room is programmed to be forwarded to the telephone operator at the switchboard by using the Do Not Disturb feature.

5. The telephone operator is able to attend to the caller adhering to the guest instruction. Should there be any incoming calls to a DND room, advise the caller that the guest does not wish to be distributed at this time and take down a message if necessary. If the incoming call is urgent, ask for the caller's name and place the caller on hold. Call the guest room immediately and provide the guest with the caller's name, advising that the call is urgent. If the guest accepts the call, connect the caller immediately. Otherwise, connect the caller to the guest room voicemail or take a message from the caller and deliver it to the guest immediately.

6. The telephone operator has to delete the Do Not Disturb program for the guest once the duration of the requested instruction is expired; the phone system will resume normal operation.

Chapter 9

Banqueting & Conferences

Study Objectives

1. To have a basic knowledge of banqueting and conferences.
2. To grasp the words and expressions used in banqueting and conferences.
3. To get the idea and information through listening and reading.
4. To handle the guests' consultation on banquet service and offer the information needed.

Lead in

A banquet is a large meal or feast, complete with main courses and desserts. It usually serves a purpose such as a charitable gathering, a ceremony, or a celebration, and is often preceded or followed by speeches in honor of someone. Think carefully and try to answer the following questions.

1. How many types of banquet have you attended?
2. What rules should the waiters follow when serving a banquet?

Part 1 Listening

Task 1 Dialogues. Listen to the dialogues and fill in the blanks with what you hear.

Dialogue 1

A: We have only 30 minutes to decorate the hall with the flowers, please hurry up!

B: ____.

Dialogue 2

A: What flowers would you like to decorate the banquet hall?

B: ____.

Dialogue 3

A: ____.

B: Yes, sir. We'll make it soon.

Dialogue 4

A: ____?

B: Yes, this way please.

Dialogue 5

A: I'd like to ________________________________.

B: Yes, sir. How long will you need it for?

Task 2 Conversations

Conversation 1 Mr. Le Fevre is calling the Hilton Hotel to book a conference room. Listen and fill in the blanks with the words or phrases provided in the box.

book	conference	charge	medium-sized	arrange a meeting

(**Hotel Clerk-C Mr. Le Fevre-F**)

C: Thank you for calling Hilton Hotel. May I help you?

F: Hello. This is Mr. Le Fevre from KPMG. I'd like to ________ for some business. Do you have a ________ room we could use?

C: Certainly, sir. How many people will be attending the meeting?

F: 160. By the way, what's the ________?

C: We have a ________ room for 150 people at $800 an hour and a larger room for 200 people at $1500 an hour.

F: I'd prefer the larger one. Can I ________ it for tomorrow morning at 9 a. m. ?

C: Sure. Could you please leave your name and phone number?

F: Yes, Mr. Le Fevre. That is L-e-f-e-v-r-e, and my phone number is 0057116883.

C: All right, thanks a lot. See you tomorrow!

F: See you!

Conversation 2 Mrs. Williams is reserving a banquet for her father's birthday party in the Continental Hotel. Listen and fill in the blanks with the words or phrases provided in the box.

approximately	receipt	excluding	in advance	celebrate his birthday

(**Banquet Reservationist-R Mrs. Williams-W**)

R: Good morning, madam. May I help you?

W: Good morning, my father is 80 years old next week; I'd like to book a hall to ________.

R: When would you like to hold the party, madam?

W: Next Sunday, say 22nd September.

R: OK, how many people will attend the party?

W: ________ 100 people.

R: I see. Then our Bamboo Hall would be big enough. It can hold up to 120 people.

W: OK, I'll take it. Can you tell me the minimum charge?

R: The minimum charge for a 100-person dinner party is 10000 yuan, ________ drinks.

W: Then how do you charge for the drinks?

R: We either charge for all the drinks ordered or agree a fixed price and let the guests drink freely within the limit.

W: Mm, I see. I'd like to take the second way.

R: OK. You have to pay a 20% deposit ________.

W: All right. Here you are.

R: Thank you. Here is your ________.

Conversation 3 Mr. Johnson is booking a wedding banquet for his daughter on the phone. Listen and fill in the blanks with what you hear.

(**Banquet Reservationist-R Mr. Johnson-J**)

R: Banqueting and Conference Section. ______________________________ ______?

J: My daughter is getting married next month. I'd like to ask ______________________________ ________.

R: Congratulations, sir! ______________________________?

J: Well, the wedding is on 1st January.

R: How many guests will be attending?

J: ______________________________.

R: Then ______________________________?

J: En, I think 1200 yuan for each table.

R: I see. Then I'll arrange the Jasmine Hall for you. It is spacious and splendidly decorated which is perfect for a wedding banquet.

J: Wow, thank you! I think I'll take it.

R: ______________________________?

J: At about 5:30 p. m..

R: ______________________________?

J: Well, I'd like pink roses with added baby's breath to decorate the banquet hall.

R: OK, ______________________________. I hope you will like it!

J: Thank you very much, bye!

R: Bye!

Part 2 Speaking

Task 1 Work in pairs. Vanessa is calling to book a banquet hall. Read and complete the following dialogue by translating the Chinese sentences in the parentheses into English.

(**Banquet Manager-M Vanessa-V**)

M: Good afternoon, Banquet Service. ________________ (请问有什么能帮您的吗)?

V: Good afternoon, this is Vanessa from Xerox. ________________ (我打电话来是想预订一个宴会厅来举行欢迎 Beckman 先生的典礼). Can you arrange it for us?

M: Definitely, madam. When would you like to have the banquet?

V: At 6:30 p. m., next Monday. ________________ (你们有空的厅吗)?

M: ________________ (请问有多少人参加宴会)?

V: 50 or so.

M: OK, then I'd like to recommend the Pearl Hall with sound set-up.

V: Wonderful! I'll take it.

M: ________________ (您每桌的预算是多少)?

V: About 2000 yuan and we'd like all the dishes to be typically Chinese. This banquet will be held to honor Mr. Beckman, as I said. He is our new CEO and I think we need to do something special for him. ________________ (你有什么建议吗)?

M: Sure. ________________ (我们可以为特别的场合制作特别的菜式). How about *All Birds Paying Homage to the Phoenix*? It's a spring chicken with boiled dumplings.

V: Great! I believe Mr. Beckman will like it.

M: Yes, ________________ (请问您需要什么酒水)? We can serve different wines, beers, and soft drinks.

V: I'd like to serve some vodka, brandy, Snow beers, mango juice and coconut milk.

M: OK, ________________ (请问您需要什么水果)?

V: I'd like some cherry, kiwi fruit, strawberry, watermelon and Hami melon.

M: I see. Let me repeat what you've ordered: a welcome banquet in the Pearl Hall at 6:30 p. m. next Monday, 2000 yuan for each table, including drinks and fruits, a special dish of *All Birds Paying Homage to the Phoenix* for each table. Is that right, madam?

V: Absolutely! Thank you!

M: It's our pleasure. Ms. Vanessa, ________________ (请问方不方便留下您的电话号码,以便我们联系您)?

V: Of course. 15962411765.

M: Thank you. We ensure it will be a wonderful evening.

V: Thank you very much.

Vocabulary

available	*adj*. 可获得的
banquet	*n*. 宴会
brandy	*n*. 白兰地酒
CEO	*abbr*. Chief Executive Officer 首席执行官

coconut n. [植]椰子
kiwi fruit n. 猕猴桃;奇异果
mango n. 芒果
occasion n. 时机;场合
recommend vt. 推荐
typical adj. 典型的
vodka n. 伏特加酒
Xerox n. 施乐公司,全球500强企业

Notes

1. Welcome Party 意为欢迎宴会,常见的宴会类型有 Farewell Dinner(告别宴会),Glee Feast(庆功宴),Reception(招待会)等。
2. I'm calling to...这个句型表示打电话的目的,类似的用法有 I'm writing to...,表示写信的目的和意图。
3. Do you have ... available? 意思是"你有空的……吗?"类似的提问"你有空的房间吗?"可以这样表达:Do you have any room available?
4. May I know how many people there will be? 这个句型是询问有多少人参加宴会,以便推荐一个合适的宴会厅,其他类似的表达有 How many guests will be attending? 或者 How many people will attend the party?
5. *All Birds Paying Homage to the Phoenix* 是杭州的一道传统名菜,取童子鸡和饺子为食材,做成一道汤,众多饺子围在童子鸡周围,意为百鸟朝凤。
6. May I have your phone number in case we need to contact you? 意为"是否可以留下您的电话号码以便联系?"一般酒店工作人员问客人要电话号码或者问对方的姓名时都用这种句型,比较委婉与礼貌。比如,询问客人姓名时可以这样问:May I have your name, please? 而"What's your name?"这样的句型,显得突兀与不礼貌,不建议使用。

Task 2 Work in pairs. Discuss and complete the conversation between a guest and a banquet service waiter by filling in the blanks with appropriate sentences given below.

A. Do you have any special requirements?
B. How many people will come to the banquet?
C. How much would you like to spend for each table?
D. May I help you?
E. What drinks would you prefer?
F. When would you like to have the banquet?

(**Waiter-W Guest-G**)

W: Good morning, Banquet Service. ______1______

G: Yes, I'd like to book a banquet in your hotel.

W: ______2______

G: Next Thursday, November 21st.

W: ______3______

G: About 300 people.

W: I see. I'd like to recommend the Queen's Hall which is spacious and luxuriously decorated.

G: Great! Then I'll take it.

W: Here is the menu. ______4______

G: About 1500 yuan.

W: All right. ______5______ We can serve brandy, Budweiser, sprite, juice, milk, etc..

G: Brandy and Budweiser, please.

W: OK. ______6______

G: Yes, I'd prefer runaway with red carpet and white Lily to decorate the hall.

W: No problem, madam. We'll get it ready before the banquet. May you enjoy it!

Task 3 Role-play. Work in pairs and make up a dialogue respectively according to the situations provided.

Situation 1 Mr. Zille is booking a birthday banquet for his grandson. Role-play his conversation with a banquet service waitress with the help of the steps provided below.

—Banquet Service Waitress

- Greet the guest.
- Ask the date of the banquet and the number of guests.
- Recommend a banquet hall and ask about the birthday cake and decoration.
- Ask about the budget for each table.
- Ask the guest to pay some deposit.
- Promise to be ready for the banquet.

—Mr. Zille

- Want to book a banquet for his grandson's 10th birthday.
- Tell the waitress that it's on June 23rd and there will be 70 guests.
- Prefer a three-layer birthday cake and cartoon decoration.
- 1000 yuan per table.
- Pay the deposit.
- Express thanks.

Situation 2 Mrs. Bretman goes to the Banquet Service Department to reserve a wedding banquet. You may use the following expressions for reference.

- Welcome to ...May I help you?
- Good morning. How may I help you?
- I'd like to hold a birthday party/wedding party for my grandson in your hotel.
- We'd like to have pink roses/white Lily/cartoons to decorate the hall.

- I wish to make something different for my grandson, and do you have any suggestions?
- When would you like to hold the party/wedding?
- May I know the date of the party/wedding?
- Do you have any special requirements?
- How many people will come to the banquet?
- How much would you like to pay for each table?
- We can provide the honey moon suite for the bride and groom if necessary.
- We'll get it ready before the banquet. May you enjoy it!

Part 3 Reading

Banquet Service

WHAT IS A BANQUET?

The **original** banquet was a **formal** meal for a large number of guests, either for a festival or to mark the occasion of a political or social event.

In view of the large amount of food to be prepared and served, the **primary** objective of such events is usually to unite people, with the secondary objective of serving **elaborate** and quality food.

Therefore, a banquet has the **distinct features** of:

Exclusive dining organized with privacy;

Food and services being **adapted** and delivered according to guests' requirements;

Large organized groups **participating in** dining, or in events **involving exhibitions**, **auctions** or **celebration** of special occasions.

WHY IS BANQUET OPERATIONS IMPORTANT?

The Banquet Department of a hotel is normally part of the **Food & Beverage Department** although in larger organizations, it may be run independently as a **Catering Services Department**, otherwise known as the **Catering & Convention Services Department.**

Whatever the organization structure may be, it is only a matter of management **perspective**, as all **hospitality** business organizations are based on very similar basic structures and operating **procedures.** This is important as Catering and Banquet is the highest contributor of **revenue** amongst all other Food & Beverage outlets, with a controllable cost structure which enables it to therefore secure the highest return in **the bottom line.**

Moreover, there is much **flexibility** and **versatility** in the banquet business where concepts and operational structures can be changed **consistently** to meet the demands and needs of clients. It would also enable management to anticipate business volumes **in advance** and to therefore **optimize** the **utility** of the space and resources to **generate** higher yields and wherever possible, other sources of non-traditional banquet **revenue.**

In view of these factors, the successful management and organization of banquet business would require skills in **coordinating** tasks and **personnel**, skills in selecting good **combi-**

nations of food and beverages which are to be served, as well as sound **judgment** in **maximizing profitability** through proper pricing and costing of events catered.

Thus, it is **imperative** for a banquet manager to have a thorough understanding of the business from the perspective of "SALES" as well as "OPERATIONS".

WHAT IS THE ROLE OF THE BANQUET DEPARTMENT?

The primary function of the Banquet Department is that it is a Food & Beverage outlet within the Food & Beverage Department and provides food and beverage for the event.

The secondary role of this department is to provide non-food-and-beverage support for the hotel's convention market.

It is also a **specialist** for organizing theme parties, weddings, dinner theatres, playhouses, **gala** dinners and any special events, which are limited only by one's **imagination**.

This department would very often **take on** the organization of outside catering functions, providing the food and beverages, set-ups as well as services in any off **premises** sites.

The events organized within or outside the hotel by the Banquet Department would indirectly provide **publicity** for the hotel through guests' attendance and their recommendations and positive remarks from the hosts of completed functions.

Vocabulary

original	*adj*. 最初的	formal	*adj*. 正式的
primary	*adj*. 首要的;主要的	elaborate	*adj*. 精心制作的
distinct	*adj*. 明显的	feature	*n*. 特征;特点
exclusive	*adj*. 专用的	adapt	*vi*. (to)适应不同情况
involve	*vt*. 包含	exhibition	*n*. 陈列;展览
auction	*n*. 拍卖	celebration	*n*. 庆祝会(仪式)
catering	*n*. 提供饮食及服务	convention	*n*. 会议
perspective	*n*. 观点;看法	hospitality	*n*. 热情好客
procedure	*n*. 程序;手续	flexibility	*n*. 灵活性
versatility	*n*. 多才多艺	consistently	*adv*. 一贯地
optimize	*vt*. 使……最优化	utility	*n*. 功用;效用
generate	*vt*. 形成;造成	revenue	*n*. 收入;收益
coordinate	*vt*. 使……协调	personnel	*n*. 全体员工
combination	*n*. 结合	judgment	*n*. 判断
maximize	*vt*. 最大化	profitability	*n*. 获利
imperative	*adj*. 不可避免的	specialist	*n*. 专家;行家
gala	*n*. 节日;庆祝	imagination	*n*. 想象力
premises	*n*. 办公场所	publicity	*n*. 宣传

Phrases and Expressions

in view of	由于;鉴于;基于
participate in	参加

the bottom line	底线
in advance	提前
take on	承担;呈现

Proper Names

Food & Beverage Department	餐饮部
Catering Services Department	宴会服务部
Catering & Convention Services Department	宴会和会议服务部

Task 1　True or false statements. Decide whether the following statements are True (T) or False (F) according to the text.

1. The first objective of a banquet is to serve elaborate and quality food. (　　)
2. In a banquet, food and services should be delivered according to guests' requirements. (　　)
3. In terms of management perspective, all hospitality business organizations are based on very similar basic structures and operating procedures. (　　)
4. Catering and Banquet is the highest contributor of revenue amongst all other Food & Beverage outlets although the cost is uncontrollable. (　　)
5. Concepts and operational structures can be changed in the banquet business to meet the demands and needs of clients. (　　)
6. The Banquet Department sometimes provides services for events outside the hotel. (　　)

Task 2　Questions. Read the text again and answer the following questions.

1. What features does a banquet have?
2. What skills should a successful management have in a banquet?
3. What concept should a banquet manager have in order to maximize the profitability of a banquet?
4. What's the function of the Banquet Department?
5. What will influence the hotel's publicity?

Task 3　Blank filling. Fill in the blanks with the words given. Change the form when necessary.

distinct	consistently	perspective	flexibility	coordinate
imperative	occasion	adapt	in advance	participate in

1. His experience abroad provides a wider ________ on the problem.
2. They appointed a new manager to ________ the work of the team.
3. We have argued ________ for a change in the law.

4. His voice was quiet, but every word was ________.
5. He was presented with the Lifetime Achievement Award on the ________ of his retirement.
6. People were evacuated from the coastal regions ________ of the hurricane.
7. It is absolutely ________ for the mineral industry and the government to attach great importance to enhancing the workers' safety in work.
8. Computers offer a much greater degree of ________ in the way work is organized.
9. Most of these tools have been specially ________ for the use by disabled people.
10. We encourage students to ________ the running of the college fully.

Part 4 Translation

Task 1 Translate the following passage into Chinese.

Table service at banquets will always be formal and will follow specific rules set down by the Food and Beverage manager. Many of these rules also apply to the service in public dining rooms. When there is a large number of guests at a banquet, staff will be trained to serve quickly but elegantly, so that guests receive the different courses at about the same time but will be made to feel that they are being individually served.

Task 2 Translate the following passage into English.

上海新国际博览中心(SNIEC)拥有17个单层无柱式(column-free)展厅,室内展览面积200000平方米,室外展览面积100000平方米。自2001年开业以来,SNIEC的业绩稳定增长,每年举办100余场知名展览会,吸引400余万名海内外客商。作为一个多功能的场馆,SNIEC也是举办各种社会、公司活动的理想场地。

Part 5 Cultural Norms

常用词汇

宴会类型

Welcome Dinner	欢迎宴会	Farewell Dinner	告别宴会
Informal Dinner	便宴	Glee Feast	庆功宴
Luncheon	午宴	Reception	招待会
Buffet	自助餐	Cocktail Party	鸡尾酒会
Return Dinner	答谢宴会	Wedding Party	婚宴

常见酒名

Grape Wine	葡萄酒	Tequila	龙舌兰
Beer	啤酒	Martell	马爹利
Brandy	白兰地	Remy Martin	人头马
Whisky	威士忌	Hennessy	轩尼诗

Rum	朗姆	Chivas	芝华士
Vodka	伏特加	Johnnie Walker	尊尼获加
Gin	杜松子酒	Jim Beam	占边

其他常用词汇

band stage	乐队舞台	candle holder	烛台
runway with red carpet	红毯过道	projector table	投影仪摆放台
registration table	签到处	cake table	蛋糕桌
tablecloth	桌布	knife	刀
bowl	碗	chopsticks	筷子
glass	玻璃杯	cup	杯子
coffee cup	咖啡杯	saucer	垫碟
hand towel	擦手巾	napkin	餐巾
tea pot	茶壶	coffee pot	咖啡壶
pepper shaker	胡椒瓶	plate	盘子
salt cellar	盐瓶	mustard pot	芥末盅
fork	刀叉	spoon	勺子
toothpick	牙签	ashtray	烟灰缸
cherry	樱桃	coconut	椰子
grape	葡萄	grapefruit	西柚
honey	蜂蜜	lemon	柠檬
mango	芒果	orange	橙子
peach	桃子	pineapple	菠萝
strawberry	草莓	watermelon	西瓜
Hami melon	哈密瓜	kiwi fruit	猕猴桃
round table	圆桌	cocktail table	鸡尾酒桌
team leader	领班	manager	经理
assistant manager	副经理	socket	插座;插口
flip chart	翻叶夹纸	LCD projector	液晶投影仪
podium	讲台	partition	屏风
whiteboard	白板	dimmer	调光器
microphone	麦克风	marker pen	记号笔
stage	舞台	dance floor	舞池

常用句子

欢迎客户

1. Welcome to Howard Johnson Jindi Plaza! 欢迎您来到金地豪生大酒店!
2. Welcome to banqueting hall! 欢迎来到宴会厅!

咨询客户信息

1. May I know how many people there will be? 请问有多少人参加宴会?
2. How many guests will be attending? 请问有多少客人参加宴会?
3. How many people will attend the party? 请问有多少人参加宴会?
4. When would you like to hold the party, madam? 女士,请问宴会定在什么时间?
5. How much would you like to spend for each table? 请问您每桌的预算是多少?
6. May I have your name please? 请问我可以知道您的名字吗?
7. May I have your phone number please? 请问我可以知道您的电话号码吗?

咨询客户需求

1. How may I help you? 请问您有什么需要帮忙的吗?
2. What would you like to drink please? 请问您要喝点什么?
3. Do you have reservation? 请问您预订了吗?
4. Do you have any special requirements? 请问您有什么特别的要求吗?
5. May I take your order now? 我现在可以为您点单吗?
6. How is everything? 您对一切还满意吗?
7. Excuse me, may I take the plates away? 打扰一下,我可以把您的盘子撤走吗?
8. Do you need any ice-blocks, please? 请问需要加冰块吗?
9. Would you like to have cold drinks or hot drinks? 请问需要冷饮还是热饮?
10. Is this table fine with you? 您认为这张桌子怎么样?
11. Where would you prefer to sit? 您想要坐在哪儿呢?
12. Would you like to have the buffet or a La carte? 您想要自助餐还是单点?

向客户致歉

1. Sorry to have kept you waiting. 对不起,让您久等了。
2. I apologize for this! 我为此道歉!

提供建议

1. It's a most popular dish. 这道菜很受欢迎的。
2. I would recommend the Queen's hall with spacious and splendid decoration, which is perfect for wedding party. 我向您推荐皇后厅,这里空间宽敞,装修豪华,非常适合举办婚宴。

与客户道别

1. I hope to see you again! 我希望再次见到您!
2. Goodbye and hope to see you again! 再见! 希望下次再见到您!
3. Have a good time! 希望您过得愉快!
4. Goodbye and thank you for coming! 再见! 谢谢您的光临!

Part 6 Supplementary Reading

The Regent Shanghai

September 28, 2014
Mr. Xia Yong
Manager/HR & General Affairs
SEGA (Shanghai) Software Co., Ltd.
16F No. 1326 YanAn Road (W)
Shanghai
Tel: 52586655 52301647
Fax: 52301648
Email: xia_yong@sega.com.cn

Dear Mr. Xia,
LETTER OF AGREEMENT

Thank you for confirming the event with us at the Regent Shanghai.

We are delighted to be the selected venue and would like to confirm the following arrangements.

MEETING/FUNCTION ROOMS

The following function rooms are assigned according to the estimated guaranteed number of persons. The hotel reserves the option to reassign function rooms should the need arise.

Date/Day	Persons	Time	Event	Venue	Set-up
October 29,2014	140	18:00—21:00	Buffet Lunch	Ballroom A & B	Round table

MINIMUM GUARANTEE

Please note that to reserve the meeting rooms indicated, the Hotel requires a minimum guarantee of 140 attendees per day. Should your actual attendance fall below the stipulated minimum guarantee, the minimum guarantee will still be charged.

BUFFET DINNER

We are pleased to confirm the meeting package at CNY 450+15% per person per day.

This package is based on a minimum guarantee of 140 attendees per day, which includes:

Special Buffet Menu;

Three hours free flow soft drink, juice and local beer.

For other beverage arrangements, kindly refer to our Banquet Bar Price List for the various charges.

SET-UP

The hotel will provide at no additional cost the following:

Dedicated Meeting Coordinator;

Flower arrangements for the reception table & dining tables;

One podium with microphone and two wireless microphones.

TERMS OF PAYMENT

Full payment CNY72450 net must reach Hotel by Friday, October 24th, 2014 by cash or telegraphic transfer. The payment must be made in Chinese Yuan.

Please make your telegraphic transfer payable to "THE REGENT SHANGHAI" or transfer your prepayment directly to our bank account.

Account Name: **Shanghai Summit Hotel Management Company The Longemont Shanghai**

Bank Name: Construction Bank of China, Shanghai Branch, Hongkou sub-branch.

Address: 3, Lane 421, Siping Road, Shanghai.

Bank Account: 31001507000050004117

All other payments are to be made at the end of the function upon presentation of the bill, which will include, but not limited to, any other charges not specified in this contract, but authorized by your company representative during the event.

This is a legal contract and must be signed by an officer empowered to sign such contracts.

THE REGENT SHANGHAI, operating for and on behalf of the Shanghai Summit Hotel Management Co. Ltd., 1090 Yan An West Road, ChangNing District, Shanghai 200052, P. R. China.

Yours sincerely

The Regent Shanghai

AUTHORIZED SIGNATORIES:

For and on behalf of	Agreed and accepted by:
____________________	____________________
The Regent Shanghai	
Suki Yu	Andy He
Assistant Catering Sales Manager	Director of Catering
Tel: 86 21 6115 9988 8672	
Fax: 86 21 6115 9739	
Email: syu@regenthotels. com	

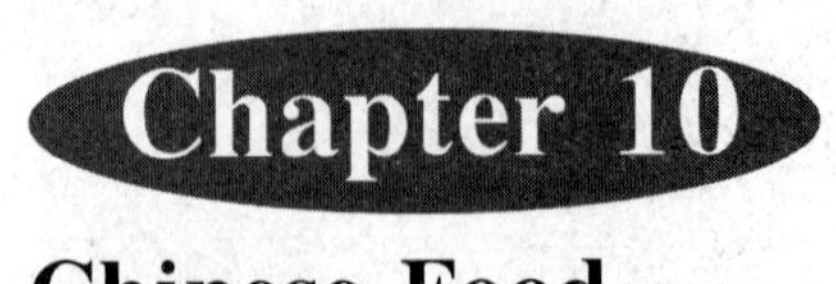

Chinese Food

Study Objectives

1. To master the service procedures of taking orders.
2. To have a good command of the sentences of taking orders in each procedure.
3. To acquaint yourself with some traditional Chinese cuisines.

Lead in

Chinese cuisine is world-famous for its perfect combination of "color, aroma, taste and appearance". China's unique culinary art owes itself to the country's long history, vast territory and hospitable tradition. Think carefully and try to answer the following questions.

1. Do you like Chinese food? What is your favorite cuisine?
2. Would you please introduce the cooking process of your favorite cuisine?
3. Do you know the 4 best-known schools of Chinese culinary tradition? What are they?

Part 1 Listening

Task 1 Dialogues. Listen to the dialogues and fill in the blanks with what you hear.

Dialogue 1

A: We have a Chinese restaurant and a Western-style restaurant. Which one do you prefer?

B: I'd like to try some Chinese ________ today.

Dialogue 2

A: Can I take your order now?

B: What do you have for today's ________?

Dialogue 3

A: Welcome to our restaurant. What kind of ________ would you like?

B: I'd like West Lake Fish in Sweet Sour Sauce and Dongpo Pork.

Dialogue 4

A: Here is the menu. What would you like, sir?

B: What would you recommend? I prefer something ________.

Dialogue 5

A: Good evening, madam. What can I do for you?

B: En, I'd like something to be ________ Chinese. Do you have any recommendations?

Task 2 Conversations.

Conversation 1 It is Jenny's first visit to China, and she wants to try some Chinese cuisine. Listen and fill in the blanks with the words or phrases provided in the box.

spicy hot	authentic	light and fresh	Cantonese cuisine	Beijing roast duck

(Jenny-J Waiter-W)

J: Oh, I'm starving. I'd like to try some ________ Chinese cuisine. What would you recommend, waiter?

W: Well, it depends. You see, there are eight famous Chinese cuisines, for instance, the Sichuan cuisine, and the Hunan cuisine.

J: They are both ________, I've heard.

W: That's right. If you like hot dishes, you can try some.

J: They might be too hot for me.

W: Then there's the ________ and the Jiangsu cuisine. They are ________. Most southerners like them.

J: What about any special Beijing dishes?

W: There's the ________.

J: Oh, yes. I've heard a lot about it. I'd like very much to try it.

Conversation 2 A guest enters a Chinese restaurant to try some Chinese food. Listen and fill in the blanks with the words or phrases provided in the box.

order	chopsticks	recommendations	tender and tasty	sweet and delicious

(Waitress-W Guest-G)

W: May I take your ________ now, sir?

G: Ur, I don't know much about Chinese food, can you recommend something?

W: Certainly. How about Cabbage in Oyster Sauce? It's ________.

G: Good, I'll take it. What's the Chicken Soup with Corn like?

W: It's soup with corn and minced chicken. It's ________.

G: En, I'll take this, too. I'd like to have some fried rice, could you make some ________?

W: How about the Chef's Fried Rice?

G: How do you make it?

W: It's fried rice with shrimp, eggs and broccoli.

G: OK, I'll try that. Thank you.

W: Anything else, sir?

G: No, thanks. That's all for now.

W: Shall I bring you a knife and fork?

G: No, thanks. ________ will do.

Conversation 3 A waiter is recommending some Chinese wine to the guest. Listen and fill in the blanks with what you hear.

(**Waitress-W Guest-G**)

W: Good evening! ________________________? Here is the wine list.

G: Yes. What would you recommend?

W: Since you've ordered Chinese food, I'd suggest you try some Chinese wine. In fact, we have Chinese ________________________ and Chinese ________________________.

G: Are there any differences between them?

W: Yes. Chinese rice wine is made from rice or ________________________, the Chinese white wine is made from barley, wheat or Chinese sorghum(高粱). People from south of China prefer rice wine while those from the north drink white liquor. If you prefer ________________________, I think ________________________ will be a good choice and ________________________.

G: Fine. We'd like some Shaoxing Jia Fan Jiu.

Part 2 Speaking

Task 1 Work in pairs. It is Mr. Hugh and Mrs. Hugh's first visit to China, and now they are in Louwailou Restaurant in Hangzhou to have their dinner. Read and complete the following dialogue by translating the Chinese sentences in the parentheses into English.

(**Waitress-W Mr. Hugh-Mr. Mrs. Hugh-Mrs.**)

W: Good evening, sir and madam. ________________________________(请问您有预订座位吗)?

Mr.: No. I'm afraid we haven't.

W: Never mind, sir. A table for two? This way, please.

Mr.: Can we sit here by the window?

W: I'm sorry, sir. ________________________________(这个位置已经被预订了). There is a sign on it. I'll seat you another table.

Mr.: OK, thanks. ________________________________(请把菜单拿给我们好吗)?

W: Here's the menu, sir. ________________________________(我过会儿来取您的点菜单).

(*Later.*)

W: Good evening, sir and madam. ______________________ (请问能点菜了吗)?

Mr.: Er, we don't understand the menu quite well. Since it's our first visit to China, ______________________ (您能给点建议吗)?

W: No problem, sir. Chinese food can be classified into Eight Cuisines. The best known and most influential are Cantonese cuisine, Shandong cuisine, Jiangsu cuisine (*specifically Huaiyang cuisine*) and Sichuan cuisine. And we serve Jiangsu cuisine in our restaurant. I'd recommend Shelled Shrimps with Dragon Well Green Tea. There are two ingredients for this dish. One looks snow white, and the other tender green. The two colors are well matched; they are pleasant to look at and fresh to taste.

Mr.: Yes, I heard it's one of the famous dishes of Huaiyang cuisine. ______________________ (这个菜色形俱佳).

W: You are quite right, sir. ______________________ (东坡肉也是我们的招牌菜). Would you like to have a try?

Mrs.: How is it cooked?

W: Well, it's pork braised in a casserole. In this dish you can find dark sauce, onion, ginger and sugar syrup. There is little water in it because too much water is likely to spoil the dish. The great thing about Dongpo Pork is that it doesn't taste fatty. It is limp and soft. It melts on the tongue. I bet you will like it.

Mrs.: It's amazing! Ah, ______________________ (我们还想来份汤). What soup do you have?

W: We have Sweet Corn and Chicken Soup, Three Fresh Delicacies Soup and Sister Song's Fish Broth. And Sister Song's Fish Broth is a mandarin fish which is steamed before the removing of its skin and bone, and then cooked with sliced ham, bamboo shoots, dried mushrooms, yolk, scallion, ginger and chicken soup seasoned with rice wine and vinegar. The thick broth prepared looks bright yellow and tastes as good as crab meat, even more tender and smooth.

Mrs.: It sounds nice. We'll have it.

W: ______________________ (您想喝点什么)? We have white liquor such as *Maotai* and *Wuliangye* as well as beers such as Tsingtao Beer.

Mr.: We'd like two bottles of Tsingtao Beer.

W: OK. You've ordered a Shelled Shrimps with Dragon Well Green Tea, a Dongpo Pork, a Sister Song's Fish Broth and two bottles of Tsingtao Beer. ______________________ (请问还有其他需要吗)?

Mr.: No, thanks.

W: Your dishes will come soon. Please enjoy your meal!

Vocabulary

cuisine	*n.* 菜肴	ingredient	*n.* (烹调的)原料
specialty	*n.* 招牌菜	braise	*vt.* 炖;焖

casserole	*n.* 焙盘；砂锅	sauce	*n.* 调味汁；酱汁
onion	*n.* 洋葱(头)	ginger	*n.* 姜；生姜
sugar syrup	*n.* 糖浆	limp	*adj.* 松软的
slice	*vt.* 切成片	mushroom	*n.* 蘑菇
yolk	*n.* 蛋黄	scallion	*n.* 青葱；大葱；韭菜
season	*vt.* 调味	vinegar	*n.* 醋
crab	*n.* 蟹；蟹肉		

Notes

1. Have you made a reservation? 请问您预订位置了吗？这一表达方式用于客人刚进餐厅时，询问是否预订了位置。如果客人已提前预订位置，则直接带客人到预留位置；如果没有，可能需要另找位置，或客已满，请顾客在等候区等待。类似的表达方式还有 Do you have a reservation? Have you booked a table?
2. Would you please give some suggestions? 您能提供一些建议吗？当客户不太了解菜品向服务员咨询意见时，可以用这一表达方式。类似的表达有 Would you please make some recommendations? Do you have any recommendations? What would you recommend?
3. Chinese food can be classified into Eight Cuisines. 中国菜有八大菜系，分别是粤菜、鲁菜、淮扬菜、川菜、徽菜、浙菜、闽菜、湘菜。其中，数粤菜、鲁菜、淮扬菜和川菜最出名。
4. Shelled Shrimps with Dragon Well Green Tea 龙井虾仁
5. Dongpo Pork 东坡肉
6. Sister Song's Fish Broth 宋嫂鱼羹

Task 2 Work in pairs. Discuss and complete the conversation between a couple and a waiter by filling in the blanks with appropriate sentences given below.

A. Which one do you prefer? B. Would you like something to drink before your meal? C. Do you have any bits to nibble? D. Is there anything else? E. How about you, dear? F. What kind would you like to have?

(**Waiter-W Mr. Morgan-Mr. Mrs. Morgan-Mrs.**)

W: Good evening, sir and madam! ______1______

Mr.: Yes, I'd like to have a cup of tea. What do you have for tea?

W: We have Dragon Well tea, Oolong tea, Jasmine tea and Chrysanthemum tea. ______2______

Mr.: I'll have a cup of Dragon Well. ______3______

Mrs.: Well, I'll have a cup of Jasmine tea. ______4______

W: Certainly, madam. We have lots of dim-sum, such as Oyster Omelet, Prawn Cracker, Shrimp Balls, Spring Rolls, Chicken Rolls, Salty Rice Pudding, Rice Tube Pudding, Red Bean and Pyramid Dumplings. ______5______

Mrs.: I'd like to try Oyster Omelet, Salty Rice Pudding and Pyramid Dumplings.

W: OK. ______6______

Mrs.: That's all for now. Thank you!

W: It is my pleasure. Please wait for a minute, I'll come back with your order in 5 minutes.

Task 3 Role-play. Work in pairs and make up a dialogue respectively according to the situations provided.

Situation 1 Ms. Norris goes to a restaurant in Hangzhou with her kids to have dinner. Practice taking orders according to the expressions given below.

—Waiter

- May I take your order now, madam?
- I'd recommend Beggar's Chicken (叫花鸡). It is a local specialty of Hangzhou and also called Hangzhou Roast Chicken. It takes four hours or so to do the roasting, and the chicken roasted is full in taste, delicious and golden-looking. It is worth a try.
- Steamed Hilsa Herring (清蒸鲥鱼) is our chef's recommendation. Fish from the Fuchun River is steamed with ham slices, dried mushrooms and bamboo shoots. The color and taste are both appealing.
- Eight-treasure Rice Pudding (猪油八宝饭) is today's special. It is a traditional food—steamed glutinous rice with choice ingredients ("eight treasures"), including bean paste, lotus seeds, red dates, preserved fruits, and pine nut kernel.
- Would you like to have a try?
- West Lake Water Shield Soup(西湖莼菜汤) looks nice. The red ham matches well with the white chicken and the green water shield which grows in the ponds of West Lake's "Three Pools Mirroring the Moon". The soup tastes delicious. It smells nice, too. The soup is highly nutritious. Water shield contains a lot of Vitamin C and a trace of iron with high medicinal value.
- What would you like to drink?
- Your dishes will be ready soon.
- May you enjoy your dinner.

—Ms. Norris

- Would you please give some recommendations?
- It sounds amazing. We'll have it.
- Yes, I heard it's one of the local people's favorite dishes.
- What soup do you have?
- We'd like some water-melon juice.

Situation 2 Ms. Norris and her kids have finished their dinner. She is going to pay the bill. Role play the conversation between Ms. Norris and the waiter.

—Ms. Norris

- Ask for the bill.
- Ask the waiter to explain the cost.
- Point out one mistake.
- Ask the ways of payment.
- Pay by credit.

—Waiter

- Bring the bill to the guest.
- Explain the cost of the meal.
- Apologize to the guest for the mistake and bring a new bill.
- Thank the guest.

Part 3 Reading

Chinese Cuisine

Chinese cuisine includes styles originating from the **diverse** regions of China, as well as from Chinese people in other parts of the world. The history of Chinese cuisine in China **stretches back** for thousands of years and has changed from period to period and in each region according to climate, imperial fashions, and local **preferences**. Over time, techniques and ingredients from the cuisines of other cultures were **integrated** into the cuisine of the Chinese people due to the trade with nearby regions in pre-modern times and with Europe and the New World in the modern period.

A number of different styles **contribute to** Chinese cuisine but perhaps the best known and most influential are Cantonese Cuisine, Shandong Cuisine, Jiangsu Cuisine (or Huaiyang Cuisine) and Sichuan Cuisine. These styles are **distinctive** from one another due to factors such as availability of resources, climate, geography, history, cooking techniques and lifestyle. One style may **favour** the use of lots of **garlic** and **shallots** over lots of **chili** and **spices**, while another may favour preparing seafood over other meats and **fowl**.

Cantonese Cuisine

Dim sum, literally "touch your heart", is a Cantonese term for small hearty dishes. These bite-sized portions are prepared using traditional cooking methods such as **frying**, **steaming**, **stewing** and **baking**. It is designed so that one person may taste a variety of different dishes at the same time. Some of these may include **rice rolls**, **lotus leaf rice**, **turnip cakes**, **buns**, Jiaozi-style dumplings, **stir-fried** green vegetables, **congee** porridge, soups, etc. The Cantonese style of dining, yum cha, combines the variety of dim sum dishes with the drinking of tea. Yum cha literally means "drink tea".

Shandong Cuisine

Shandong Cuisine is commonly and simply known as Lu Cuisine. With a long history,

Shandong Cuisine once formed an important part of the **imperial** cuisine and was widely promoted in North China. However, it isn't so popular in South China (including the more embracing Shanghai).

Shandong Cuisine features a variety of cooking techniques and seafood ingredients. The typical dishes on local menu are **braised abalone**, **braised trepang**, **sweet and sour carp**, **Jiuzhuan Dachang** and **Dezhou Chicken**.

Jiangsu Cuisine

Jiangsu Cuisine, also known as *Su* (*Cai*) *Cuisine* for short, is one of the major components of Chinese cuisine, which consists of the styles of Yangzhou, Nanjing, Suzhou and Zhenjiang dishes. It is very famous all over the world for its distinctive style and taste. It is especially popular in the lower reach of the Yangtze River.

Sichuan Cuisine

Chuan Cai, is a style of Chinese cuisine originating from the Sichuan Province of southwestern China famed for bold flavors, particularly the **pungency** and **spiciness** resulting from liberal use of garlic and chili peppers, as well as the unique flavor of the Sichuan **peppercorn** and **facing heaven pepper**. Peanuts, sesame paste and ginger are also prominent ingredients in this style.

Styles and tastes also varied by class, region, and **ethnic** background. This led to an **unparalleled** range of ingredients, techniques, dishes and eating styles in what could be called Chinese food, leading Chinese to pride themselves on eating a wide variety of foods while remaining true to the spirit and traditions of Chinese food culture.

Vocabulary

diverse	*adj*. 多种多样的	preference	*n*. 偏爱;优先权
integrate	*vt*. 使……完整	distinctive	*adj*. 有特色的
favour	*vt*. 喜爱	garlic	*n*. 大蒜;蒜头
shallot	*n*. 葱	chili	*n*. 红辣椒
spice	*n*. 香料;调味品	fowl	*n*. 鸡;家禽
fry	*vi*. 用油煎;油炸	steam	*vt*. 蒸煮
stew	*vt*. & *vi*. 炖;煨	bake	*vt*. 烤;烘焙
congee	*n*. 粥	imperial	*adj*. 帝国的
pungency	*n*. 辛辣	spiciness	*n*. 香馥;香味
peppercorn	*n*. 胡椒子;花椒	ethnic	*adj*. 种族的
unparalleled	*adj*. 无比的;无双的;空前的		

Phrases and Expressions

stretch back...	追溯到……
contribute to	导致

Proper Names

Dim Sum	点心	Rice Rolls	饭卷

Lotus Leaf Rice	荷叶饭	Turnip Cake	腊味萝卜糕
Braised Abalone	红烧鲍鱼	Braised Trepang	烩海参
Sweet and Sour Carp	糖醋鲤鱼	Jiuzhuan Dachang	九转大肠
Dezhou Chicken	德州扒鸡	Facing Heaven Pepper	朝天椒

Task 1 True or false statements. Decide whether the following statements are True (T) or False (F) according to the text.

1. Chinese cuisine has changed over the time due to climate, imperial fashions, and local preferences. ( )
2. Chinese people adopted techniques and ingredients from the cuisines of other cultures while doing trade with people from other countries. ( )
3. Cantonese may enjoy a variety of dim-sum dishes with the drinking of tea. ( )
4. Shandong Cuisine is quite popular both in North China and South China. ( )
5. Jiangsu Cuisine is only welcomed by those living in the lower reach of the Yangtze River. ( )
6. The liberal use of different peppers results in the unique flavor of Sichuan Cuisine. ( )

Task 2 Questions. Read the text again and answer the following questions.

1. What brought about the change of the history of Chinese Cuisine over the period?
2. What causes the different styles of the four cuisines in China?
3. How many ways are there to make dim sum in Cantonese Cuisine?
4. Why could Shandong Cuisine be widely promoted in North China in the course of history?
5. What contributes to the unique flavor of pungency and spiciness of Sichuan Cuisine?

Task 3 Blank filling. Fill in the blanks with the words given. Change the form when necessary.

ethnic	unparalleled	distinctive	diverse	integrate
imperial	favour	preference	stretch back	contribute to

1. The policy is to ________ children with special needs into ordinary schools.
2. In 1959, Akihito broke with ________ tradition by marrying a commoner.
3. India has always been one of the most religiously ________ countries.
4. Medical negligence was said to have ________ her death.
5. Cooking with the lid on gives the food that ________ smoky flavor
6. Many countries ________ a presidential system of government.
7. The Pentagon will give ________ to companies which do business electronically.
8. The book explores the connection between American ________ and regional literatures.

9. The country is facing a crisis ________ since the Second World War.
10. Warnings that curiosity can be destructive ________ to the very beginning of civilization.

Part 4 Translation

Task 1 Translate the following passage into Chinese.

In the 19th century, Chinese in San Francisco operated sophisticated and sometimes luxurious restaurants patronized mainly by Chinese, while restaurants in smaller towns served what their customers requested, ranging from pork chop sandwiches(猪排三明治) and apple pie to beans and eggs. These smaller restaurants developed American Chinese cuisine when they modified their food to suit a more American palate(味觉). First catering to miners and railroad workers, they established new eateries in towns where Chinese food was completely unknown, adapting local ingredients and catering to their customers' tastes. In the process, cooks adapted southern Chinese dishes such as chop suey, and developed a style of Chinese food not found in China.

Task 2 Translate the following passage into English.

说起中餐,人们都知道中餐烹饪以其"色、香(aroma)、味、形"俱全而著称于世。中国悠久的历史、广袤的疆土、好客的习俗,这些都孕育了中餐烹饪的独特艺术。中餐烹饪讲究原料的选配、食物的质地(texture)、佐料(seasonings)的调整、切菜的刀工、适时的烹调,以及装盘艺术。最负盛名的中餐菜系有南方的粤菜、北方的鲁菜、东部的淮扬菜和西部的川菜,素有"南淡北咸,东甜西辣"之特点。

Part 5 Cultural Norms

中餐菜名翻译技巧

随着全球化大趋势的发展,餐饮业日趋国际化。作为餐饮业的从业人员,了解餐饮方面的专业英语是非常必要的,而掌握中餐英文菜单则是最基本的要求。

由于中英两种语言差异较大,在把中餐菜名译成英文时,应采用写实命名法,尽量将菜肴的原料、烹制方法、菜肴的味型等翻译出来,让客人一目了然。下面简单介绍几种方式供大家参考。

1. 以主料开头的翻译方法。

(1) 介绍菜肴的主料和辅料。

公式:主料(形状)+(with)辅料

例:杏仁鸡丁 chicken cubes with almond
牛肉豆腐 beef with bean curd
西红柿炒鸡蛋 scrambled egg with tomato

(2) 介绍菜肴的主料和味汁。

公式:主料(形状)+(with/in)味汁

例：芥末鸭掌 duck webs with mustard sauce

葱油鸡 chicken in scallion oil

米酒鱼卷 fish rolls with rice wine

2. 以烹制方法开头的翻译方法。

(1) 介绍菜肴的烹法和主料。

公式：烹法＋主料(形状)

例：软炸里脊 soft-fried pork fillet

烤乳猪 roast suckling pig

炒鳝片 stir-fried eel slices

(2) 介绍菜肴的烹法和主料、辅料。

公式：烹法＋主料(形状)＋(with)辅料

例：仔姜烧鸡条 braised chicken fillet with tender ginger

(3) 介绍菜肴的烹法、主料和味汁。

公式：烹法＋主料(形状)＋(with/in)味汁

例：红烧牛肉 braised beef with brown sauce

鱼香肉丝 fried shredded pork with sweet and sour sauce

清炖猪蹄 stewed pig hoof in clean soup

3. 以形状或口感开头的翻译方法。

(1) 介绍菜肴的形状(口感)和主料、辅料。

公式：形状(口感)＋主料＋(with)辅料

例：芝麻酥鸡 crisp chicken with sesame

陈皮兔丁 diced rabbit with orange peel

时蔬鸡片 sliced chicken with seasonal vegetables

(2) 介绍菜肴的口感、烹法和主料。

公式：口感＋烹法＋主料

例：香酥排骨 crisp fried spareribs

水煮嫩鱼 tender stewed fish

香煎鸡块 fragrant fried chicken

(3) 介绍菜肴的形状(口感)、主料和味汁。

公式：形状(口感)＋主料＋(with)味汁

例：茄汁鱼片 sliced fish with tomato sauce

椒麻鸡块 cutlets chicken with hot pepper

黄酒脆皮虾仁 crisp shrimps with rice wine sauce

4. 以人名或地名开头的翻译方法。

(1) 介绍菜肴的创始人(发源地)和主料。

公式：人名(地名)＋主料

例：麻婆豆腐 Mapo Dofu

四川水饺 Sichuan boiled dumpling

(2) 介绍菜肴的创始人(发源地)、烹法和主料。

公式：人名(地名)+烹法+主料

例：东坡煨肘 Dongpo stewed pork joint

北京烤鸭 Beijing Roast Duck

在中餐菜名翻译成英文的过程中，可以采用多种方法，并且每一道菜都可以从不同的角度翻译。例如，川菜中的"宫保鸡丁"这道菜就有以下几种译法：

—Sautéed Chicken Cubes with Peanuts

—Gongbao Chicken Cubes

—Diced Chicken with Chili and Peanuts

由此可见，中餐菜名的英译方法是灵活多变的。至于我们在翻译中应该采用哪种方法，可根据个人的习惯和具体情况确定。不过根据笔者的经验，只要掌握了第一种以主料开头的翻译方法，对其他种类的翻译方法便可以触类旁通，我们只需根据文中所列出的翻译公式去做一些相应替换即可。

常用句子

解释菜品

1. Generally speaking, Cantonese cuisine is light and clear; Sichuan cuisine is strong and hot; Shanghai cuisine is sweet and Beijing cuisine is spicy and a bit salty. 总地来说，广东菜比较清淡、爽口；四川菜口味偏重、偏辣；上海菜口味偏甜；北京菜偏辣、偏咸。
2. It's crisp/tasty/tender/clear/strong/spicy/aromatic. 它很酥脆/可口/鲜嫩/清淡/浓烈/辣/香味扑鼻。
3. It looks good, smells good and tastes good. 这道菜色、香、味俱全。
4. It's a well-known delicacy in Chinese cuisine. 它是中国菜里一道有名的佳肴。
5. It's very popular among our guests. 它非常受客人欢迎。
6. The chicken soup with cream corn is the soup with corn and minced chicken. It's sweet and delicious. 鸡茸玉米羹是用甜玉米和鸡茸做的，很鲜甜。
7. The stewed mutton is stewed in wine with carrot and onion. 炖羊肉是用酒炖的，还配有萝卜和洋葱。
8. It's for 4 persons. 这是四个人吃的量。
9. How many ways are there to cook chicken soup? 这道鸡汤有几种烹制方法？
10. Is there any other way to cook pigeon other than roasted? 乳鸽除了烤之外还有其他的烹制方法吗？
11. Would you tell me how to cook the steamed pork wrapped with rice flour? 你能告诉我们粉蒸肉是怎么做的吗？
12. What is the best way to cook scallops? 请问用什么方法烹制扇贝最好？

推荐菜品

1. The set course will not take so much time. I would recommend that you order a set course for 2 persons. It is cheap and delicious. 套餐很快就能上，我推荐你们点一份两人套餐，经济又实惠。
2. I'm afraid it is not enough for four persons. It would be better to add two dishes. 恐怕这

不够四个人吃。最好再加两个菜。

3. This course is for a minimum of 5 to 6 persons. I think the portions will be too large for two. 这道菜至少是 5～6 个人吃的。我想这分量对两个人来说太多了。
4. Today's special is..., with a 40% discount. 今天的特价菜是……有 6 折优惠。
5. If you are in a hurry, I would recommend... 如果您赶时间,我推荐您……
6. The beef BBQ is terrific! You'll love it. 牛肉烧烤棒极了！您一定会喜欢的。
7. Goose Wings and Feet in Soy Sauce is very typical of Chaozhou style. "卤水鹅掌翼"很有潮州风味。
8. Hand Shredded Chicken of Dongjiang style is a very old traditional dish. "东江手撕鸡"已经有很悠久的历史了。
9. May I suggest the ...? It's our house specialty/the latest recommendation/the latest style. 我推荐……,这是我们的招牌菜/最新推介/最新菜品。
10. Spring is the best season for carp. 春天是吃鲤鱼的最佳时节。
11. The spinach is in season now. Would you like to try it? 菠菜刚上市。您要试一下吗?
12. Have you tried fried garoupa with mayonnaise sauce? It's our chef's special. 您尝过红斑鱼配蛋黄酱吗? 这是我们大厨的拿手菜。
13. Would you like to try our mutton hot pot? It will keep you warm in winter. 您要试下我们的羊肉火锅吗? 冬天吃可以让您很暖和。
14. If you are entertaining important guests, our braised sea cucumber with mushroom in abalone sauce is a very luxurious dish. 如果您是招待贵客的话,我建议您点一个比较名贵的鲍汁海参炖花菇。
15. Would you like to try our House Specialty? 您要试下我们店的招牌菜吗?

没有客人需要的食物时

1. It's out of season. How about ...? 这道菜已经过季了。试试……怎么样?
2. I'm sorry, there is no ... today. 抱歉,今天没有……了。
3. I'm afraid ...is not on our menu. But I'll ask our chef if it is available.
   抱歉,菜单上没有……。我问一下主厨看看是否能做出来。
4. I'm afraid ... is sold out. 抱歉,……已经卖完了。
5. That dish is not available now. May I suggest ...? It is also tasty.
   那道菜已经卖完了。我为您推荐……怎么样? 这道菜也很美味。
6. I'm afraid it is out of season, sir. Would you like to try something else?
   抱歉,先生,这道菜已经过季了。您要不要尝尝其他菜?

Part 6 Supplementary Reading

Regional Cuisine in China

Chinese cooking is recognized as one of the greatest cuisines in the world. There is an ever increasing interest in and appreciation of Chinese food in the West. The fact that Chinese restaurants are growing quickly in the West is evidence of the variety and quality of

Chinese food.

The most well-known cuisines in China are so called "Eight Cuisines", namely, Anhui Cuisine, Cantonese Cuisine, Fujian Cuisine, Hunan Cuisine, Jiangsu Cuisine, Sichuan Cuisine, Shandong Cuisine and Zhejiang Cuisine.

Jiangsu Cuisine favours cooking techniques such as braising and stewing, while Sichuan Cuisine employs baking, just to name a few. Hairy crab is a highly sought after local delicacy in Shanghai, as it can be found in lakes within the region. Peking duck and dim-sum are other popular dishes well known outside of China. Based on the raw materials and ingredients used, the method of preparation and cultural differences, a variety of foods with different flavors and textures are prepared in different regions of the country. Many traditional regional cuisines rely on basic methods of preservation such as drying, salting, pickling and fermentation.

Anhui Cuisine

Anhui Cuisine is derived from the native cooking styles of the Huangshan Mountains region in China and is similar to Jiangsu Cuisine, but with less emphasis on seafood and more on a wide variety of local herbs and vegetables. Anhui province is particularly endowed with fresh bamboo and mushroom crops.

Fujian Cuisine

Fujian Cuisine is influenced by Fujian's coastal position and mountainous terrain. Woodland delicacies such as edible mushrooms and bamboo shoots are also utilized. Slicing techniques are valued in the cuisine and utilized to enhance the flavor, aroma and texture of seafood and other foods. Fujian Cuisine is often served in a broth or soup, with cooking techniques including braising, stewing, steaming and boiling.

Hunan Cuisine

Hunan Cuisine is well known for its hot spicy flavor, fresh aroma and deep color. Common cooking techniques include stewing, frying, pot-roasting, braising, and smoking. Due to the high agricultural output of the region, there are many varied ingredients for Hunan dishes.

Zhejiang Cuisine

Zhejiang Cuisine derives from the native cooking styles of the Zhejiang region. The dishes are not greasy, heavy but instead a fresh, soft flavor with a mellow fragrance.

The cuisine consists of at least four styles, each of which originated from different cities in the province:

Hangzhou style, characterized by rich variations and the use of bamboo shoots.

Shaoxing style, specializing in poultry and freshwater fish.

Ningbo style, specializing in seafood.

Shanghai style, a combination of different Zhe styles, is also very famous for its dim sum.

Chapter 11

Western Food

Study Objectives

1. To master the whole procedure for serving Western food.
2. To have a good command of the sentences of taking orders in each procedure.
3. To acquaint yourself with table manners in Western countries.

Lead in

Western cuisine is a generalized term collectively referring to the cuisines of Europe and other Western countries. The cuisines of Western countries are diverse by themselves, although there are common characteristics that distinguish Western cooking from cuisines of Asian countries and others. Think carefully and try to answer the following questions.

1. Do you like Western food?
2. Do you know the whole procedure for serving Western food?
3. What table manners should we pay attention to while having Western food?

Part 1 Listening

Task 1 Dialogues. Listen to the dialogues and fill in the blanks with what you hear.

Dialogue 1

A: May I take your order, please?

B: Er, I'd like ________ and meat dish.

Dialogue 2

A: Good morning, madam. Would you prefer ________ or a la carte?

B: A la carte, please.

Dialogue 3

A: How do you like your steak?

B: ________, please.

Dialogue 4

A: How do you want your eggs?

B: ________, please.

Dialogue 5

A: What would you like for ________?

B: I'll have ice cream.

Notes

1. Buffet 自助餐
2. A la carte 零点餐，是根据客人的选择提供菜式，花费比套餐高。

Task 2 Conversations

Conversation 1 A couple is waiting to be seated in a crowded restaurant. Listen and fill in the blanks with the words or phrases provided in the box.

available	reservation	by the window	step this way	a table for two

(**Waitress-W Guest-G**)

W: Do you have a ________, sir and madam?

G: No, I'm afraid we don't.

W: I'm sorry. The restaurant is full now. You have to wait for about half an hour. Would you care to have a drink at the lounge until a table is ________?

G: No, thanks. We'll come back later. May I reserve ________?

W: Yes, of course. May I have your name, sir?

G: Bruce. By the way, can we have a table ________?

W: We'll try to arrange it but I can't guarantee, sir.

G: That's fine.

(*Half an hour later, the couple comes back.*)

W: Your table is ready, sir. Please ________.

Conversation 2 Bill is having an American breakfast in the restaurant. Listen and fill in the blanks with the words or phrases provided in the box.

prefer	strong	black coffee	sign this bill	with fried eggs

(**Waitress-W Bill-B**)

W: Good morning. Can I help you?

B: I'd like an American breakfast ________, sunny side up.

W: What kind of juice do you ________, sir?

B: Grapefruit juice and please make my coffee very ________.

W: Yes, sir. American breakfast with fried eggs, sunny side up, grapefruit juice and a ________. Am I correct, sir?

B: Yes, that's right.

W: Is there anything else, sir?

B: No, that's all.

(*Later.*)

W: Good morning, sir. I've brought the breakfast you ordered.

B: Just put it on the table, please.

W: Do you need anything else, sir?

B: No thanks. Ah, yes! Can I have some more juice for the mini-bar?

W: What kind of juice would you like, sir?

B: Tomato, orange and apple juice, please.

W: Yes, sir. I'll get them for you right away. Would you please ________ first? Thank you, sir.

Notes

西式早餐的鸡蛋有五种不同的制作方法：煮蛋(boiled egg)、煎蛋(fried egg)、炒蛋(scrambled egg)、荷包蛋(poached egg)和蛋饼(omelet)。一定要问清客人的需求，以免不合口味。煎蛋一般分两种：单面煎(sunny side up)和双面煎(over easy)。

Conversation 3 A couple is ordering their dishes in a restaurant. Listen and fill in the blanks with what you hear.

(Mr. Clark-A Waitress-B Mrs. Clark-C)

A: Waitress, a table for two, please.

B: Yes. This way, please.

A: ________________________________, please?

B: Here you are.

A: What's good today?

B: ________________________________.

A: Well, it is too greasy. Perhaps ________________________________ followed by some seafood and chips.

B: ________________________________?

C: No dessert, thanks. Just coffee.

(*After a few minutes.*)

A: I can have the check, please.

B: Cash or charge, sir?

A: Charge, please. Put it on my American Express.

Part 2 Speaking

Task 1 Work in pairs. Mr. and Mrs. Wilson go to a Western restaurant to have dinner. Read and complete the following dialogue by translating the Chinese sentences in the parentheses into English.

(Waiter-W Mr. Wilson-Mr. Mrs. Wilson-Mrs.)

W: Good evening, sir and madam. Welcome to Parkland Western Restaurant. ________________________________ (你们喜欢坐吸烟区还是无烟区呢)?

Mrs.: No-smoking.

W: Follow me, please. I'll seat you. ________________________ (这张桌子可以吗)?

Mrs.: Fine. Lovely view! Thank you!

W: You are welcome. Here's the menu. We have both table d'hote and a la carte. Take your time please. ________________________ (我一会儿来为您点餐).

Mr.: Thank you. May I have a glass of Dubonnet first?

W: Yes, sir. And how about you, madam? Would you like an aperitif?

Mrs.: Yes, thank you. I'd like a dry vermouth, please.

W: Certainly.

(*Later, the waiter comes back with drinks.*)

W: May I take your order now, sir?

Mr.: ________________________ (今天的招牌菜是什么)?

W: There are two: Grilled Salmon Fillet and Lobster Thermidor.

Mr.: (*To Mrs. Wilson*) What would you like, honey?

Mrs.: I'd like the chicken liver pate to start, followed by the grilled salmon fillet and a green salad.

W: And would you like a dessert, madam? ________________________ (我们有很多的甜品可供选择).

Mrs.: Oooh yes please! I'll have the cheese cake. Thank you.

W: OK. And you, sir?

Mr.: I'll try the mushroom soup please.

W: I'm sorry, sir. I'm afraid that the mushroom soup is finished. How about French onion soup?

________________________ (这是我们厨师的招牌菜之一).

Mr.: Oh, OK, I'll have that followed by a steak for the main course with a mixed salad.

W: How would you like the steak done, sir?

Mr.: Medium, please.

W: ________________________ (您想要点酒来配您的晚餐吗)? Here is the wine list.

Mrs.: What do you suggest?

W: I would suggest Californian red wine or Chateau Latour for the beef steak and Sauvignon Blanc or ______________________ (香槟配鱼吃).

Mrs.: That's great. We will have half bottle of Californian red wine and half bottle of champagne.

W: Thank you, sir. You've ordered a chicken liver pate followed by the grilled salmon fillet and a green salad, a cheese cake, a French onion soup, a steak (medium) with a mixed salad, half bottle of Californian red wine and half bottle of champagne. Am I correct?

Mr.: Absolutely!

W: Would you need anything else?

Mr.: No. That's all for now.

W: OK, I'll bring your starters along in just a few minutes.

Mr.: Good. Thank you.

W: You are welcome.

Vocabulary

aperitif	*n.* (餐前)开胃酒	vermouth	*n.* 味美斯酒;苦艾酒
pate	*n.* 鱼酱;肉酱	grill	*vt.* & *vi.* 烧烤
salmon	*n.* 鲑鱼;三文鱼	fillet	*n.* 肉片;鱼片
mushroom	*n.* 蘑菇	specialty	*n.* 招牌菜
steak	*n.* 牛排	champagne	*n.* 香槟酒

Proper Names

Lobster Thermidor	热月龙虾,酿龙虾
Dubonnet	杜邦内葡萄酒
Californian red wine	加州红葡萄酒
Chateau Latour	拉杜堡红葡萄酒
Sauvignon Blanc	(加利福尼亚)白索维农酒

Notes

1. Would you like to sit smoking or non-smoking? 你们喜欢坐吸烟区还是无烟区呢?
   在英国及其他很多国家,餐厅一般划分为吸烟区和无烟区。一进餐厅,服务员会主动征询客人的意见,然后引领客人前往所选择的区域就餐。
2. We have both table d'hote and a la carte. 我们有套餐也可以照菜单点菜。
   table d'hote 套餐;a la carte 照菜单点菜(每道菜分别定价,有别于套餐)。
3. I'm afraid that the mushroom soup is finished. 抱歉,蘑菇汤已经卖完了。
   当客户点的菜已经卖完时,可以用这一表达方式回答。其他类似的表达还有 I'm sorry, there is no ... today. 抱歉,今天没有……了。I'm afraid ... is sold out. 抱歉,……已经卖完了。That dish is not available now. May I suggest ...? It is also tasty. 那道菜已经卖完了。我为您推荐……怎么样? 这道菜也很美味。

4. How would you like your steak done, sir? Medium. 请问您点的牛排要几成熟呢？五成。去西餐厅就餐吃牛排时，服务员会问你需要几成熟，你可以根据自己的喜好做出选择。一成熟 extra-rare or blue (bleu)，三成熟 rare，四成熟 medium rare，五成熟 medium，七成熟 medium well，全熟 well done。

Task 2 Work in pairs. Discuss and complete the conversation between a guest and a banquet service waiter by filling in the blanks with appropriate sentences given below.

A. How would you like your eggs, sir?
B. And I'd like to have a black tea.
C. Please take your time, sir.
D. May I take your order now?
E. That's right.
F. Which kind of juice would you like?

(Waiter-W Guest-G)

W: Good morning! ______1______

G: Please give me a few minutes. I'm not yet ready.

W: ______2______

G: Waiter, I'd like to have a full breakfast.

W: Certainly, sir. ______3______

G: Orange.

W: Would you like sausage, bacon or ham?

G: Sausage, please.

W: ______4______

G: Two fried eggs, fried over.

W: Certainly. Would you like toast, breakfast rolls, croissants or Danish pastries?

G: Croissants, please. ______5______

W: Certainly, sir. So that's orange juice, sausage and eggs, fried over, croissant and a black tea.

G: ______6______

W: Thank you, sir.

Task 3 Role-play. Work in pairs and make up a dialogue respectively according to the situations provided.

Situation 1

—Waitress
- Would you like to order now?
- Veal cutlet is not available.

—Mr. Simpson
- Shrimp cocktail, veal cutlet, coffee with cream, etc.

- Recommend sirloin steak.
- How do you like your steak done?
- Would you like some wine to go with the dinner?
- Would you like anything else?
- Repeat the order.
- Will go place the order.

- Take the steak.
- Rare.
- Gin and tonics with lemon and ice.
- That's all.
- Thank you.

Situation 2

—Waiter

- We have both table d'hote and a la carte. What would you prefer?
- Today's specialty: Brazilian Style Rib Eye Steak and Australian Sirloin Steak.
- How would you like the steak done, madam?
- Would you like some dessert? We have a good selection of desserts.
- Would you like some wine to go with your dinner?
- I would suggest Botter Chianti or Wolf Blass White Label Cabernet for the Rib Eye Steak.

—Ms. Curtis

- A la carte, please.
- What is today's specialty?
- Medium well, please.
- I like the Parfait with Cream Caramel Flavor.
- Would you please make some recommendations?
- Perfect! I will have a glass of Botter Chianti.

Part 3 Reading

Table Manners in Western Countries

Manners in every country are different. What is polite in China may not be polite in the West. These basic rules will help you enjoy Western food with your friends from other cultures.

Always put the **napkin** on your lap first. Before you leave the table, **fold** your napkin and put it beside your plate.

As the meal is served, use the **silverware** farthest from the plate first. When eating something in a **bowl**, do not leave the **spoon** in the bowl. Put it on the plate beneath the bowl. Soup, as well as all American food is eaten quietly. Do not **slurp** the soup. The soup spoon is used by moving the spoon away from you. Do not over fill the spoon. The bowl may be **tipped** slightly away from you to allow the last bit of soup to be collected on the spoon. Do not pick the bowl up to hold it closer to your mouth. When you have finished your meal, place your knife and fork side by side on the plate. This **signals** that you have finished eating.

Wait until everyone has been served to begin eating. Everyone begins to eat at the same time. The host or hostess may invite you to start eating before everyone is served. Some foods may be cold if you are required to wait until everyone is served. If invited to begin before others are served, wait until three or four people have been served before starting to eat.

While eating, remember not to talk with your mouth full of food.

During the meal, the **host** or **hostess** will offer you a second helping of food. Sometimes they will ask you to help yourself. When they offer you food, give a direct answer. If you **refuse** the first time, they might not ask you again.

At the table, ask others to pass you dishes that are out of your reach. Good phrases to know are"Please pass the..." or "Could you hand me the ..., please?" If asked to pass the salt to someone, you should pass both the salt and pepper which are placed on the table together. Hand the salt and pepper to the person seated next to you. Do not reach over the person next to you to pass anything to others.

Sit up straight at the table. Bring the food up to your mouth. Do not **lean down** to your plate.

Cut large pieces of meat, potatoes and vegetables into bite size pieces. Eat the pieces one at a time.

When eating **spaghetti**, **wind** the noodles **up** on your fork. You may use your spoon to assist in winding the noodles on your fork. The spaghetti on your fork should be eaten in one bite. It is very impolite to eat half your noodles and allow the other half to fall back on your plate.

Some foods may be eaten with your fingers. If you are not sure if it is proper to eat something by picking it up with your fingers, watch what others do before doing so yourself. Examples of foods which can be eaten with your fingers include: **bacon** which has been cooked until it is very **crisp**; bread should be broken rather than cut with a knife; cookies; sandwiches; and small fruits and **berries** on the stem. Most fast foods are intended to be eaten with your fingers.

Do not lean on your arm or **elbow** while eating. You may rest your hand and **wrist** on the edge of the table.

In America, people do not use toothpicks at the table.

Some of the rules mentioned here may be somewhat relaxed in informal settings.

The best way to learn good manners is to watch others. **Observe** the way your Western friends eat. This is the best way to avoid making mistakes when you **are** not **sure of** what to do.

Vocabulary

manner	*n.* 方式;礼貌	napkin	*n.* 餐巾;餐巾纸
fold	*vt.* 折叠;合拢	silverware	*n.* 银器
bowl	*n.* 碗	spoon	*n.* 匙;调羹

slurp	v. 啜食	tip	vt. 倾斜;翻倒
signal	vt. 用动作(手势)示意	host	n. 主人
hostess	n. 女主人	refuse	v. 拒绝;回绝
spaghetti	n. 意大利面	bacon	n. 培根;熏猪肉
crisp	adj. 脆的;干冷的	berry	n. 浆果
elbow	n. 肘部	wrist	n. 腕;手腕
observe	vt. & vi. 观察;研究		

Phrases and Expressions

lean down	向下弯
wind up	卷起
be sure of	确信

Task 1 True or false statements. Decide whether the following statements are True (T) or False (F) according to the text.

1. Generally speaking, you may use the silverware farthest from the plate first when the meal is served. ( )
2. When you've done with your meal, the proper placement of the silverware is to lay them parallel to each other. ( )
3. At the table, when the dishes are out of your reach, you may ask others to pass them to you or stand up to fetch them. ( )
4. When served a large piece of meat, you may cut the entire meat up into pieces or cut more than one at a time. ( )
5. When eating spaghetti, you may eat half your noodles and allow the other half to fall back on your plate if they are too long. ( )
6. It is impolite to lean on your arm or elbow while eating. ( )

Task 2 Questions. Read the text again and answer the following questions.

1. If the host invites you to begin the dinner before other guests, what should you do?
2. If the dishes are out of your reach, what should you do?
3. What's the proper manner for eating spaghetti?
4. What should you do when you are not sure whether the food is eaten with fingers?
5. What's the best way to learn good manners?

Task 3 Blank filling. Fill in the blanks with the words given. Change the form when necessary.

fold	signal	refuse	host	crisp
observe	napkin	lean down	wind up	be sure of

1. The patients were ________ over a period of several months.
2. He stood up, ________ to the officer that he had finished with his client.
3. She was taking tiny bites of a hot dog and daintily wiping her lips with a ________.
4. The bed can be ________ away during the day.
5. I've always had a loud mouth, and I ________ to be silenced.
6. In 2010, Shanghai played ________ to the World Expo.
7. The air was thin and ________, filled with hazy sunshine and frost.
8. Tony was so tall that he had to ________ to get through the doorway.
9. She looked over her shoulder to ________ her footing.
10. He started ________ the window ________ but I grabbed the door and opened it.

Part 4 Translation

Task 1 The restaurant needs a Chinese menu. Translate the menu into Chinese, using a dictionary when necessary.

Soup

Masala Beef Soup

Cream of Chicken Mushroom Soup

Cold Starters

Black Forest Ham with Rye Bread

Smoked Salmon with Toast and Butter

Main Courses

Brazil Style Rib Eye Steak

Jumbo Shrimp Wrapped in Bacon with Basil Pesto

Gratin Lasagna Bolognaise

Spaghetti with Shrimp in Italian Style Basil Sauce

Baked Seafood Rice with Eggs Frittata

Baked Rice with Chicken in Provencal Style Sauce

Desserts

Hot Cherries Doused in a Cognac and Served with a Scoop of Vanilla Ice Cream

Apple Strudel Warm and Served with Vanilla Sauce

Walnut Ice Cream two scoops of walnut ice cream with fresh gigs and cream

Parfait with Chocolate Flavor

Task 2 Translate the following passage into English.

在正式场合中，所有的银器(silverware)、杯具(glassware)和碟盘(cups and saucers)都摆放在桌面上，所以通常很难分辨出该用哪一把叉子，或哪个是你的水杯。一般来讲，刀叉是按照人们用餐顺序从外向内摆放。比如，吃沙拉的刀叉摆放在餐具的最外层(outermost)。吃甜点的刀叉会摆放在你主餐盘(entree plate)上面。玻璃杯、茶杯和碟子都摆放在你的右侧，而餐巾、面包盘和黄油刀(butter spreader)摆放在你的左侧。

Part 5 Cultural Norms

西餐上菜顺序

在西餐厅就餐，菜单一般由三类不同的菜别组成。The First Course 或者 Starters 是指第一道菜，往往是汤、一小碟色拉或其他小吃。第二道菜是主菜 Entrée，最后一道菜是 Dessert 甜食——或冷或热，但都是甜的。西方饮食习惯是先吃咸的，后吃甜的。就餐时服务员会问你各类酒和主菜的搭配。一般而言，红酒宜佐红肉，白酒宜佐鱼或白肉(如鸡肉)。

常用词汇

coffee pot	咖啡壶	coffee cup	咖啡杯
paper towel	纸巾	napkin	餐巾
table cloth	桌布	tea-pot	茶壶
tea set	茶具	tea tray	茶盘
caddy	茶叶罐	dish	碟子
plate	盘子	mug	马克杯
rice bowl	饭碗	chopstick	筷子
soup spoon	汤匙	knife	餐刀
cup	杯子	glass	玻璃杯
picnic lunch	便当	fruit plate	水果盘
toothpick	牙签	saucer	小碟子

常用句子

1. 询问是否可以开始点餐。

(1) Here is the menu/wine list/dessert menu, sir. The waiter will be here to take your order. 先生，这是菜单/酒单/甜品单。服务员稍后为您点餐。

(2) Please take your time, and I'll be back to take your order. 请慢慢选择，我一会儿来为您点餐。

(3) Are you ready to order, sir? 先生，请问能点餐了吗？

(4) Excuse me, sir. May I take your order now? 打扰一下，先生，现在能为您点餐了吗？

(5) Would you like to order now? 您现在想点餐吗？

(6) Are you ready to order or you need another minute? 您准备现在点餐还是再过一会儿？

2. 关心客人的饮食禁忌、喜好及特殊需要。

(1) Would you like to have table d'hote or a la carte? 您选择套餐还是零点呢？

(2) We have both buffet style and a la carte dishes, which would you prefer? 我们有自助式和点菜式，您喜欢哪一种？

(3) Why not try our buffet dinner? 要不要试下我们的自助餐？

(4) How would you like your egg/steak/coffee? 您希望鸡蛋/牛排/咖啡怎么做？

(5) Would you like your fried eggs sunny-side up? 您点的煎蛋是只煎一面吗?

(6) Which sauce would you like for the steak? 您的牛排想配什么汁?

(7) Are you allergic to any particular food, sir? 先生,请问您对某些食物过敏吗?

(8) How would you like your steak done, sir/madam, medium, medium well or well done? 请问您点的牛排要几成熟呢,半熟、七成熟或全熟?

(9) What kind of dressing would you prefer with your steak? We have black pepper sauce, red wine sauce, mushroom sauce and onion sauce. 您的牛排想要配什么汁呢? 我们有黑椒汁、红酒汁、蘑菇汁和洋葱汁。

(10) Would you like to have your steak with rice, French fries, baked potatoes or spaghetti? 您的牛排是配饭还是配薯条、焗薯或意大利面?

Part 6 Supplementary Reading

Table Manners in America

Table manners are the rules of etiquette used while eating, which may also include the appropriate use of utensils. Different cultures observe different rules for table manners. Many table manners evolved out of practicality. For example, it is generally impolite to put elbows on tables, since doing so creates a risk of tipping over bowls and cups. Each family or group sets its own standards for how strictly these rules are to be enforced.

American Table Manners

Before dining

Men's and unisex hats should never be worn at the table. Ladies' hats may be worn during the day if visiting others.

Before sitting down to a formal meal, gentlemen stand behind their chairs until the ladies are seated.

A prayer or blessing may be customary in some households, and the guests may join in or be respectfully silent. Most prayers are made by the host before the meal is eaten. Hosts should not practice an extended religious ritual in front of invited guests who have different beliefs.

One does not start eating until every person is served or those who have not been served request that you begin without waiting.

Napkins are placed in the lap. On more formal occasions, diners will wait to place their napkins on their laps until the host places his or her napkin on his or her lap.

On more formal occasions, all diners should be served at the same time and will wait until the hostess or host lifts a fork or spoon before beginning.

Even if one has dietary restrictions, it is inappropriate for non-relatives to request food other than that which is being served by the host at a private function.

General manners while dining

When a dish is offered from a serving dish (a. k. a. family style), as is the traditional manner, the food may be passed around or served by a host or staff. If passed, you should pass on the serving dish to the next person in the same direction as the other dishes are being passed. Place the serving dish on your left, take some, and pass to the person next to you. You should consider how much is on the serving dish and not take more than a proportional amount so that everyone may have some. If you do not care for any of the dish, pass it to the next person without comment. If being served by a single person, the server should request if the guest would like any of the dish. The guest may say "Yes, please" or "No, thank you".

When serving, serve from the left and pick up the dish from the right. Beverages, however, are to be both served as well as removed from the right-hand side.

Dip your soup spoon away from you into the soup. Eat soup noiselessly, from the side of the spoon. When there is a small amount left, you may lift the front end of the dish slightly with your free hand to enable collection of more soup with your spoon.

If you are having difficulty getting food onto your fork, use a small piece of bread or your knife to assist. Never use your fingers or thumb.

It is acceptable in the United States not to accept all offerings, and not to finish all the food on your plate. No one should ask why another doesn't want any of a dish or why he has not finished a serving.

There should be no negative comments on the food nor on the offerings available.

Chew with your mouth closed. Do not slurp, talk with food in your mouth, or make loud or unusual noises while eating.

Say "Excuse me" or "Excuse me. I'll be right back" before leaving the table. Do not state that you are going to the restroom.

Do not talk excessively loudly. Give others equal opportunities for conversation.

Refrain from blowing your nose at the table. Excuse yourself from the table if you must do so.

Burping, coughing, yawning, or sneezing at the table should be avoided. If you do so, say, "Excuse me."

Never slouch or tilt back while seated in your chair.

Do not "play with" your food or utensils. Never wave or point silverware.

You may rest forearms or hands on the table, but not elbows.

Do not talk on your phone or "text" at the table, or otherwise do something distracting, such as read or listen to a personal music player. Reading at the table is permitted only at breakfast. If an urgent matter arises, apologize, excuse yourself, and step away from the table so your conversation does not disturb the others.

If food must be removed from the mouth for some reason, it should be done using the same method which was used to bring the food to the mouth, i. e. by hand, by fork, etc., with the exception of fish bones, which are removed from the mouth between the fingers.

Before asking for additional helpings, always finish the serving on your plate first.

Gentlemen should stand when a lady leaves or rejoins the table in formal social settings.

Using utensils

The fork is used to convey solid food to the mouth. Do not use your fingers unless eating food customarily eaten as such, such as bread, asparagus spears, chicken wings, pizza, etc.

Do not make unnecessary noises with utensils.

The fork may be used either in the American style (use the fork in your left hand while cutting; switch to right hand to pick up and eat a piece) or the European "Continental" style (fork always in left hand).

Unless a knife stand is provided, the knife should be placed on the edge of your plate when not in use and should face inward.

As courses are served, use your silverware from the outside moving inward toward the main plate. Dessert utensils are either above the main plate or served with dessert.

At the end of the meal

When you have finished your meal, place all used utensils onto your plate together, on the right side, pointed up, so the waiter knows you have finished. Do not place used utensils on the table.

Except in a public restaurant, do not ask to take some uneaten food or leftovers home, and never do so when attending a formal dinner. A host may suggest that extra food be taken by the guests, but should not insist.

Leave the napkin on the seat of your chair only if leaving temporarily. When you leave the table at the end of the meal, loosely place the used napkin on the table to the left of your plate.

Chapter 12

Beverage Service

Study Objectives

1. To have a basic knowledge of beverage service.
2. To grasp the words and expressions used in beverage service.
3. To get the idea and information through listening and reading.
4. To handle the guests' consultation on beverages and offer the information needed.

Lead in

Drinks, or beverages, are liquids specifically prepared for human consumption. In addition to basic needs, beverages form part of the culture of human society. Think carefully and try to answer the following questions.

1. Do you happen to know any places where beverages are served?
2. Suppose you are a waiter in a hotel, and your guest needs a kind of wine to match their meals, what suggestions will you make?

Part 1 Listening

Task 1 Dialogues. Listen to the dialogues and fill in the blanks with what you hear.

Dialogue 1

A: What sort of drink would you like?

B: Um, I'd like a nice cold beer, ________________________________ ____.

Dialogue 2

A: Do you serve soft drinks?

B: Certainly, madam. ________________________________.

Dialogue 3

A: How do you like your whisky?

B: ________________________________.

Dialogue 4

A: ________________________________ and a tin of Seven Up.

B: Right away, Mrs. Parrish.

Dialogue 5

A: Could you mix them up for me?

B: Certainly, Mrs. Brown. ________________________________?

Task 2 Conversations.

Conversation 1 Fred and Helen enter a bar and the barman is greeting them. Listen and fill in the blanks with the words or phrases provided in the box.

alcoholic	non-alcoholic	liqueur	brandy	cocktails

(Barman-B Fred-F Helen-H)

B: How are you, madam and sir?

F&H: Fine.

B: What can I do for you?

F: What shall we enjoy tonight, Helen?

H: What do you think of ________?

F: That's a good idea. Waiter, two cocktails, please.

B: Both are ________ cocktails, aren't they?

H: A ________ one for me, please.

F: One with ________ for me.

B: What about brandy Alexander, sir? There is mint ________, lemon juice, ice and brandy.

F: That's OK.

B: One brandy Alexander and one non-alcoholic cocktail.

F: Yes.

Conversation 2 A sommelier is recommending the wine to the guest. Listen and fill in the blanks with the words or phrases provided in the box.

house wine	delicate body	with your meal
go very well with	allow it to breathe	

(Sommelier-S Guest-G)

S: Good evening, sir. Would you like to order some wine ____________ ____________?

G: Um, yes. What would you recommend?

S: I think that Chablis or a Muscatel would ____________________ your oysters.

G: We'd like one which is very dry. The Muscatel is OK.
S: How much would you like?
G: We'll take a half bottle of that then.
S: And what would you like with your steak?
G: Let me see, do you have a very full-bodied wine which is not too fruity?
S: Our own ____________________ which we import specially, the Chateau de lescours, would be very suitable. It is Burgundy with a rich but ____________________ which is not too dry.
G: That sounds just right. We'll have a full bottle of that.
S: Certainly, sir. Just a moment, please.
(*Later.*)
S: (*Shows the brand to the guest*) Your Red Burgundy. May I serve it now?
G: Yes, please.
S: I'll put the cork here. (*Pours wine*) May I decant it now to ____________________? How is it, sir?
G: Excellent!
S: (*Give a sip to the guest*) Please taste it, sir. Is it all right?
G: Wonderful!
S: Thank you, sir. Please enjoy your meal.

Conversation 3 A barman is serving the tea to a guest. Listen and fill in the blanks with what you hear.

(Barman-B Guest-G)
B: What can I do for you, madam?
G: I'd like some tea, please.
B: ____________________?
G: Green tea, please.
B: We have got Dragon Well tea, which is from Hangzhou and Bi Luo Chun from Jiangsu.
G: I've heard a lot about Dragon Well tea. So, Dragon Well tea, please. By the way, is there any ____________________ in China?
B: Of course there is. The most famous one is Oolong. It's said that ________________.
G: Really? You mean I should drink some Oolong, don't you?
B: No. I should say ____________________.
G: Thank you. What's jasmine tea?
B: Oh, it's a kind of green tea with the smell of jasmine. People from Beijing like it very much. ____________________.
G: I see.
B: Would you like to have your tea now, madam?
G: Yes, please.
B: A cup of Dragon Well tea, right?
G: Yes.

Part 2 Speaking

Task 1 Work in pairs. Mr. William entered a bar to have a drink, and the barman is greeting him now. Read and complete the following dialogue by translating the Chinese sentences in the parentheses into English.

(Barman-B Mr. William-W)

B: Hello, Mr. William. Glad to see you again.

W: Glad to see you.

B: ______________________________(您想喝什么酒)?

W: White wine, please.

B: Here you are, sir.

W: Good. ______________________________(有什么较好的中国酒吗)?

B: Most Chinese people like spirits. When we have dinner, the most popular one is white spirit. It's very common, ______________________________(尤其是在中国的北方地区,而且味道也不错). The best Chinese liquor is Maotai, which is special for national banquets. It is strong yet doesn't go to the head.

W: Maotai, is my pronunciation right? ______________________________(我下次去中国餐馆的时候要尝一下). What other Chinese wine, please?

B: ______________________________(最典型的是绍兴米酒), which is made from rice and is not as strong as Maotai, ______________________________(一种温和的酒). It's popular in the south part of China. ______________________________(有些人喜欢在喝之前热一下).

W: To drink warm wine? It's first time I have heard of that. It sounds very interesting. ______________________________(我很少喝不加冰的酒,干杯)!

Vocabulary

spirit	*n*. 烈酒	liquor	*n*. 酒;烈性酒

Notes

1. The best Chinese liquor is Maotai, which is special for national banquets.
   最好的白酒是茅台,它是国宴用酒。
2. It is strong yet doesn't go to the head. 茅台劲大但不上头。

Task 2 Work in pairs. Steven is serving three ladies from Britain in the bar. Discuss and complete the conversation between them by filling in the blanks with appropriate sentences given below.

A. Would you like that with a slice of lemon?
B. It's a type of strong spirit.
C. What would you like to drink?

D. I'll have a larger one, please.
E. How about a wheat beer?
F. I'd like a soft drink.

(Steven-S Manny-M Laura-L Jenny-J)

S: Good evening. ______1______

M: Ah, we are not sure really, because we can't work out the menu.

S: That's OK. I'll help you. What sort of drink would you like?

M: Um, I'd like a nice cold beer, but not too bitter.

S: ______2______ It isn't too bitter. It's lighter and more refreshing than other beers. There are two kinds: Kristall, which is clear, and Hefe, which is cloudy. They are both delicious. That's Kristall, over there in that tall glass.

M: Mmm, that looks great! I'll have one of those, please.

S: ______3______ Some people drink it that way. I think it tastes better without, personally.

M: Er, no. I'll have it without lemon, then, please.

S: So, that's one Kristallweizen without lemon. What about you, madam?

L: What's your strongest beer?

S: Salvator. It's stronger and darker than other beers. It's a local specialty and you can only get it at this time of year.

L: I'll have one of those, please.

S: And you, madam? What would you like?

J: ______4______ What about cherry water?

S: Oh, it's the most alcoholic drink on the menu! ______5______

J: Oh! Not quite what I had in mind.

S: Our soft drinks are... here. I'd recommend apple juice and mineral water.

J: Mm, yes, that sounds nice. I'll have apple juice, please.

S: Would you like a small glass—point two of a litre or a larger glass—point four of a litre?

J: ______6______

S: OK, ladies, I'll be back with your drinks shortly.

Task 3 Role-play. Work in pairs and make up a dialogue respectively according to the situations provided.

Situation 1 Mr. Gary goes to a restaurant with his friends to have dinner.

—Waitress	—Mr. Gary
• Ask the customer whether they would like to order some wine to go with the meal.	• Ask for recommendations.
• Recommend that Sauvignon Blanch or Muscatel would go very well with the fish.	• Sounds great. Order half a bottle of Muscatel.

• Ask if open the bottle right now.	• Yes.
• Ask the customer whether to have a taste at the moment.	• Sure.
• Wish a good meal.	• Thank you.

Situation 2 A customer is seeking some recommendations for the dinner in a restaurant. Now try to make the dialogue with the sentences given below.

—Waiter

- Would you like to have some wine with your dinner/meal?
- I think... goes quite well with your steak/fish/lamb/oyster. It is delicate/smooth/tasty.
- Shall I open it now or later?
- Would you like to taste it right now/now/for the moment?
- How is it? /How do you like it?
- Enjoy your dinner/meal. /May you have a nice dinner.

—Customer

- Would you please give us some suggestions? /What do you recommend?
- It sounds a good/great idea. I'll take a glass/half a bottle/a bottle of it.
- Yes, please. /Sure. /Of course.
- Quite well. /Great! /Perfect! / Fabulous! /Wonderful!
- Thank you. /Thanks a lot. /Thank you very much.

Part 3 Reading

The World in a Glass: Six Drinks that Changed History

Tom Standage **urges** drinkers **to savor** the history of their favorite beverages **along with** the taste.

The author of *A History of the World in 6 Glasses* (Walker & Company, June 2005), Standage **lauds** the **libations** that have helped shape our world from the **Stone Age** to the present day.

"The important drinks are still drinks that we enjoy today," said Standage, a technology editor at the London-based magazine *the Economist*. "They are **relics** of different historical periods still found in our kitchens."

Take the six-pack, whose contents first **fizzed** at the dawn of **civilization.**

Beer

The ancient **Sumerians**, who built advanced city-states in the area of present-day **Iraq**, began **fermenting** beer from **barley** at least 6000 years ago.

"When people started agriculture, the first crops they produced were barley or wheat. You consume those crops as bread and as beer," Standage noted. "It's the drink **associated with** the dawn of civilization. It's as simple as that."

Beer was popular with the masses from the beginning.

"Beer would have been something that a common person could have had in the house and made whenever they wanted." Said Linda Bisson, a **microbiologist** at the **Department of Viticulture and Enology** at the **University of California, Davis.**

"The guys who built the pyramids were paid in beer and bread." Standage added, "It was the defining drink of Egypt and **Mesopotamia.** Everybody drank it. Today it's the drink of the working man, and it was then as well."

Wine

Wine may be as old or older than beer—though no one can be certain.

Paleolithic humans probably sampled the first "wine" as the juice of naturally fermented wild grapes. But producing and storing wine was proved difficult for early cultures.

"To make wine you have to have fresh grapes," said Bisson, the U. C. Davis microbiologist. "For beer you can just store grain and add water to process it at any time."

Making wine also demanded **pottery** that could **preserve** the precious liquid.

"Wine may be easier to make than beer, but it's harder to store," Bisson added. "For most ancient cultures it would have been hard to catch fermenting grape juice as wine on its way to becoming vinegar."

Such **caveats** and the expense of producing wine helped the beverage quickly gain more **cachet** than beer. Wine was originally associated with social **elites** and religious activities.

Wine **snobbery** may be nearly as old as wine itself. Greeks and Romans produced many grades of wine for various social classes.

The quest for quality became an economic engine and later drove cultural expansion.

Spirits

Hard liquor, particularly brandy and rum, **placated** sailors during the long sea voyages of the Age of Exploration, when European powers **plied** the seas during the 15th, 16th, and early 17th centuries.

Rum played a crucial part of the **triangular** trade between Britain, Africa, and the North American **colonies** that once dominated the Atlantic economy.

Standage also suggests that rum may have **been** more **responsible** than tea **for** the independence movement in Britain's American colonies.

"**Distilling molasses** for rum was very important to the New England economy," he explained. "When the British tried to tax molasses it struck at the heart of the economy. The idea of 'no taxation without representation' originated with molasses and sugar. Only at the end did it **refer to** tea."

Great Britain's longtime superiority at sea may also owe a debt to its navy's drink of rum-based choice—**grog**, which was made a **compulsory** beverage for sailors in the late 18th century.

"They would make grog with rum, water, and lemon or lime juice," Standage said. "This improved the taste but also reduced illness and **scurvy. Fleet physicians** thought that this had doubled the efficiency of the fleet."

Coffee

The story of modern coffee starts in the **Arabian Peninsula**, where roasted beans were first brewed around A. D. 1000. Sometime around the 15th century, coffee spread throughout the Arab world.

"In the Arab world, coffee rose as an alternative to alcohol, and coffeehouse as alternatives to **taverns**—both of which are banned by Islam." Standage said.

When coffee arrived in Europe, it was similarly hailed as an "anti-alcohol" that was quite welcome during the **Age of Reason** in the 18th century.

"Just at the point when the **Enlightenment** is getting going, here's a drink that sharpens the mind," Standage said. "The coffeehouse is the perfect **venue** to get together and exchange ideas and information. **The French Revolution** started in a coffeehouse."

Coffee also fuelled commerce and had strong links to the **rituals** of business that remain to the present day.

Tea

Tea became a daily drink in China around the third century A. D.

Standage says tea played a leading role in the expansion of imperial and industrial might in Great Britain many centuries later. During the 19th century, the East India Company enjoyed a **monopoly** on tea exports from China.

"Englishmen around the world could drink tea, whether they were a colonial administrator in India or a London businessman," Standage said. "The sun never set on the British Empire—which meant that it was always teatime somewhere."

As the **Industrial Revolution** of the 18th and 19th centuries gained steam, tea provided some of the fuel. Factory workers stayed alert during long, **monotonous** shifts thanks to welcome tea breaks.

The beverage also had unintended health benefits for rapidly growing urban areas. "When you start packing people together in cities, it's helpful to have a water-purification technology like tea, which was brewed with boiling water." Standage explained.

Coca Cola

In 1886 pharmacist John Stith Pemberton sold about nine Coca Colas a day.

Today his soft drink is one of the world's most valuable brands—sold in more countries than the United Nations' members.

"It may be the second most widely understood phrase in the world after 'OK'." Standage said.

The drink has become a symbol of the United States—love it or hate it. Standage notes that East Germans quickly reached for Cokes when the Berlin Wall fell, while Thai **Muslims** poured it out into the streets to show **disdain** for the U. S. in the days leading up to the 2003 **invasion** of Iraq.

"Coca Cola **encapsulates** what happened in the 20th century: the rise of consumer capitalism and the emergence of America as a superpower." Standage said. "It's globalization in a bottle."

While Coke may not always produce a smile, a survey by the *Economist* magazine (Standage's employer), suggests that the soft drink's presence is a great indicator of happy citizens. When countries were polled for happiness, as defined by a United Nations index, high scores **correlated** with sales of Coca Cola.

"It's not because Coke makes people happy, but because its sales happen in the dynamic free-market economies that tend to produce happy people." Standage said.

Vocabulary

savor	*vt*. 品尝	laud	*vt*. 称赞;赞美
libation	*n*. 奠酒;饮酒	relics	*n*. 遗产;遗物
fizz	*vi*. 发嘶嘶声	civilization	*n*. 文明;文化
ferment	*vt*. & *vi*. 使……发酵	barley	*n*. 大麦
viticulture	*n*. 葡萄栽培	microbiologist	*n*. 微生物学家
enology	*n*. 葡萄酒酿造学	paleolithic	*adj*. 旧石器时代的
pottery	*n*. 陶器	preserve	*vt*. 保护;保存
caveat	*n*. 警告;附加说明	cachet	*n*. 特征;威信
elite	*n*. 精英	snobbery	*n*. 势利
placate	*vt*. 安抚	ply	*vt*. & *vi*. 经常供应(食物、饮料)
rum	*n*. 朗姆酒	triangular	*adj*. 三角(形)的
colony	*n*. 殖民地	distill	*v*. 蒸馏;提取
molasses	*n*. 糖浆	grog	*n*. 掺水烈酒
compulsory	*adj*. 强制性的	scurvy	*n*. 坏血病
physician	*n*. 内科医生	fleet	*n*. 舰队
venue	*n*. 犯罪地点;会场	tavern	*n*. 小旅馆;酒馆
monopoly	*n*. 垄断	ritual	*n*. (宗教等的)仪式
disdain	*n*. 鄙视;轻蔑	monotonous	*adj*. 单调的
encapsulate	*vt*. 封装;概述	invasion	*n*. 入侵;侵略
correlate	*v*. 联系		

Phrases and Expressions

urge...to...	鼓励(某人)朝着(某方向努力)
along with	和……一起
take sth. (for example)	以……为例
associate with	与……交往;联系
be responsible for	对……负责
refer to	涉及;指的是……

Proper Names

Stone Age	石器时代
Sumerian	苏美尔人;苏美尔语

Iraq	伊拉克共和国
University of California, Davis	(美国)加利福尼亚大学戴维斯分校
Mesopotamia	美索不达米亚(西南亚地区)
Arabian Peninsula	阿拉伯半岛
Age of Reason	理性时期(通常指 18 世纪)
Enlightenment	启蒙运动
The French Revolution	法国大革命
Industrial Revolution	工业革命(18 世纪 60 年代在英国开始)
Muslim	穆斯林;伊斯兰教信徒

Task 1 True or false statements. Decide whether the following statements are True (T) or False (F) according to the text.

1. It is believed that beer is associated with the dawn of civilization of human beings. ( )
2. Like bread, beer once was used as the pay for work. ( )
3. The caveats and the expense of producing wine made it less popular than beer. ( )
4. Standage suggests that rum may have been more responsible than tea for the independence movement in Britain's American colonies. ( )
5. Starting in the Arabian Peninsula, coffee spread throughout the Arab world around the 15th century. ( )
6. Coca Cola is so popular that it becomes the most widely understood phrase in the world. ( )

Task 2 Sentence completion. Complete the following sentences with the words or phrases from the text.

1. The ancient Sumerians began fermenting beer from ________ at least 6000 years ago.
2. It is difficult to store the wine because it is hard to catch ________ on its way to becoming vinegar.
3. The navy's drink— ________ contributed greatly to Great Britain's longtime superiority at sea.
4. Around the third century A. D. , ________ became a daily drink in China.
5. Coca Cola has become a symbol of ________.

Task 3 Blank filling. Fill in the blanks with the words given. Change the form when necessary.

invasion	placate	disdain	civilization	distill
ritual	colony	compulsory	associate with	urge ...to

1. It seemed to him that Western ________ was in grave economic and cultural danger.

2. Even a written apology failed to ________ the indignant hostess.
3. The newly-occupied Italian ________ of Libya rose in revolt in 1914.
4. The factory ________ and bottles whisky.
5. Britain did not introduce ________ primary education until 1880.
6. What can we do to ________ these lazy workers ________ increase production?
7. The centuries-old ________ seems headed for extinction.
8. If you feel ________ for someone or something, you dislike them because you think that they are inferior or unimportant.
9. Is reading a child's diary always a gross ________ of privacy?
10. Mother warned the boys not to ________ bad companions.

Part 4 Translation

Task 1 Translate the following passage into Chinese.

Drinks, or beverages, are liquids specifically prepared for human consumption. In addition to basic needs, beverages form part of the culture of human society. Although most beverages, including juice, soft drinks, and carbonated drinks, have some form of water in them, water itself is often not classified as a beverage, and the word "beverage" has been recurrently defined as not referring to water. An alcoholic beverage is a drink containing ethanol, commonly known as alcohol, although in chemistry the definition of an alcohol includes many other compounds. Alcoholic beverages, such as wine, beer, and liquor, have been part of human culture and development for 8000 years. Non-alcoholic beverages often signify drinks that would normally contain alcohol, such as beer, but are made with less than 5 percent alcohol by volume.

Task 2 Translate the following passage into English.

销售酒精饮料(alcoholic beverages)的场所有好几种,最常见的是酒吧,通常有一个长吧台(counter),客人在吧台取酒。酒吧和小酒馆通常开在居民区,也常常被人们简单地称为"当地酒吧"。小酒栈(tavern)是小酒馆的一种古老说法。鸡尾酒会或酒吧间通常设有一个吧台、几张小桌子,气氛非常轻松,还会有一些小演出。夜总会除了酒水服务外,还提供额外的服务项目,比如,舞蹈、音乐、餐点和文艺表演。

Part 5 Cultural Norms

中国的"酒文化"源远流长,英语中的"酒"也无处不在。其中,最常用的"酒"的说法有以下四种。

1. drink 是指酒类,相当于 alcohol 或 strong drink(烧酒);有时也指其他饮料,指其他饮料时前面应加 soft。
2. liquor 是指经过蒸馏而酿成的酒。
3. spirits 主要是指酒精含量很高的烈性酒,如 whisky(威士忌)、brandy(白兰地)等。

4. wine 是指果汁经发酵而制成的酒，多指葡萄酒，如 white wine、red wine 等。

下面介绍几种常见酒供大家了解。

威士忌(Whisky)——以大麦、黑麦、燕麦、小麦、玉米等谷物为原料，经发酵、蒸馏后放入橡木桶中陈酿、勾兑而成的一种酒精饮料。它主要生产国为英语国家。依照生产地和国家的不同，可将威士忌酒分为苏格兰威士忌酒、爱尔兰威士忌酒、美国威士忌酒和加拿大威士忌酒四类。其中，尤以苏格兰威士忌酒最为著名。饮用时，可以加冰块、苏打水和其他饮料。

金酒、杜松子酒(Gin)——世界第一大类的烈酒。以杜松子酒为基酒，可以调制出千种以上的鸡尾酒，所以被称为“鸡尾酒的心脏”。

朗姆酒(Rum)——是以甘蔗糖蜜为原料生产的一种蒸馏酒，也称为兰姆酒、蓝姆酒。原产地在古巴，口感甜润、芬芳馥郁。

白兰地(Brandy)——意为可燃烧的酒，是指葡萄发酵后经蒸馏而得到的高度酒精，再经橡木桶储存而成的酒。白兰地是一种蒸馏酒，以水果为原料，经过发酵、蒸馏、储藏后酿造而成。

伏特加(Vodka)——以多种谷物(马铃薯、玉米)为原料，用重复蒸馏、精炼过滤的方法，除去酒精中所含毒素和其他异物的一种纯净的高酒精浓度的饮料。伏特加无色无味，没有明显的特性，但很提神。

龙舌兰酒(Tequila)——是墨西哥独有的名酒，它由热带作物龙舌兰的发酵浆液蒸馏而成，常作为鸡尾酒的基酒。

雪利酒(Sherry)——法国的葡萄酒加上白兰地，就是雪利酒，常被用作餐前酒，有增加食欲的作用。

香槟(Champagne)——法国出产的名酒，用于增添宴会喜庆气氛。

鸡尾酒(Cocktail)——鸡尾酒是由两种或两种以上的酒和果汁、香料等混合而成的酒，多在饮用时临时调制。

利口酒(Liqueur)——餐后甜酒，是餐后饮用的，糖分很高，有帮助消化的作用。

味美思(Vermouth)——以葡萄酒为酒基，用芳香植物的浸液调制而成的加香葡萄酒。

苦艾酒(Bitter)——一种有茴芹、茴香味的高酒精度蒸馏酒，主要原料是茴芹、茴香及苦艾。酒液呈绿色，加入冰水时变为混浊的乳白色。此酒芳香浓郁，口感清淡而略带苦味。

常用句子

1. Would you like to try some Chinese alcohol? 您想不想试一试中国酒呢？
2. Maotai is the best Chinese spirit. 茅台是中国最好的烈酒。
3. It's rather strong, but never goes to the head. 它度数高(劲大)，但从不上头。
4. What would you like to drink? 您想喝些什么？
5. Have you decided what you would like to drink? 您决定喝什么了吗？
6. Which vintage would you prefer? 您喜欢哪种葡萄酒？
7. Would you like... (recommended drink)? 您喜欢……(推荐的饮料)吗？
8. How about Champagne? 来点香槟怎么样？
9. Would you like to try the dry Sherry? 您想不想尝尝不甜的雪利酒呢？

10. I would recommend ...我想向您推荐……
11. Would you like to have some snacks with your wine? 您要不要叫一点小吃来下酒呢?
12. Here is the wine list. 这是酒水单。
13. We have a very extensive cellar. 我们的藏酒非常丰富。
14. I think that a Chablis would go very well with your oysters. 我想夏布利白葡萄酒和您点的生蚝很搭配。
15. What is your "house wine"? 你们的"本店特饮"是什么?
16. It is Burgundy with a rich but delicate body which is not too dry. 这是勃艮第葡萄酒,浓郁香醇,也不至于一点甜味都没有。
17. I'll put the cork here. 我把软木塞放在这儿。
18. How is the taste/color/bouquet/temperature/... of the wine? 酒的味道/颜色/香味/温度/……如何?
19. There is a lot of sediment in the bottle. 这酒瓶子里有很多沉淀物。
20. This wine is not chilled enough. 这酒不够凉。
21. If we add ice, the taste will be spoiled. 如果我们加冰,会破坏它的味道。

Part 6 Supplementary Reading

Chef's Pride Catering

Bars & Beverages

Punch, lemonade or ice tea $1.50 per guest.

Coffee service: Includes regular and decaffeinated coffee, sugar, creamer, 10 oz foam cups, straws, beverage napkins and restocking throughout the event $1.75 per guest.

Wine Punch (Wine supplied by client)

Plastic cups, beverage napkins, fruit and ice can be supplied for additional $1.50 per guest.

Wine glasses $1.75 per guest.

Bar Tending Service

Chefs Pride Catering will only supply our bar tenders if food is being served.

Bar Tenders Charges: $45.00 per hour per bartender, 4-hour minimum (Client will be billed for travel and setup time).

—1 hour minimum setup time is needed for bars

—2 bartenders must be hired per event

While Chef's Pride bartending only service is pricey, it is due to high liability involved. Therefore, clients may find that it is more cost effective to handle their own bar, or go with a service upgrade.

Larry Burdek

President/Chef

Chef's Pride Catering Inc.
Traverse City, Michigan
Phone (231) 943-9683
fehc@moc. kedrubl
www. leelanaucatering. com

Chapter 13

Room Service

Study Objectives

1. To learn useful expressions and patterns in helping guests with room service.
2. To practice situational dialogues and translation fluently.
3. To know more about the procedure for taking a room service order.

Lead in

Room Service is a service in a hotel by which meals or drinks are provided for guests in their rooms. It is essential in a full-service hotel especially for breakfast. Room Service is a small department in a big hotel, but necessary. It can even affect the guests' whole impression of the whole hotel. Think carefully and try to answer the following questions.

1. What room types do you know?
2. What do you think room service should include?

Part 1 Listening

Task 1 Dialogues. Listen to the dialogues and fill in the blanks with what you hear.

Dialogue 1

A: Room Service, can I help you?

B: I'm going to New York early tomorrow morning. So I would like to ______________________________, please.

Dialogue 2

A: Hi, I'm in Room 222. I would like to _______________. Please try to hurry, I cut my finger.

B: No problem, I'll come up ______________________________.

Dialogue 3

A: What does a Continental breakfast have?

B: ______________________.

Dialogue 4

A: Should I tip for room service?

B: Yes. When ordering food or drinks, ______________________.

Dialogue 5

A: ______________________, grapefruit or orange?

B: Orange, thanks.

Vocabulary

bandage	*n.* 绷带	grapefruit	*n.* 西柚汁
chilled	*a.* 冰冻的	minimum tip	最少小费
expect	*v.* 预期		

Task 2 Conversations. Listen and fill in the blanks with the words or phrases provided in the box.

master controller	insert	flat hole	panel	doorframe
automatically	Continental breakfast	confirm	refrigerator	supplement
contact	complete	room account	unseal	beverage

(**Clerk of Room Service-C Guest-G**)

Conversation 1 A guest is calling the Room Service for how to operate lights in the room.

C: Good afternoon, Room Service. May I help you?

G: I wonder how to ________?

C: Certainly sir. Guest rooms are equipped with ________. Lights in the room will be turned on if the key is ________ on ________ which is ________. When you leave the room, please take the key card of the door, and lights will be ________.

G: Oh, thanks.

C: Alright.

Conversation 2 A guest is calling the Room Service for a meal in his room.

C: Good morning, Room Service. May I help you?

G: I'd like to have a meal in my room.

C: Certainly sir. We offer two types of breakfast, ______________. Which one would you prefer?

G: What does Continental breakfast have?

C: ______________, coffee or tea.

G: That would be fine, I will take it. I'd like a white coffee with two sugars, please.

C: I see. May I have your name and room number, please?

G: Sure, It's Jefferson Black in Room 1506.

C: ______________. Mr. Jefferson Black in Room 1506, Continental breakfast, white coffee with two sugars. Is that right?

G: Exactly.

C: ______________. Thank you for calling.

Conversation 3 A guest is calling the Room Service for the drinks and food in minibar and refrigerator.

C: Good evening, Room Service. May I help you?

G: Can I use drinks and food in the minibar and refrigerator?

C: Certainly sir. You may help yourself to the food and drinks in the minibar and refrigerator. Drinks and food will be ______________. If there is an urgent need, please ______________ and contact with the Service Center.

G: How should I pay for them?

C: Please ______________, the bill will be added to your ______________ and will be (______________).

G: I see, thanks.

C: My pleasure.

Part 2 Speaking

Task 1 Work in pairs. Discuss with your partners and try to think about some more courteous expressions to replace the following sentences.

1. Just read the Service Information Booklet. Everything is in it.
2. Sorry, that's not my department.
3. My English is poor. What did you say?
4. Just take a taxi! You can certainly afford it.
5. Don't you see I'm busy cleaning this room?
6. I can't do it. Just ask somebody else.

Task 2 Role-play. Work in pairs and make up a dialogue respectively according to the situations provided.

Situation 1 A guest wants to have breakfast in his room. Try to make up a conversation with your partner with the information provided.

English breakfast	ham	croissant	sausage	bacon	sunny-side up

Situation 2 Mrs. White calls the Room Service to send a dinner for her room. Make up the conversation with your partner. You may need the following words and expressions to help you.

steak	green beans	Brussels sprouts	salad

Part 3 Reading

Room Service

Room Service is the service of food or beverages in guests' room in hotels or order from **accommodation establishments**, such as **motels** or serviced apartments. In all-suite hotels it is often referred to as "in-suite service".

In establishments of any size there is usually a **specialist** Room Serviced Department responsible to the Food and **Beverage** manager. Room Service Department must work closely with the Kitchen, Front Office and Housekeeping departments to make sure that the standard of service satisfies, or more than satisfies, guests' **expectations.** Hotels are often judged, as much as anything else, by the standard of the room service they provide. A five-star property will be expected to provide room service for at least 18 hours of the day, if not all hours of the day and night, and that service must at all times be friendly, quick and **efficient.**

Most room service orders are given by telephone. The telephone is therefore the first point of contact with room service staff and good telephone technique is vital in creating that all important **favorable** first impression.

The person answering the telephone must have a good knowledge of the menu and a **professional** telephone manner.

The telephone must be answered quickly. The benchmark for a five-star hotel is no more than three rings before it is answered. Then pay special attention to the greeting, introduction to department and self, and use of the guest's name. These can be **achieved** by an answer on these lines:

"Good morning. Mr. Stephens. This is Room Service Mark speaking. May I help you?"

The use of guest's name has the **advantage** of ensuring that the items requested are **delivered** to the right guest and charged to the right account as well as making the guest feel known and valued. Continue to use the guest's sure name at all stages of room service.

After greeting the guest and **confirming** his or her name, continue as follows:

Write the order down carefully on an order **docket** as you speak to the guest. Don't forget to record the room number—often forgotten!

Always seek opportunities to "up-sell", that is to use suggestive selling techniques to increase the value of the order.

Be flexible and helpful if the guest requests items not on the menu.

Repeat the order to the guest, **clarifying** the **doubtful** details.

Tell the guest **approximately** how long it will take for the order to be delivered. It should not be more than 30 minutes.

Check that all the details (including the room number) are correctly recorded on the docket. Include the time when the order was taken.

Enter the order in POS.

Promptly distribute the order to the appropriate personnel both in room service department and in other departments if necessary, most obviously the kitchen.

Vocabulary

accommodation	*n.* 住宿	achieve	*v.* 达成
establishment	*n.* 设施	advantage	*n.* 优势
motel	n. 汽车旅馆	deliver	*v.* 传达
specialist	*n.* 专家	confirm	*v.* 确认
beverage	*n.* 饮料	docket	*n.* 记事本
expectation	*n.* 期望	clarify	*v.* 解释;澄清
efficient	*adj.* 有效率的	doubtful	*adj.* 怀疑的
favorable	*adj.* 喜爱的	approximately	*adv.* 大约
professional	*adj.* 专业的		

Task 1 Questions. Read the text and answer the following questions.

1. What is room service?
2. What's the relationship between room service section and other departments?
3. Why should room service staff use guests' names when speaking to them?

Task 2 Translation. Read the text again and translate the underlined parts into Chinese.

Part 4 Translation

Task 1 Translate the following sentences into Chinese.

1. The service time is 6:30 a.m. to 10:00 a.m..
2. We have different sizes, 7 inches, 9 inches, and 11 inches. Which do you prefer?
3. Good morning, here is the Continental breakfast you ordered.
4. It won't take long to prepare your breakfast.
5. It will take 20 minutes to prepare your lunch.
6. Your food and drinks will be sent up in a few minutes.
7. I will send someone up with your breakfast immediately.
8. I am sorry, we don't start serving lunch until 11 a.m..
9. Is there anything else that you want?
10. The room service menu is on the back of the door.
11. When shall I send the cake to your room?
12. How many eggs and how would you like them done?

13. Do you want to pay cash or sign the bill?
14. Please sign your name and room number on the bill.
15. Some of my friends will come and see me this afternoon. Would you please bring me some more tea cups?

Task 2 Translate the following sentences into English.

1. 您如果还需要别的什么,尽管告诉我好了。
2. 您想喝点什么,茶还是咖啡?
3. 客房服务,有什么可以帮您?
4. 您希望什么时候把您的早餐送来?
5. 除了欧式早餐,你还想要点别的吗?
6. 请问要送几人餐?
7. 如果想在房间里用餐,可与房间服务台联系。
8. 我将随时为您服务。
9. 哪些服务是需要额外付费的?
10. 如果有最低消费或服务费,应事先说明。
11. 这里有个小册子介绍饭店的各项服务。
12. 您可以从您房间里打电话。
13. 我马上把它送上来。
14. 请您在账单上签名,好吗?
15. 谢谢,请慢用,再见。

Part 5 Cultural Norms

常用词汇

cuisine 菜系,烹饪
table d'hôte(fixed price meal) 套餐
on a diet 节食
take orders 点菜
done by orders 即点即做
specialty 特色菜
sauce 调味汁
pea 豆角
roast 烤的
tender 鲜嫩的
clear 清淡的
spicy/hot 辣的
oily 油重的
a la carte 按菜单点菜(与套餐相对)
have a try 试一试;尝一尝
delicious 美味的
tasty 美味的
typical 典型的;地道的
sauté 煎的,炒的
Brussels sprouts 椰菜花
porridge 麦片粥
jam 果酱
sweet & sour 酸甜的
salty 咸味的
crisp 酥脆的

常用句子

订餐服务说明

1. Breakfast is served from 7:30 to 10:00 a. m. , and lunch and dinner served from 11:00 a. m. to 11:00 p. m.. 早餐是从上午 7:30 到 10:00,午餐和晚餐是从上午 11:00 到晚上 11:00。
2. Room Service is available 24 hours a day. 客房送餐服务 24 小时提供。
3. You may dial 6, then ask for Room Service. 请您先拨 6,然后转接客房服务台。
4. If you like, we can make a note of your list and send it to them. What would you like us to do? 如果您愿意,我们可以替您记下来,再转告他们。您希望我们怎么做?
5. There is an extra charge of 15% for Room Service. 客房送餐服务要加收 15%的服务费。

询问客人的喜好

1. Which kind of juice would you prefer, grapefruit or orange? 您喜欢哪种果汁,是西柚汁还是橙汁?
2. How would you like your eggs/steak? 您点的蛋/牛排要怎么做呢?
3. Would you like ham or bacon with your eggs? 您喜欢火腿还是咸肉夹蛋?
4. Would you prefer rolls or toast? 您想要早餐包还是烤面包?
5. A Continental breakfast or an American breakfast? 您是要欧式早餐还是美式早餐?

Part 6 Supplementary Reading

Taking the Order

Servers should greet the guest by identifying himself by name and inform the guest of the soup of the day and any specials that are available. Proceed to take a drink order and inquire about taking a food order upon delivery of the drink order. If guest is not ready to place and order yet, suggest an appetizer or more time to decide. Room Service calls must be answered within five rings. Calls to Room Service should not be put on hold for more than thirty (30) seconds. The person taking Room Service orders must ask the guest's name and room number, ask the appropriate food preparation questions, repeat the order back to the guest to confirm accuracy, quote an estimated time of arrival, and thank the guest while using his/her name for the order.

Delivering the Order

Food delivered to guest should be at temperature and should have everything needed for the meal on the plate or already at the table by the time it comes out. Example: steak knife should be set at the table after the order is taken and before the food comes out. Food should be served from the left and retrieved from the right side of the guest when possible (booths). If a guest orders two items off the menu, they should never come out at the same time unless specified by the guest.

Food delivered to guest rooms must be delivered at an appropriate temperature. Room

Service meals must be served with appropriate plate covers. Plastic wrap/foil is not allowed for the entrée.

When delivering the order, the server must knock on the door and identify himself/herself as "Room Service", greet the guest when the door is opened and ask for permission to enter the room. (If the guest does not give the server permission to enter the room, the guest must be provided with a clean tray and a clean tray liner.)

Upon receiving permission from the guest to enter the room, the server must bring the order into the guest room and place the tray on an appropriate surface as specified by the guest. The server must then review with the guest each item of the order and the guest check total. if the automatic gratuity is added to the guest check, the server must disclose this when reviewing the check total.

If Room Service is ordered, and a "Do Not Disturb" sign is in place, the Room Service attendant should follow standard delivery procedures. When the guest answers the door, the Room Service attendant should acknowledge that the Room Service request is being honored over the "Do Not Disturb" signage in the event that the guest forgot to remove the "Do Not Disturb" sign.

Dish and Tray Removal

Trays will be dropped off in housekeeping closets on each floor to be picked up by the restaurant servers. There will be a tray run performed by servers before and after each shift. (Breakfast, Lunch and Dinner.)

Task: Read the text, and try to summarize how to serve the guests with their orders.

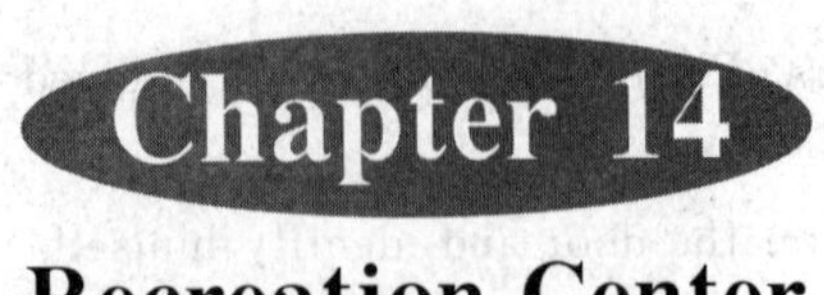

Chapter 14

Recreation Center

Study Objectives

1. To learn useful expressions and patterns about recreational facilities and services.
2. To practice situational dialogues and translation fluently.
3. To know more about the services and facilities provided by the Recreation Center.

Lead in

The Recreation Center is the place where the guests can enjoy various entertainment services such as karaoke, bar and so on. In addition, at the Recreation Center, the guests can also go to some health clubs to do some exercises or just have a relax. Think carefully and try to answer the following questions.

1. What kind of services do the recreation centers usually provide?
2. Can you list more words about recreational facilities and services?
3. What do you think are the duties of the recreation staff?

Part 1 Listening

Task 1 Dialogues. Listen to five short dialogues and mark (√) which service is mentioned in each dialogue.

	Body Building	Ball Games	Beauty Salon	Entertainment	Outdoor Activities
Dialogue 1					
Dialogue 2					
Dialogue 3					
Dialogue 4					
Dialogue 5					

Task 2 Conversations.

Conversation 1 A couple goes to the Bowling Center of a hotel. Listen and fill in the blanks with the words or phrases provided in the box.

injury	spacious	regulations	registered guests
sizes	Bowling Center	alleys	warm-up

(**Recreation Clerk-C Guest-G**)

C: Good evening, sir and madam. Welcome to the ________________.

G: Good evening. Could you please tell me your opening hours?

C: Yes, from 9:00 a.m. to 12:00 p.m..

G: It looks very ________________ and bright.

C: Yes, we also have first-class equipment. How many people altogether?

G: Just my wife and I. Are there any ________________ available?

C: Let me see. We have six bowling alleys altogether. You can use the third alley.

G: How much do you charge for ________________?

C: We give a 20% discount, so that's 200 yuan per hour. Could you please tell me your name and room number?

G: Bill Douglas, D-o-u-g-l-a-s. Room 1606.

C: Thank you, Mr. and Mrs. Douglas. What about the ________________ of your shoes?

G: Size 42 for me, and 37 for my wife.

C: Here you are. May I suggest you do some ________________ exercises so as to avoid ________________?

G: Yes, thank you. By the way, can I bring my twelve-year-old son in with me to the bowling room?

C: I'm afraid not, Mr. Douglas. According to the ________________, children under 16 cannot bowl.

G: OK.

C: The game is ready for you. When the game is over, please return the shoes and sign the bill.

G: Thank you so much.

Conversation 2 Mr. Green goes to the indoor swimming pool of a hotel. Listen to the conversation and complete the sentences with what you hear.

1. The water temperature is ________________.
2. If you are not good at swimming, you can choose the ________________ to swim.
3. We change the water ________________.
4. We open at ________________ and close at ________________.

Listen again and decide whether the following statements are true (T) or false (F).

(　　)1. Mr. Green thinks the water temperature is too cold to swim in.

(　　)2. Mr. Green will choose the deep area of the pool to swim.

(　　)3. The water is very clean and clear because clerks just changed it last night.

(　　)4. There is a lifeguard standing by the pool in case of needs.

Conversation 3　Listen to the following conversation and fill in the blanks.

(**Guest-G　Recreation Clerk-C**)

G: Is there any place in the hotel where we can ________________?

C: If you want to ________________, you can go to the garden. It is very ______________ there.

G: That sounds good. But is that the only place to go?

C: No, sir. There is a ____________________. You can play ____________________, and ________________.

G: Is there a place where we can listen to some music?

C: Yes, sir. There is a ________________ where you can enjoy both ________________ such as Beethoven, Bach, Mozart, Liszt, and ________________, while having some Chinese tea or other drinks.

G: Oh, great. Thank you very much.

C: It's a pleasure.

Vocabulary

spacious	*adj*. 宽敞的	shallow	*adj*. 浅的
alley	*n*. 小路	billiards	*n*. 桌球
injury	*v*. 受伤	bridge	*n*. 桥牌

Part 2　Speaking

Task 1　Work in pairs. Read and practice the following conversation. Pay more attention to the bold type.

(**Clerk-C　Mr. White-Mr.**)

C: Good evening, sir. Welcome to our **Fitness Center**. How may I assist you?

Mr.: I want to do some exercises. Could you **show me around**?

C: Yes, sure. This way, please. Our gym is **well-equipped with all the latest recreational sports apparatus**. Here're dumb bells, bar bells, chest expanders and stationary bikes. They are all for **body building**.

Mr.: What are those machines over there?

C: Oh, they are our **world-famous brand facilities**: a race apparatus, rowing machine, and **stairmaster** as well.

Mr.: Very well. Do we need to pay for using them?

C: We don't charge registered guests, sir.

Mr. : Sounds good. By the way, can you **recommend** some traditional Chinese exercises to me?

C: Have you ever heard of Taijiquan or Qigong exercises?

Mr. : What is Taijiquan?

C: We also call it Chinese Shadow Boxing. It's **an important branch of Chinese martial arts.** The movements are even and slow. It's used for **life enhancement and health building.** Many Chinese are fond of it.

Mr. : I see. And what about Qigong?

C: Qigong is a kind of breathing exercise.

Mr. : Is it **similar** to yoga?

C: Right you are. **Which one do you prefer**, Taijiquan or Qigong?

Mr. : Do you have a coach here to **supervise the exercises**?

C: Yes, we have a **resident** coach standing by to show you exactly what to do. If you need any help or **instructions**, just call him.

Mr. : OK. I think I'll **get registered** in your Taijiquan training class.

Task 2 Work in pairs. Miss Bellow wants to lose weight and goes to a gym. Make up a conversation as in Task 1 with the help of the expressions in the box, and then act it out.

Welcome to our gym. The best way is to do some exercises in the gym every day. Our gym is well-equipped with all the latest sports apparatus. We have aerobics and Taijiquan classes every evening. Taijiquan is used for life enhancement and health building. We have an experienced coach.

Task 3 Work in pairs. A recreation clerk is introducing sauna & massage services to Mr. Lee. Some of his introductions are listed in the following box. Make up a conversation between Mr. Lee and the clerk and act it out.

Our center provides several kinds of sauna baths, such as dry sauna, wet sauna and salt sauna. The temperature in the sauna proper (桑拿浴室) is about 80 degrees Centigrade. Chinese-style massage has a long history and can prevent and treat many kinds of diseases by improving the blood circulation. I'm sure the massage can relax your muscles and ease your pain.

Task 4 Work in pairs. Mr. Black goes to the Recreation Center of a hotel. Role play the situation according to the steps provided in the boxes.

Clerk	Mr. Black
• Greet and welcome the guest. • Ask if he needs any help. • Reply to the guest's inquiry. • Show the guest to the locker room. • Advise the guest to cool off under a shower after sauna. • Introduce Chinese massage. • Say goodbye to the guest.	• Greet. • Ask about the sauna baths. • Show his interest in the Finnish dry sauna. • Take the Finish sauna. • Agree and ask what can ease the pain in his shoulders. • Agree to have a Chinese massage. • Express thanks.

Task 5 Role-Play. Two guests come to the coffee bar. They want the waitress to give them some recommendations. Finally, one chooses coffee and the other juice. Make up a conversation and act it out.

Vocabulary

latest	*adj.* 最近的	martial arts	*n.* 武术
recreational sports	*n.* 娱乐运动	enhancement	*n.* 加强
apparatus	*n.* 仪器	similar	*adj.* 相似的
brand	*n.* 品牌	resident	*n.* 居民
facility	*n.* 设备	instruction	*n.* 指示
stairmaster	*n.* 登山机	register	*v.* 注册

Part 3 Reading

Passage 1 The following is an ad. of Shangri-La Singapore's Health Club. Complete the ad. with the words or phrases given below.

complimentary	sign up	equipped	surrounded	coach
private	ease	revitalize	range	relaxation

The Shangri-La Hotel, Singapore offers many opportunities to relax, play or exercise.

Health Club

Located near the outdoor pool in the Lower Lobby level, Shangri-La's Health Club offers a fully ____________ gymnasium with steam, shower, Jacuzzi and ____________ areas.

Outdoor Pool

The outdoor pool is ____________ by lush tropical landscaping. The pool area also offers a

Jacuzzi, a children's play pool, and graceful fountains. It's the place where you can ______ ______ your mind and tone your body.

Tennis

The hotel offers four tennis courts. Our expert ____________ is available for advice and training. Tennis equipment can be obtained from the Fitness Center.

Spa Services

Aromatherapy, beauty and spa services are available at the ____________ massage and treatment rooms. A wide ____________ of massages, from reflexology to post-flight therapy and spa treatments, ____________ the busy travelers.

Singapore residents are invited to ______________ for Health Club membership.

Benefits include:

—Access to all fitness center facilities

—10% discount at all restaurants and bars

—15% discount on massage and spa services

—20% discount on all services at Brown's beauty salon

—____________ car parking facilities

Contact us at (65) 6737 3644 for more details.

Passage 2

Recreation Center

Today, the Recreation Center has become one of the **integral** parts of a successful hotel. More and more hotels make complete recreational facilities a feature of their **operation.** In a hotel, the Recreation Center usually provides the following services.

1. Body Care Service, which refers to **a series of** service items that meet the demands of guests on keep-fit exercising and health care. It mainly includes basketball, badminton, tennis, golf, shuffle board, table tennis, billiards, bowling, gymnastics, arrow shooting, etc.

2. Bathing Service, which refers to a series of service items that meet the demands of guests on relaxing. It mainly includes bathing, sauna, massage, spa, swimming, **fragrant** herbal bath, etc.

3. Health Care Service, which refers to a series of service items that meet the demands of guests for beauty and body care. It mainly includes hairdressing, body care, physical **therapy**, medical examinations, etc.

4. Entertainment Service, which refers to a series of service items that meet the demands of guests on recreation and amusement. It mainly includes singing, dancing, KTV, net bar, cards & chess, etc.

Because of all these recreational activities, many hotels hire a number of people to give lessons to guests on tennis, golf, swimming, etc. For example, lifeguards are often necessary at swimming pools; there is always a **coach** in yoga lessons.

The recreation staff should keep the following in mind when they provide service for guests:

—Greeting the guest in a warm and polite manner;

—Introducing the main service items and facilities to the guest, and replying to his inquiries;

—Introducing the charge of items and knowing the way of payment;

—Leading the guest to the service place;

—Introducing how to use the facilities and reminding them of points for attention;

—Settling accounts with the guest;

—Inviting the guest to come again.

Vocabulary

integral	*adj*. 完整的;不可或缺的	fragrant	*adj*. 芬芳的;香的
operation	*n*. 运转;操作;生效	therapy	*n*. 治疗
a series of	一系列;许多	coach	*n*. 教练

Task 1 Translation. Try to translate the underlined sections into Chinese.

Task 2 Choices. Read again and tick off the service items mentioned in the passage.

□ table tennis	□ cupping
□ singing & dancing	□ sauna & massage
□ surfing	□ horse riding
□ squash	□ golf
□ skiing	□ hairdressing

Task 3 Order. Put the job procedure of the recreation staff into the correct order.

(　　)A. Settling accounts with the guest.

(　　)B. Leading the guest to the service place.

(　　)C. Introducing the using methods of facilities and reminding him of the points for attention.

(　　)D. Inviting the guest to come again.

(　　)E. Greeting the guest warmly.

(　　)F. Introducing the main service items to the guest and replying his inquiries.

Task 4 Match. Match the following phrases with their Chinese meanings.

1. body care service	a. 保健服务
2. bathing service	b. 射箭
3. health careservice	c. 沙弧球
4. entertainment service	d. 香薰泡浴
5. arrow shooting	e. 娱乐服务
6. medical examinations	f. 洗浴服务
7. recreational facilities	g. 体检
8. shuffle board	h. 康体服务
9. fragrant herbal bath	i. 康乐设施

Part 4 Translation

Task 1 Write the Chinese names of the following recreational areas.

1. karaoke bar
2. billiards room
3. fitness center
4. ballroom
5. golf course
6. bowling room
7. night club
8. beauty parlor

Task 2 Choose the best Chinese translation for each sentence.

1. More and more hotels make complete recreational facilities a feature of their operation.
   A. 越来越多的酒店拥有完整的娱乐设施,这是它们运营的特点。
   B. 越来越多的酒店把拥有完备的康乐设施作为其经营的一大特色。
   C. 越来越多的酒店设有完整的娱乐设施,这成为其操作的特征。
   D. 越来越多的酒店康乐设施齐全,这成为其主要卖点之一。
2. In such weather, I'm afraid the water is too cold to swim in.
   A. 在这样的天气下,恐怕游泳使人感到很凉爽。
   B. 在这样的天气下,恐怕游泳时我会感到水凉。
   C. 在这样的天气下,我恐怕水太凉而不能在里面游泳。
   D. 在这样的天气下,我害怕去游泳,因为水会很凉。
3. Our gym is well-equipped with all the latest sports apparatus.
   A. 我们有装备完善的健身房,拥有最新式的运动器材。
   B. 我们的健身房装备有崭新的运动器材。
   C. 我们的体育馆装备很好,拥有最高级的健身器材。
   D. 我们的体育馆配备有各式各样的健身器材。

4. Taijiquan is an important branch of Chinese martial arts, which is used for life enhancement and health building.

   A. 太极拳是中国文化艺术的重要分支,用来延年益寿和强身健体。

   B. 太极拳是中国军事艺术的重要组成部分,用来提高军队的战斗力。

   C. 太极拳是中华传统文化的瑰宝,用来提高寿命和强壮身体。

   D. 太极拳是中华武术的重要分支,用来延年益寿和强身健体。

Task 3 Read the dialogues and translate the Chinese parts into English.

Situation 1 介绍酒店设施。

A: Could you tell me something about ________________(酒店的设施) in your hotel?

B: Of course, sir. There's ________________(全套一流的餐厅和酒吧) of course. We also have ________________(健身和美容设施), including a health centre and sauna and a beauty salon.

There is also a ________________(标准游泳池), and tennis and squash courts as well. You can of course look up the directory for information about room service and ________________(怎样使用客房设施) in your room.

Situation 2 介绍残疾人设施。

A: OK. How about ________________(残疾人设施)? You see, my husband's in a wheelchair.

B: Er, what do you mean?

A: Well, ________________(你们除了楼梯还有坡道吗)? In some hotels, my husband has real problems.

B: Mm. Yes, I understand, madam, but I'm afraid there are ________________(没有可以供残疾客人使用的专门设施).

Situation 3 介绍商务中心。

A: Excuse me, where is ________________(商务中心)?

B: It's on the fourth floor. ________________(请乘大厅电梯上去) and then turn right. ________________(商务中心在走廊尽头). But sir, I'm afraid it is closed.

A: What! ________________(这里不提供24小时服务吗)?

B: I'm sorry, sir. ________________(商务中心只服务至晚上11点). Now it is already half-past eleven.

Situation 4 介绍游泳馆。

A: Excuse me, how can I get to the swimming pool from here?

B: ________________(乘这个电梯到顶楼就可以了). You can't miss it. After you get out of the elevator, ________________(跟着路标走就行了). ________________(游泳池旁边还有桑拿浴室、健身房和更衣室).

A：OK. Thank you very much.

B：You're welcome. And ______________________(祝您游泳愉快)！

Part 5 Cultural Norms

常用词汇

sauna	桑拿	shower	冲凉
massage	按摩	masseur	男按摩师
masseuse	女按摩师	foot	足
manicure	修指甲	pedicure	修趾甲
ear cleaning	采耳	back scrub	擦背
facial	面部的	VIP	贵宾
relax	放松;修养	healthy	健康的
sauna attendant	桑拿室服务员	house bill	房账
20% discount	八折	cash	现金
credit card	信用卡	exchange rate	汇率
shoes closet	鞋柜	gymnasium	健身房
steam room	蒸汽室	swimming pool	游泳池
timer	计时员	import	进口
locker	更衣柜	Jacuzzi	水流按摩池
equipment	器材	beauty care	美容
remote control	遥控器	price list	价格表
body building	健身;健美	Taiji/shadow boxing	太极拳
locker room	更衣室	resident coach	常驻教练
spring grip	弹簧握力计	chest expander	扩胸器
aerobic stair climber	爬楼器	sauna proper	桑拿浴室
yoga	瑜伽	Pilates	普拉提
bowling court	保龄球馆	badminton court	羽毛球场
golf course	高尔夫球场	baseball diamond	棒球场
skating rink	溜冰场	cricket court	板球场

常用句子

美容美发

1. Good afternoon. I want a haircut and a shave, please. 下午好，请替我理发并修面。
2. How would you like your hair cut? 您想剪什么发式？
3. Would you like to have a shampoo? 您要洗头吗？
4. Do you want me to shave off your beard? 胡须要不要给您刮掉？
5. Do you want me to trim your moustache? 要不要把您的胡须修剪一下？
6. How would you like your hair done, madam? Permanent, cold wave, or washed and

dressed? 女士,您的头发是想电烫、冷烫,还是洗一洗再做?

7. Can you show me some patterns of hair styles? 您能否给我看一些发型的式样?

酒吧

1. What can I prepare for you, sir? 先生,您想喝杯什么?
2. Your usual, sir? 先生,还是和每天一样吗?
3. Your beer, sir. Enjoy your drink. 先生,您的啤酒,希望您喜欢。
4. Here is your bill, sir. 先生,这是您的账单。
5. Here is your change, sir. 先生,这是找您的零钱。
6. If you don't like this drink, how about that one? 如果您不喜欢这种饮料,那种怎么样?
7. If you prefer something milder, there is Shaoxing rice wine, which is a real Chinese specialty in South China. 您如果想喝点温和些的酒,有绍兴加饭酒,它是中国南方的特产酒。
8. Would you like your coffee with milk and sugar? 您想在咖啡里加点牛奶和糖吗?
9. What would you like to drink? We've a great variety of wines. Which kind of them do you prefer? 您要喝什么? 我们有好多种酒。您想喝哪种?

运动中心

1. We have a well-equipped gym with all the latest recreational sports apparatus—exercise bicycles, weights, swimming pools, tennis courts—that sort of thing. You may find more details in this map. 我们体育馆有许多先进的运动设施,像运动自行车、哑铃、游泳池、网球场之类的。您从这张地图能了解更多细节。
2. We have an excellent sauna, with a free supply of towels and soap. 我们有一个不错的桑拿浴室,免费提供毛巾和浴皂。
3. You'd better do some stretches before you work out. 在健身前,您最好做做伸展运动。
4. Please wipe off the machine after use. 健身器材使用后请擦干净。
5. Do you need some help using that machine? 您使用那台机器需要帮助吗?
6. This exercise will help build your shoulders. 这项运动能让您的肩膀更有型。
7. How often do you work out? 您多久运动一次?
8. I would suggest you try a yoga/an aerobics class. 我建议您上瑜伽课/有氧运动课。
9. Our gym has all the latest exercise equipment, including stairmasters, exercise bikes, and nautilus machines. 我们的健身房拥有所有最新的运动器材,包括台阶器、运动自行车和全身型健身器。
10. There's an area for exercise machines, one area for free weights, and a completely separate area for stretching and special classes. 健身房有一个健身器材区、一个自由重量训练区和一个完全隔开的区域,用于伸展运动和特殊课程。
11. We offer yoga, Pilates, martial arts, and Tai ji classes. 我们有瑜伽、普拉提、武术和太极课程。
12. We have hot mineral springs here. 我们这里有温泉。
13. We have sauna, the mineral mud SPA and fragrant milk SPA. 我们有桑拿、矿泥 SPA

和芳香牛奶 SPA。

14. We have dry and wet sauna. 我们有干蒸和湿蒸。
15. Do you need a massage? 您需要按摩吗?
16. We have body massage, point massage and foot massage. 我们有全身按摩、穴位按摩和足底按摩。
17. Massage not only helps relax the muscles but also eases the pain. 按摩不但能放松肌肉,而且能缓解疼痛。

Part 6 Supplementary Reading

"All work and no play makes Jack a dull boy" is a popular saying in the United States. Other countries have similar sayings. It is true that all of us need recreation. We cannot work all the time if we are going to keep good health and enjoy life.

Everyone has his own way of relaxing. Perhaps the most popular way is to take part in sports. There are team sports, such as baseball, basketball, and football. There are individual sports, also, such as golf and swimming. In addition, hiking, fishing, skiing, and mountain climbing have a great attraction for people who like to be outdoors.

Not everyone who enjoys sports events likes to take part in them. Many people prefer to be on lookers, either watching them on television, or listening to them on the radio. When there is an important baseball game or boxing match, it is almost impossible to get tickets; everyone wants to attend.

Chess, card-playing, and dancing are forms of indoor recreation enjoyed by many people. It doesn't matter whether we play a fast game of ping-pong, concentrate over the bridge table, or go walking through the woods on a brisk autumn afternoon. It is important for everyone to relax from time to time and enjoy some form of recreation.

Shopping

Study Objectives

1. To learn useful expressions and patterns in helping guests with shopping.
2. To practice situational dialogues and translation fluently.
3. To know more about Chinese products and culture.

Lead in

Shopping arcade in hotel aims at providing a convenient and relaxed shopping experience for the guests. As far as the customers are concerned, they find that in the arcade they can buy what they want in a short time and the goods there are usually of great quality. Think carefully and try to answer the following questions.

1. What kinds of Chinese products do you think foreign tourists are most interested in?
2. What kind of products do hotel shops in China offer to foreign tourists?
3. What should the shop assistants do in order to satisfy the customers?

Part 1 Listening

Task 1 Dialogues. Listen to the dialogues and fill in the blanks with what you hear.

Dialogue 1

A: Good morning, sir. Can I help you?

B: Good morning. You see, I'm ____________________________.

Dialogue 2

B: Ah, they look rather ____________________________.

A: Sure! They're the ____________________________.

Dialogue 3

B: Any ____________________________?

A: How about this one? ____________________________, what do you think?

Dialogue 4

A: By the way, is there a cinema near here?

B: Yes. ________________. Then turn right. ________________.

Task 2 Conversations. Listen and fill in the blanks with the words or phrases provided in the box.

silk scarf	recommendation	Chinese knots	souvenir shop	mascot
Olympic Games	Paralympic Games	collection	preserved fruits	

Conversation 1 Mr. Benson wants to buy some gifts in the shopping arcade.

(Salesgirl-S Mr. Benson-Mr.)

S: Good morning. Welcome to the ________________. Can I help you?

Mr.: Yes. I just want to ________________.

S: Do you have ________________?

Mr.: Yes. I want to buy some gifts for my daughter and son, ________ ________, and some ________________.

S: OK. For kids these ________________ are very popular. For ladies, we have ________________, ________________, ________________ and so on. For men, these ________________, ________________, are good choices.

Mr.: I'd like to take the green car and the red car for my kids, and this ________________ for my wife. But I have no idea for my friends. Can you give me some ________________?

S: We have many ________________, and you may take a look first.

Mr.: OK. I will ________________. How much are they?

S: It's 300 yuan for the ________________, 100 yuan for the ________________, and 100 yuan for the two ________________. The total is 500 yuan. You may pay over there.

Mr.: Thank you very much.

Conversation 2 Miss Emily wants to choose some gifts for her friends.

(Salesgirl-S Miss Emily-Miss)

S: Good morning. Welcome to the ________________. Can I help you?

Miss.: Yes. I'd like to buy some ________________.

S: We have Fuwa, ________________; Funiu, ________________.
Many people are ________________ about them.

Miss.: Great. That's a good idea. How much is the Fuwa?

S: For the big size one, it's 500 yuan.

Miss.: Wow, It ________________. I have six good friends, and I need to buy one for each of them. Oh, my god!

S: ________________, I suggest you buying the small size ones. Six of them will be 600 yuan.

Miss.：That's OK. How much is the small Funiu?

S：It's 80 yuan.

Miss.：OK，I will ________________ of Fuwa and two Funius.

S：I will ________________ them for you. You may pay over there.

Miss.：Thank you very much.

Conversation 3 A guest is choosing some gifts for his family.

(Salesman-S Guest-G)

S：Good morning. Welcome to the ________________. Can I help you?

G：Yes. I'd like to have some ________________ for my family.

S：________________?

G：I don't have anything in mind. Can you introduce something in your food shop?

S：Sure. We have very famous ________________ and ________________ here.

G：I have heard a lot about that.

S：Do you like preserved fruits? There are many preserved fruits from different ____________.

G：Which one is more famous?

S：The popular ones here are Xufuji，Daoxiangcun and so on. They are ______________.

G：I have heard of Daoxiangcun before. ________________.

S：You may pay over there.

G：Thank you very much.

Part 2 Speaking

Task 1 Work in pairs. Discuss with your partner and put the job procedure of a shop assistant into the correct order.

(　　)A. Explain the products to the guest (quality，color，size，feature，etc.).
(　　)B. Greet and welcome the guest.
(　　)C. Show the sample.
(　　)D. Pack the products.
(　　)E. Offer cautions.
(　　)F. Accept the payment.
(　　)G. Recommend the products.

Task 2 Work in pairs. A guest wants to buy something for his wife in the hotel shopping arcade. Read the following dialogue with your partner and fill in the blanks with the words or phrases provided in the box.

cultured pearls	attended to	label	latest style
pearl producing area	luster	value	string

(Shop Assistant-A Guest-G)

A: Good afternoon, sir. Are you being ________________?

G: Not yet. I'd like to buy something special for my wife.

A: I see. We have pearl, gold and cloisonné necklaces and bracelets. Would you like to have a look?

G: OK. Can you show me the ________________ of pearl necklaces?

A: Sure. We have both sea pearls and ________________. Which do you prefer?

G: Could you tell me the difference?

A: Yes. This is a sea pearl, the ________________ is particularly fine and it is very round. Compared with cultured pearls, sea pearls are of much higher ____________.

G: Looks nice. How much is it?

A: 2900 yuan. It's from the South China Sea.

G: May I have a look at the cultured pearls?

A: Certainly. This necklace is made with cultured pearls. You see, cultured pearls have equal luster and are just as beautiful. Part of their attraction is their various shapes.

G: Oh, I see. Where do they come from?

A: They come from Hepu, a very famous ________________ in China. The price is marked on the ________________.

G: 200 yuan. I think I prefer the sea pearls but they are very expensive.

A: Yes, they are. What about these cultured pearls—they are very shiny and quite round. They cost 500 yuan a strand.

G: OK, I'll take those. Can you ________________ them for me please?

A: Yes, of course. Thank you, sir. I'm sure your wife will like them.

Task 3 Work in pairs. Make up a dialogue respectively according to the situations provided.

Situation 1 Mrs. Lee wants to buy a china tea set in the hotel shop. Practice recommending products and act it out. The expressions given in the box are for your reference.

Shop Assistant	Guest
Would you like a tea set for four, six or eight persons?	I'd like to buy a china tea set for my friends.
How about...?	A set for six persons will be all right.
It's a traditional Chinese design.	It is really beautiful.
This brown china tea set is quite unusual.	Where does it come from?
You've made a good choice, madam.	Would you give me a discount?
Shall I wrap it up for you?	I see. Then I'll take it.
Please handle the china tea set carefully.	

Situation 2 Make up the conversation between Mr. Tony Brown and a shop assistant with the help of the steps provided in the box.

Greet.
Want to buy a set of Chinese tableware.
Show interest in the blue-and-white tableware with the bamboo design.
Want to buy tablecloth to go with it.
Ask about the tablecloth which is hand-embroidered.
Ask about the discount.
Take the two items.
Express thanks.

Vocabulary

apartment store	*n.* 百货商店	show window	*n.* 橱窗
children's goods store	*n.* 儿童用品商店	show case	*n.* 玻璃柜台
antique shop	*n.* 古玩店	cash desk, cashier's desk	*n.* 收银处
second-hand store	*n.* 旧货店	shelf	*n.* 货架
counter	*n.* 柜台	price tag	*n.* 标价签
stall, stand	*n.* 售货摊		

Situation 3 A customer wishing to buy her sister a birthday present comes to the hotel shop. Make up a conversation between them. The words and expressions below are for your reference.

Vocabulary

curiosity	*n.* 好奇心	charge	*v.* 赊账;记账
amazingly	*adv.* 令人吃惊地	necklace	*n.* 项链
affordable	*adj.* 买得起的		

Part 3 Reading

Hotel Shops

Every year millions of foreigners visit China on business, for sightseeing or exchanges in the fields of economy, trade, sports, science and culture. They are not only **fascinated** by the beautiful scenery, but also fond of the local specialties. Shopping, therefore, becomes a must of their **itineraries.** Many of them return home **loaded with** Chinese souvenirs and gifts.

In China, hotel shops offer a wide range of goods to foreign tourists. Many foreign tourists cannot resist the temptation of the products when they visit China. Chinese arts and crafts are the main products in hotel shops, which are the favorite goods for foreign buyers. The **cloisonné**, which enjoys a high reputation at home and abroad, is beautiful and elegant in molding, splendid and graceful in design and **dazzling** and brilliant in colors. The **jade carving** is characterized by its distinct national style of simplicity, gracefulness and delicate lucidity. **Lacquerware**, **exquisite** in workmanship, is noted by elegant modeling, beautiful figuration, and **lustrous** color. **Porcelain** is perhaps the greatest invention Chinese people made for the world. The chinaware made in Jingdezhen—the capital of porcelain—is known to be "as white as jade, as thin as paper, as bright as mirror and as **melodious** as *qing* (an ancient Chinese musical instrument)". Silk products and **embroidery**, exquisite in workmanship, harmonious in color scheme, and **distinctive** in national style, are really good buys in China. In fact, tourist shopping has become one of the **pillars** that support China's tourism industry.

In order to meet the increasing shopping needs of the customers, shop assistants should not only be familiar with the products and have a good command of languages and job procedures, but also have a warm desire to serve the customers heart and soul. They need to try every means to make every customer feel the value of every coin they spend.

Vocabulary

fascinate	*v*. 使……入迷;吸引住
itinerary	*n*. 旅行日程;路线
loaded with	装满
cloisonné	*n*. (法)景泰蓝瓷器
dazzling	*adj*. 令人眼花缭乱的;耀眼的
jade carving	玉雕
lacquerware	*n*. 漆器;陶器
exquisite	*adj*. 精挑细选的;精致的
lustrous	*adj*. 有光泽的;光辉的
porcelain	*n*. 瓷;瓷器
melodious	*adj*. 旋律美妙的;调子优美的
embroidery	*n*. 刺绣;刺绣品
distinctive	*adj*. 独特的;有特色的
pillar	*n*. 柱子;支柱;核心(人物)
calligraphy	*n*. 书法
antique	*n*. 古董;古玩
stationery	*n*. 文具;信纸
chopsticks	*n*. 筷子

Task 1 Choices. Tick off the Chinese products mentioned in the passage.

□embroidery	□stationery
□paper-cut	□lacquerware
□porcelain	□jade carving
□jewelry	□antique
□arts and crafts	□cloisonné
□calligraphy	□chopsticks

Task 2 True or false statements. Decide whether the following statements are True (T) or False (F) according to the text.

( )1. Foreign tourists like to buy Chinese souvenirs and gifts when they visit China.

( )2. Chinese garments are the main products sold in hotel shops, which are the favorite goods for foreigners.

( )3. Nowadays tourist shopping plays an important role in China's tourism industry.

( )4. Shop assistants should be good at languages and job procedures.

Task 3 Match. Match the following phrases with their Chinese meanings.

1. local specialty	a. 便宜货
2. resist the temptation	b. 工艺品
3. enjoy a high reputation	c. 精通语言
4. a good buy	d. 当地特产
5. color scheme	e. 丝织品
6. have a good command of languages	f. 抵制诱惑
7. silk product	g. 享有盛名
8. arts and crafts	h. 色彩设计

Task 4 Translation. Try to translate the underlined sections into Chinese.

Part 4 Translation

Task 1 Translate the following passages into Chinese.

1. Look! This is a Qing-style three-board wooden screen. Such screens used to be made up of three to five boards. It is foldable, used in the house to keep the wind out, or to stop others from seeing in. There are different designs painted on each screen, see, flowers, fish, birds and mammals, and ancient beauties.
2. About in the 12th century, Chinese kites spread to the West and Oriental and Western kite cultures were formed after years of development. In this process, the traditional

culture integrated with the kite craft, and finally formed the kite culture with unique characteristics.

Task 2 Translate the following passages into English.

1. 在种类繁多的民间手工艺品中，潮州绣香包(也称绣玩具)是多姿多彩且独具特色的一种。它是一种富于地方风采、玩赏和装饰兼备的手工艺品。它们大多是玲珑的小玩具，也有些是大型的饰品和实用的工艺品。这些独具风格的工艺品，以其造型优美、色彩斑斓、极富乡土艺术韵味而受到人们的喜爱。
2. 虎头鞋是为学步儿童设计的一种鞋子，因鞋头呈虎头模样，故称虎头鞋。凡在中原地区生活的人，对学步儿童穿的虎头鞋都非常熟悉。它给家庭带来欢乐，给父母带来希望。它既有实用价值，又有吉祥的含义，人们还希望它能驱鬼辟邪。

Part 5 Cultural Norms

常用词汇

Fifth Avenue (New York)	纽约第五大道
Avenue des Champs-Elysees (Paris)	巴黎香榭丽舍大道
Causeway Bay (Hong Kong)	香港铜锣湾
Times Square (New York)	纽约时代广场
Ginza (Tokyo)	日本东京银座
Oxford Street (London)	英国伦敦牛津大街
Madison Avenue (New York)	纽约麦迪逊大道
H. Bond Street (London)	英国邦德街
shopping arcade	商场部
carving	雕刻
inkstone	砚石
colored ceramics	彩瓷
lacquer ware	漆器
woven item	编织品
folk music instrument	民间乐器
sandal wood fan	檀香扇
seal	印章
four treasures of Chinese handwriting	文房四宝
clay figurine	泥人
earthen figurine	陶俑
puppet show	木偶戏
lacquer painting	漆画
shadow show	皮影戏
clay modeling	泥塑

sculpture	雕塑
ironwork	铁铸品
cloth ornament	服饰
antique	古玩
twelve year animals	十二生肖
jadeite	翡翠
ruby	红宝石
agate	玛瑙
diamond	钻石
ivory	象牙
pearl	珍珠

常用句子

1. Su embroidery formed its own unique characteristics: smooth, bright, and neat. 苏绣具有平、亮、齐的特点。
2. Yue embroidered pictures are mainly of dragons and phoenixes, and flowers and birds. 粤绣的图案主要由龙凤和花鸟组成。
3. Double-sided embroidery is an excellent representative of Su embroidery. 双面绣是苏绣中的代表作。
4. Kites were invented by the Chinese people over 2000 years ago. 风筝是两千年前由中国人发明的。
5. Jingtailan is classified into two categories: Common Jingtailan and Flower-strip Jingtailan. 景泰蓝分为普通景泰蓝和花纹景泰蓝两种。
6. Do you have anything specific in mind? 你心中有什么特别的要求吗?
7. Do you have any other colors? 有没有别的颜色?
8. Many country women are good at papercutting. 许多农村妇女擅长剪纸。
9. It is said that there is a legend behind each year animal. 据说每个生肖的背后都有一个传说。
10. Brisk carving requires elaborate and complicated process. 砖雕需要非常精致和复杂的工艺。
11. Sandalwood furniture is popular in Guangdong. 在广东,红木家具深受人们喜爱。
12. Jade is always cool to the touch and is resistant to being scratched by metal. 真玉摸上去有点凉的感觉,而且不怕金属刮擦。
13. Are you being attended to? 有人接待您了吗?
14. It is sold by the yard by a package. 这个按码成包出售。
15. Sorry, it's out of stock. 对不起,卖完了。
16. What size and color do you take, sir? How about this one? 先生,您穿多大号? 要什么颜色? 这双怎么样?
17. How about this color and this size? How do you like this one? 这种颜色、尺寸怎么样? 您看这个怎么样?

18. We are open from 9 a. m. to 9 p. m. every Monday to Saturday. 我们每周一到每周六营业，时间是从早上 9 点至晚上 9 点。
19. Here is your charge, sir, thank you and here is your receipt. 这是找您的钱，先生，谢谢，这是您的收据。
20. You look lovely in this overcoat. 您穿上这件外套真漂亮。
21. May I try this on? 我可以试穿这个吗？
22. Can you cut me a deal? 你可以算便宜一点吗？
23. Can I pay by credit card? 我可以用信用卡结账吗？
24. What time do you open/close? 你们几点开始营业/打烊？
25. Please wrap this for me. 请帮我把这个包起来。

Part 6 Supplementary Reading

Chinese folk handicrafts are closely related to the Chinese people's daily life. Throughout the long history, there have been developed hundreds of types and thousands of varieties of folk handicrafts. These works have greatly enriched Chinese people's life.

Chinese **ceramics** has a long history. The ancient people over 7000 years ago were already able to make colored **pottery** (which requires a temperature under 1050°C), and people of the Eastern Han Dynasty could make ceramics over 1900 years ago, 1700 years earlier than the people in Western countries. With the culture advances, the use of pottery and ceramics has gradually turned from **utensils** to **ornamental** works of art.

Chinese **lacquer** ware boasts a history of over 5000 years. It is made with a mixture of various refined colorful natural lacquer through such procedures as **polishing**, carving, filling, painting etc. **Contemporary** lacquer ware bases mainly include Beijing, Hangzhou, Yangzhou, and Sichuan, etc.

Chinese jade carving enjoys the reputation of "the essence of **oriental** arts" in the world. The jade carvings have different kinds of forms, mainly in the shape of human figures, birds, animals, flowers, and utensils. Chinese crafts masters make use of natural **texture**, shape, and **luster** of the jades and carve them into masterpieces of carving with excellent skills.

Vocabulary

ceramics	*n.* 陶瓷
pottery	*n.* 陶器
utensil	*n.* 器具
ornamental	*adj.* 装饰的
lacquer	*n.* 漆；漆器
polish	*v.* 擦亮；擦光
contemporary	*adj.* 同时代的；同时
oriental	*adj.* 东方人的

texture n. (材料等的)结构;质地

luster v. 有光泽;发亮;使……发光

Notes

1. The use of pottery and ceramics has gradually turned from utensils to ornamental works of art. 陶器和瓷器的使用逐渐由生活器皿向艺术装饰品转变。
2. It is made with a mixture of various refined colorful natural lacquer through such procedures as polishing, carving, filling, painting etc. 它是由各种彩色的天然漆混合,并经过如打磨、雕刻、填料、绘画等一系列的工艺才制成的。把漆涂在各种器物的表面所制成的日常器具及工艺品、美术品等,一般称为"漆器"。
3. Chinese jade carving enjoys the reputation of "the essence of oriental arts". 中国玉雕享有"东方艺术精髓"的美誉。在中国,玉是纯洁、富贵的代名词,冰清玉洁、琼楼玉宇、金玉满堂等涉及玉的美好词汇不胜枚举。中国也是用玉最早的国家之一。
4. The jade carvings have different kinds of forms, mainly in the shape of human figures, birds, animals...玉雕的造型多种多样,主要模仿人物、鸟兽……
5. Chinese crafts masters make use of natural texture, shape, and luster of the jades and carve them into masterpieces of carving with excellent skills. 中国的手工艺人利用玉石的天然质地、形状和光泽,用精湛的工艺将它们雕刻成艺术精品。

Chapter 16

Complaints Handling

Study Objectives

1. To learn useful expressions and patterns in helping guests with their problems.
2. To practice situational dialogues and translation fluently.
3. To know more about methods for handling customer complaints.

Lead in

As a service business, all hotels will receive complaints and compliments all the time. To handle the problems well will show the communicative skills of the staff in charge of the case. Therefore, patience and nice communicative skills will be necessary. Think carefully and try to answer the following questions.

1. What do you think guests may complain about the hotel?
2. Have you ever been dissatisfied with hotel service? What happened and how was the problem solved?
3. What steps do you think the hotel staff should follow in order to solve guests' problems?

Part 1 Listening

Task 1 Dialogues. Here are pieces of complaining. Listen carefully, fill in the blanks according to what you hear and learn some similar expressions.

Dialogue 1

A: Ah, yes. The room is too cold for me. I feel ________________ when I sleep. Can you ________________ the air conditioner.

B: (*Checks*) The air conditioner is already off, madam.

Similar expressions

Maybe I'm ________________.

Would you like an ________________?

OK. And would you please get me some hot water, too? I think I need to ____________.

Certainly, madam. I'll be right back...Here is a blanket and hot water for you. Anything else?

Dialogue 2

A: Yes, I'd like to ____________. This bill is wrong. I've been ____________. It says I sent two ____________ from your Business Center, but I've nevereven been to the business center. I don't even know where it is!

B: I see. Mr. Hendrickson. So you've been charged for faxes you didn't send?

Similar expressions

Well, sir, I'm terribly sorry, but it appears we've made a mistake. The Business Center ____________ you with a Mr. H-e-n-d-e-r-s-o-n who is staying in the hotel at the moment. I must ____________, Mr. Hendrickson.

That's all right. Everyone makes mistakes, I suppose. Now, can I ____________ please? I've got ____________

Dialogue 3

A: I wonder what has happened to my room. You said it would be ready in ten minutes, but I've waited for ____________. Can you tell me exactly when I can get in?

B: I'm terribly sorry, sir. Because the ____________ has ____________, so our house maid is still ____________. It will be ready in a few minutes.

Similar expressions

I'm so tired now. I don't mind ____________.

Sorry for keeping you waiting, sir. But we insist on ____________ for our guests. I can ____________ it won't take long.

I ____________ but please think about how tired one is after ____________.

Maybe you could take a seat ____________, sir.

Dialogue 4

A: That's ____________! I won't pay the ____________ anyway.

B: Then, please wait a moment, sir. I'll get the manager to take care of your ____________.

Similar expressions

Wait a minute. Why three and a half day? I have ____________ the room for three days only.

I'm sorry, sir. But because you ____________ at six o'clock, so there is an ____________.

But no one told me there is an extra charge. Besides, I just stay a little bit longer.

We've tried to ____________ you, sir, but you're not in your room.

Dialogue 5

A: ____________ and ____________. There are no ____________ in the bathroom.

B: I'm terribly sorry to hear that. I'll ________________ right away. We usually check every room before guests move in. But we have been ________________ with a large ______________. What's more, it's the ________________. We might have ________________ some points. I'll send a ________________ to your room right now.

Similar expressions

That's not all. The worst thing is that ________________ and when I ________________ it, it ________________.

Oh, dear, we are terribly sorry for all this ________________. You see, the hotel has just opened and the kinks haven't been worked out yet. So if you please ________________, we will move you to another room. I'll send a ________________ up to your room and help you with the luggage.

Task 2 Conversations. Listen and fill in the blanks with the words or phrases provided in the box.

smelly	inconvenience	hesitate	elevator	corridor	spare room

Conversation 1 A guest is complaining about her room.

(Front Office Clerk-C Guest-G)

C: Good evening. Front Office. Can I help you?

G: This is Mrs. Stevenson, Room ________________. I've just checked in and I'm not happy with my room.

C: May I know what is wrong?

G: The room is ________________ and there is someone's hair on my bed! I didn't expect such things would happen in your hotel.

C: I'm sorry to hear that. Mrs. Stevenson. I'll send a housemaid to your room at once. She will bring ________________ and make up the bed again for you. We do apologize for the ________________.

G: That's fine. Thank you.

C: You're welcome, Mrs. Stevenson. My name is Simon, and if there is anything else I can do for you, please don't ________________ to call me.

Conversation 2 Mr. Brown complains about his room.

(Front Office Clerk-C Mr. Brown-Mr.)

C: Good morning, sir. What can I do for you?

Mr.: I'm Brown. I'm in Room 608. Can you change the room for me? It's too noisy. I was woken up several times by the noise ________________, It was too much for me.

C: I'm awfully sorry, sir. I do apologize. Room 608 is ________________. It's possible that the noise is heard early in the morning when all is quiet.

Mr.: Anyhow, I'd like to change my room.

C: No problem, sir. We'll manage it, but we don't have any ________ today. Could you wait till tomorrow? The American Education Delegation will be leaving tomorrow morning. There'll be some rooms for you to choose from.

Mr.: All right. I hope I'll be able to enjoy my stay ________ tomorrow evening and ________.

C: Be sure. I'll make a note of that. Everything will be taken care of. And if there is anything more you need, please let us know.

Conversation 3 A guest calls the Room Service.

(Guest-G Clerk of Room Service-C)

G: Hello, this is room ________. I've just ________ and have found some problems.

C: What can we ________ today?

G: It seems ________.

C: We'll ________.

G: Thank you.

C: We're very sorry for ________ we've caused you.

G: That's ________.

C: Bye.

Part 2 Speaking

Task 1 Work in pairs. Practice the following dialogues. Pay more attention to the underlined parts.

Situation 1 A customer complains about his steak.

(Manager-M Customer-C)

M: You asked to see me, Mr. Smith?

C: Yes, I did. I'm very upset at the way I have been treated.

M: Perhaps you could tell me what exactly the matter is.

C: It's my steak.

M: What is wrong with your steak, sir?

C: It is too raw. I can't eat it. But when I complained to your waitress, she just ignored me.

M: I'm very sorry, sir. I'm sure the waitress didn't mean to be rude. You see, she just started out as a waitress a week ago and doesn't understand English very well. She should have changed your steak.

C: Except she didn't.

M: It's been a misunderstanding, sir. I'll have the steak returned to the kitchen right away.

C: That's more like it. Well, there is something else. This wine here, I think it is corked.

M: Are you sure, sir? The Chianti has been very popular with our guests.

C: Well, here you are. Try it for yourself.

M: No, sir. It doesn't taste wrong at all. Perhaps it is a little too sour for your taste. I would recommend that you try the Burgundy next time.

C: Right. Perhaps I will.

M: Well, I hope you enjoy your dinner.

Vocabulary

medium	*adj*. 中等的;适中的	recommend	*v*. 推荐;介绍
cork	*v*. 用软木塞塞住		

Situation 2 A guest wants to change a room. He goes to the assistant manager.

(**Manager-M Guest-G**)

M: Good morning. sir. What can I do for you?

G: I'm Bell. I'm in Room 908. Can you change the room for me? It's too noisy. My wife was woken up several times by the noise the baggage elevator made. She said it was too much for her.

M: I'm awfully sorry, sir. I do apologize. Room 908 is at the end of the corridor. It's possible that the noise is heard early in the morning when all is quiet.

G: Anyhow, I'd like to change our room.

M: No problem, sir. We'll manage it, but we don't have any spare room today. Could you wait till tomorrow? The American People-to-people Education Delegation will be leaving tomorrow morning. There'll be some rooms for you to choose from.

G: All right. I hope we'll be able to enjoy our stay in a quiet suite tomorrow evening and have a sound sleep.

M: Be sure. I'll make a note of that. Everything will be taken care of. And if there is anything more you need, please let us know.

Vocabulary

elevator	*n*. 电梯	delegation	*n*. 代表团
corridor	*n*. 走廊;回廊	extra	*adj*. 额外的;外加的

Situation 3 A guest rings for service.

(**Assistant Manager-A Guest-G**)

A: Good evening, madam. Did you ring for service? What can I do for you?

G: Yes. The light in this room is too dim. Please get me a brighter one.

A: Certainly, madam. I'll be back right away. Do you mind if I move your things?

G: Oh, no. Go ahead.

A: Thank you. How is the light now?

G：It's much better now. Thank you.

A：You're welcome. And if you need any other things，please let us know.

G：Ah，yes，the room is too cold for me. I feel rather cold when I sleep. Can you turn off the air-conditioning?

A：(*Checks*) The air-conditioning is already off，madam.

G：Maybe I'm getting a cold.

A：Would you like an extra blanket?

G：OK. And would you please get me some hot water，too? I think I need to take some medicine.

A：Certainly，madam. I'll be right back. Here is a blanket，and hot water for you. Anything else?

G：No，thanks.

A：Good night，madam.

Task 2　Complete the following dialogue according to the Chinese in brackets.

(Guest Stephen Nobel-G　Waitress Jane-W)

G：Excuse me，waiter.

W：________________(您对一切满意吗)?

G：No. The fish was recommended，but it is not very fresh.

W：________________(真对不起，我给您换一盘).

G：So what? It is not fresh and I am not happy about it.

W：________________(很抱歉，先生。您想要试其他东西吗？我们可免费送您食物).

G：No. I don't want to try something else，and find it is not fresh again.

W：________________(来一份美味的甜食，免费送您，好吗)?

G：I am not so keen on desserts as a habit. They are fattening.

W：________________(好，先生，这是您的账单。请在账单上签名，我保证您下次来的时候一切都会好的).

G：Don't be so sure of it yet. I am very critical and demanding.

W：I have very confidence in our chef. Just give us another chance.

G：________________(好的，我会再来的).

W：________________(非常感谢，先生).

Task 3　Practice the conversations and translate the sentences into English.

Situation 1　物品被盗时

A：Just a moment，madma. Let me read the tape of the door lock to see ________________(有没有人在您不在的时候进过您的房间). The tape showed that only a housekeeper had entered the room in your absence，but ________________(录像证实不是她偷了您的衣服).

B：_______________(我可以亲自看一下录像带吗)?

A：Of course. Please come with me to _______________(保安经理办公室).

B：_______________(真是蹊跷)! It seemed that _______________(房屋管理员离开房间的时候,手上并没有拿包裹).

A：I'm sorry, madma. _______________(不管是谁偷了您的东西,都是由于我们的疏忽大意造成的). _______________(我们会负责,并在3天之内给您赔偿).

Situation 2 空调故障

A：I'm from the _______________(维修部). Did you call us?

B：Yes. _______________(这个空调有些问题).

A：What's the problem?

B：____________(遥控器有问题). I turned on the air conditioner, but I ____________(无法调节温度).

A：Let me have a look. I think ____________(可能电池该换了). Let me ____________(换上两节新的). Now, it's working.

Task 4 Role-play.

Situation 1 Mr. Lee calls to the Duty Manager to complain the impolite room attendant who comes into the guest room without knocking at the door. The following expressions provided in the box may be of help to you.

open the door without pressing the button or knocking at the door
investigate this case and give you feedback
pay me back some money because of the rude action made by your employee
give you our dinner coupon valued at...
it is very impolite
thank you for your understanding
the room I am staying in is not private
guarantee that such things will not happen again

Vocabulary

impolite	*adj*. 不礼貌的	dinner coupon	晚餐券
private	*adj*. 私人的	carelessness	*n*. 粗心
incident	*n*. 事件		

Situation 2 A guest named Turner calls the Concierge to complain the slow delivery of the luggage. The Concierge asks Mr. Turner to describe the luggage's features. After checking, the Concierge tells Mr. Turner that his stuff is on the way. The following expressions provided in the box may be of help to you.

May I have your name and room number please?
I will check them for you and call you back in five minutes.
I am sorry to keep you waiting.
Why hasn't my luggage been sent up yet?
Your luggage is on the way.
Would you please give me some features of your luggage?
Is your name tag attached to them?
a big blue suitcase and a medium-sized black suitcase

Vocabulary

delivery	*n.* 派送	feature	*n.* 特征
luggage	*n.* 行李	name tag	名字标签
concierge	*n.* 礼宾		

Situation 3 Mr. White checks out at the Reception Desk. When the room attendant checks the room, she finds two bath towels are missing. The following expressions provided in the box may be of help to you.

have you seen two bath towels from the bath room
we need to charge you 100 yuan for the two towels
show you my bag
call our Duty Manager to handle it
I've already told your staff
trust our guests, but it is our job to account for all the items
should I pay for my final bill
charge you

Vocabulary

complaint	*n.* 抱怨	bath towel	*n.* 浴巾
uncomfortable	*adj.* 不舒适的	account for	负责
discount	*n.* 折扣	item	*n.* 物品
Duty Manager	值班经理		

Situation 4 A customer complains to the Reception Desk about getting the crank call at night. The following expressions provided in the box may be of help to you.

an annoying call asking me if I need a massage
check our phone records and give you feedback
the crank call was from an internal customer
checked the operator system
sorry for bringing you trouble

Vocabulary

crank call	骚扰电话	massage	*n.* 按摩

operator	*n.* 电话接线员	security	*n.* 安全
put through	接通	investigate	*v.* 调查
feedback	*n.* 反馈		

Part 3 Reading

Passage 1

There are many **unique** hotels around the world. In Greenland, there is a hotel made out of ice, open between December and April every year. In Turkey, there is a **cave** hotel with a television, **furniture**, and a bathroom in each room. And in Bolivia, there is the Salt Palace Hotel.

Thousands of years ago, the area around the Salt Palace Hotel was a large lake. But over time, all the water disappeared. Today, the area has only two small lakes and two salt **deserts**. The larger of the two deserts, the Uyuni salt desert, is 12000 square kilometers. During the day, the desert is bright white because of the salt. There are no roads across the Uyuni desert. So local people must show guests the way to the hotel.

In the early 1990s, a man named Jusan Quesada built the hotel. He cut big blocks of salt from the desert and used the blocks to build it. Everything in the hotel is made of salt: the walls, the roof, the tables, the chairs, the beds, and the hotel's bar. The sun heats the walls and roof during the day. At night the desert is very cold, but the rooms stay warm. The hotel has twelve rooms. A single room costs \$40 a night, and a double room costs \$60. A sign on the hotel's wall tells guests: Please don't **lick** the walls.

Vocabulary

unique	*n.* 独一无二的人或物 *adj.* 独特的
cave	*n.* 洞穴;窑洞
furniture	*n.* 家具;设备
desert	*n.* 不毛之地
lick	*v.* 舔

Task 1 Multiple Choices. Read the text and find the correct choice for each of the following questions.

1. What is unique about the Salt Palace Hotel?
   A. Its long history. B. The price of the rooms.
   C. The guests that stay here. D. What it is made of.
2. Which sentence about the area around the Salt Palace Hotel is NOT true?
   A. It was a lake many years ago.
   B. It is white during the day.
   C. There are several roads to the hotels.

D. It is more than 10000 square kilometers.

3. Where did the salt used for the hotel come from?

A. A salt factory. B. The ground.

C. Turkey. D. The walls of the hotel.

4. Who is Jusan Quesada?

A. A hotel guest. B. A guide.

C. The hotel's owner. D. An expert on salt.

5. What keeps the rooms warm at night?

A. Heat from the walls. B. The desert air.

C. The sun. D. The furniture.

Task 2 Translation. Try to translate the underlined sections into Chinese.

Passage 2

Sure, they all have beds and a bathroom (we hope!), but when it comes to business travel, all hotels are not created equal. Check out these features that might come in handy before you book your next hotel for business travel.

1. High-Speed Internet in Your Room

Whether it's wireless or via an Ethernet line, in-room Internet service is essential for staying on top of emails, working on presentations and curbing on-the-road boredom.

2. **Business Centers**

Need to fax or print something? Lost your computer and need to get online? Though not available in every hotel chain, a business/office center can be indispensable for on-the-road workers.

3. Room Service

Yes, it's expensive and not always good (or good for you), but when you're tired from a long day of meetings, the last thing you want to do is to drive around town looking for something to eat. At the very least, you'll want the hotel to have some sort of mini-mart where you can pick up water, soda, and small bites to tide you over.

4. Workout Facilities

After too many nights of said room service meals, you may notice that your pants are feeling a little snug. Stay healthy on the road by checking yourself into hotels that have some sort of exercise equipment.

5. **Shuttle Services**

Avoid having to take a cab or rent a car by booking rooms in hotels with shuttle service to/from the airport.

6. **Location**

Do some research before you travel, so you can find a hotel in the best location relative to your meetings or the airport, depending on your schedule.

7. Concierge Service

Available generally in major cities, concierge service can help you with everything from finding a restaurant to flagging a cab.

8. **Conference Rooms**

If you need to prepare for a large presentation, or just need a place for a team to work before a meeting, a conference room can be helpful. In addition, if you require significant time to set up before a meeting or have lots of samples, you might want to have clients come to your hotel for the meeting instead of schlepping large items around town.

Vocabulary

Conference Room	会议室	Business Center	商务中心
Shuttle Service	航班服务	location	*n.* 定位

Task 1 Summary. Summarize the passage in your own words.

Task 2 Translation. Try to translate the underlined sections into Chinese.

Part 4 Translation

Task 1 Translate the following sentences into Chinese.

1. Do believe we understand your frustration at this moment and try all our best to help you.
2. Cheer up! There is always a way out!
3. No problem, sir. We will manage it for you. But we don't have any vacancy available. Do you mind if...?
4. I'm afraid I can't do that for you. It's against our regulation.
5. Don't get me wrong. What I mean is that if we both parties can remain cool and make a reasonable agreement to remove the complaints.
6. My wife was woken up several times by the noise the baggage elevator made.
7. I'm sorry. You should have deposited valuables with the reception.
8. I'm sure the waiter didn't mean to be rude. Perhaps he didn't understand you correctly.
9. I'm sorry sir, and there must be some misunderstandings.
10. I'm terribly sorry, but that is the situation. Please take a seat. I'll soon have something arranged for you.

Task 2 Translate the following sentences into English.

1. 真的很抱歉,先生。我会马上联系酒店看看如何解决您的问题。请您给我提供更多的详细情况,好吗?
2. 我会让人立刻去调查此事,看看谁该为这个差错负责任。

3. 对不起,我们马上采取措施。请不要担心。
4. 如果有火警,您可以通过紧急出口和楼梯逃生。
5. 很抱歉发生这样的事情。但我向您保证:我们会尽一切努力使您的损失减少到最低限度。
6. 我们会尽力办到,但是今天我们没有空余房间。
7. 恐怕您误会了我的意思,我能解释一下吗?
8. 很抱歉我不能这么做,这是违反我们宾馆规定的。
9. 抱歉,您的要求超越了我的权限。
10. 我们无法同意您的要求,实在对不起。
11. 请您把事情的经过仔细地讲一下,好吗?
12. 对此非常抱歉,我们将尽快处理此事。
13. 请您不要着急,我们将尽一切努力尽快找到您的行李。
14. 您如果还有什么需要,请通知我们。
15. 请您稍等,我们马上派人过去修理。
16. 很抱歉,我马上与餐饮部联系。
17. 谢谢您为我们提供的这些情况,我们立即派人去调查一下。
18. 我们一找到您的手表会马上通知您。
19. 对不起,厨房今天可能缺人手。我马上叫人给您送去。
20. 非常抱歉,很可能因为客人太多,行李送错地方了。

Part 5 Cultural Norms

常用句子

1. 顾客投诉问题。

(1) There is no hot water/water boiler. 没有热水/热水器。

(2) The room is in a mess/too noisy. 房间一团糟/太吵了。

(3) The window curtain is full of dust. 窗帘积满了灰尘。

(4) The pillow cases are stained. 枕套上有污渍。

(5) The bathtub/water closet is dirty. 浴缸/抽水马桶是脏的。

(6) The water closet is clogged and when I flushed it, it overflowed. 抽水马桶堵住了。我一冲水,水就冒出来。

(7) There are no towels/toiletry items/toilet paper in the bathroom. 卫生间没有浴巾/洗浴用品/厕纸。

(8) My necklace/watch/wallet is missing. 我的项链/手表/钱包不见了。

(9) Get me your manager! 把你们经理叫来!

2. 表示歉意和关注。

(1) I'm terribly sorry to hear that. 听到这样的事情,我真的非常抱歉。

(2) I'll attend to /take care of this right away. 我马上处理这件事。

(3) I'll look into this matter at once. 我马上去查清这件事情。

(4) I'll send a chambermaid immediately. 我马上派一个房间服务员过去。

(5) We might have overlooked some points. 我们可能忽略了一些细小的地方。

(6) We do apologize for the inconvenience. 我们为给您带来不便深表歉意。

(7) There could have been some mistake. I do apologize. 可能是出了什么差错，实在对不起。

3. 解释原因。

(1) The previous guest checked out late and you demanded immediate access to your room. So the chambermaid didn't have time to make up the room. 上一位客人很迟才退房，而您要求马上入住，所以服务员没时间来整理房间。

(2) You put the "DND" sign on the knob, so the chambermaid didn't make up the room. 您把"请勿打扰"的牌子放在把手上了，所以服务员没来整理房间。

(3) Sorry, it is beyond our rules and we cannot help. 很抱歉，但是这件事情是违反我们饭店的规定的，我们无法帮忙。

4. 提供解决方案。

(1) If you get your luggage ready, we would move you to another room. 您如果把行李整理好，我们安排您到别的房间。

(2) I will send a porter to help you with the luggage. 我派个行李员帮您搬行李。

(3) To express our regret for all the trouble, we offer you a 10% discount/complimentary flowers. 我们给您带来这么多麻烦，为了表示歉意，特为您提供 9 折优惠/免费花束。

(4) Please allow me to send a chambermaid to your room to help you look for it again. 请允许我派一位服务员来帮您再仔细找找。

(5) Shall I call the police for you? 我帮您报警，好吗？

(6) I will speak to our manager about it. 我会向我们经理报告这件事。

(7) This is really the least we can do for you. 我们能为您做得实在太有限了。

(8) Our manageris not in town. Shall I get our assistant manager for you? 我们的经理不在本地。我帮您叫经理助理来，好吗？

(9) Just a minute, we will call for the manager right now. 请您稍等一下，我现在就去找我们的经理来。

重要提示

(1) Use polite service language. 使用礼貌服务用语。

(2) Be patient to listen to what the guest complains and take notes. 耐心聆听并做记录。

(3) Say "sorry" or make an apology to the guest. 向客人道歉。

(4) Tell the guest what will be done at once. 告诉客人酒店马上要采取的措施。

(5) Tell the guest the time in which the problem will be solved. 告诉客人解决问题所需时间。

(6) Ask the guest to tell the name and room number. 询问客人的姓名和房号。

(7) Say "Thank you" to the guest. 向客人道谢。

(8) Follow up the other staff to do at once. 追踪其他相关员工立即处理投诉。

(9) Check the result and make a record. 检查结果并做记录。

(10) On the guest's request, you can say: "I'm sorry to hear that, but I will send someone to...at once."在回应客人的要求时,可以说:"听到这样的事,我感到很抱歉,我马上派人去……"

(11) When a guest makes a complaint against something to you, be sure not to argue with the guest. But you can try your best to make clear what it is. Certainly you can ask the guest some questions, so the guest can have a chance to explain. 当客人因某事向你投诉时,一定不要同客人争论。不过,你可以尽力去弄清事情的真相。当然你还可以向客人提问题,这样客人可以有机会解释。

Say sorry to the guest with the following 向客人表示道歉时说:

I'm sorry to hear that...

We do apologize for...

We do apologize for the inconvenience.

Show sincerity to the guest with the following 向客人表示诚意时说:

Thank you for bringing the matter to our attention.

I assure you that it won't happen again.

Part 6 Supplementary Reading

Methods for Handling Customer Complaints

Customers are the most important element of any business since they can directly attribute to your success or not. However, even the best of businesses will have unhappy customers at one point or another; what can distinguish you from the pack is how you deal with them. Here are five methods for handling customer complaints that will keep customers happy and encourage repeat patrons.

Ask How to Make Things Right

So many businesses have canned responses when it comes to handling customer complaints (such as offering a refund or taking money off a bill), but there's not a one-size-fits-all solution for every complaint. Take initiative and show the customer you are willing to do what it takes to make things right by asking outright what you can do. Be genuine and polite and you may be surprised to find that most people don't want much, they simply want to make their feelings known and be heard.

The Customer Is Always Right...Once

It can often be difficult for businesses to know whether or not a complaint is valid; there are dishonest people who will make false claims in order to get some kind of bonus or free ride. For example, a customer may return an article of clothing to a retail store stating they changed their mind or decided they did not like it even though they may have already worn it. The store will often refund the money since there's no way to know whether the customer is being truthful or not. That being said, take most customer complaints for face-value and adopt the adage "the customer is always right once". You may need to implement a process or strategy to handle customers with suspicious repeat complaints.

Let Them Know You Understand

Customers like to know that businesses understand exactly why they are upset. Listen to the customer's complaint than politely reiterate the situation to them to illustrate you fully comprehend. Being understanding is a great way to diffuse the situation with an angry customer and begin to make amends.

Respond ASAP

Delaying a response or a resolution to a customer's complaint will likely only result in an even angrier and more resentful customer. Take the necessary steps needed to resolve the situation as soon as possible. When a business can demonstrate to a customer that they are doing everything they can to accommodate them, customers are more willing to forgive and move on.

Thank Them

It may seem odd but thank customers for their honest and direct feedback no matter what it is. Without it, you have no idea if you are delivering the experience and level of service your customers want and it provides an opportunity to improve.

Following these five simple steps can breed a loyal customer base which in turn gives you the foundation for a successful, credible business.

Key to the Exercises

Chapter 1 Reservation

Part 1 Listening

Task 1 Dialogues.

Dialogue 1

B: I'd like to book a room

Dialogue 2

B: I'd like to make a group reservation if possible

Dialogue 3

B: I'm afraid that I have to cancel the reservation I made yesterday

Dialogue 4

B: Yes, there is a 20 percent discount

Dialogue 5

B: By telephone and in the name of Mr. Charles Green

Task 2 Conversations.

Conversation 1

reservations; single room; front view; per night; How long; What time; expect; confirm; look forward to; settled

Conversation 2

R: May I know how many people there will be in the party

R: What kind of rooms would you like

R: Sorry to have kept you waiting, madam

G: How much is the room rate, then

R: 480 yuan per night per room, with breakfast

R: May I book the rooms under your name

Conversation 3

R: Room Reservations

G: I'd like to cancel a reservation

R: in whose name the reservation was made

R: How do you spell that, please

R: And what was the date of the reservation

R: may I have your name and phone number, please

R: I'll cancel Mr. Black's reservation from April 5th to 8th for three nights
We look forward to another chance to serve you

Part 2 Speaking

Task 1 Work in pairs.

G: I'd like to reserve a room for next Tuesday

R: How many nights will you need the room for

G: I'm booking the room on behalf of a business client

R: What type of room does your client need

G: A twin

G: What's the difference in price

R: Both include buffet breakfast

R: May I have your name, please

R: Could you please spell that please

R: And may I have your telephone number

Task 2 Work in pairs.

1. C 2. E 3. A 4. D 5. F 6. B

Task 3 Role-play.

Situation 1

(Reservationist-R Guest-G)

R: Good evening, Room Reservations. How can I help you?

G: Good evening. I'd like to reserve a room.

R: For which dates, sir?

G: For the nights from March 3rd to 5th.

R: How many guests will there be?

G: Two.

R: What kind of room would you like, sir?

G: A double room.

R: Wait a moment, please. Let me check... Sorry to have kept you waiting. We do have double rooms available for those days. May I have your name, please?

G: Michael Ford. By the way, how much is the room rate?

R: The room rate is 380 yuan per night per room, including breakfast. Could I know if you have any special requests, please?

G: If possible, I'd like to have a room with a street view.

R: No problem, Mr. Ford. So that's a double room for Mr. Michael Ford with a street view for the nights from March 3rd to 5th at 380 yuan per night per room including breakfast. Is that correct?

G: Exactly. Thanks.

R: You're welcome, Mr. Ford. We're looking forward to seeing you at our hotel. Goodbye.

Situation 2

(Reservationist-R Guest-G)

R: Room Reservations. May I help you?

G: Yes, my name is George Smith. I made a reservation last week. Now I'd like to modify it.

R: One moment, please. Let me have a check... You booked a single room for two nights from February 15th to 16th. How would you like to change it?

G: I'd like to change the single room into a family suite and extend my reservation for two more nights till February 18th.

R: Wait a moment, please... Sorry to have kept you waiting. So that's a family suite for four nights from February 15th to 18th. Is that right?

G: Exactly.

R: Now the room rate has changed from 290 yuan to 420 yuan. Could you pay 200 yuan more to guarantee your revised reservation?

G: OK.

Part 3 Reading

Task 1 True or false statements.

1. T 2. F 3. F 4. T 5. F 6. T

Task 2 Questions.

1. Because a majority of hotel guests make reservation in advance of their stay.
2. Five steps.
3. The guest makes request for reservation through different means such as by telephone, fax, letter, telex, and telegram etc.
4. Non-guaranteed and guaranteed.
5. From the time or date the hotel receives the guests' notification in writing.

Task 3 Blank filling.

1. at his discretion 2. in person 3. procedure 4. instantaneous 5. In the event of
6. vacancies 7. Additionally 8. achieved 9. confirmed 10. on average

Part 4 Translation

Task 1

对联是中国特有的一种文学形式,是中华民族文化和民间文化融合的产物。由于汉语语言独特的特点,对联无法被其他任何一种语音字母直接重现。每副对联有两联,它们通常言简意赅、主题广泛,如政治、经济、军事、历史、宗教、人物、山水及风景和历史名胜等。对联兴起于唐代(618—907),是中华民族文化宝库中的重要组成部分。许多知名的对联都是优秀的文学作品。

Task 2

The house has an ancient screen standing in the middle and the four treasures of the study (writing brush, ink stick, ink slab, and rice paper) and old furniture displayed around. The left room is a tearoom. It is really a nice place for reading or enjoying landscape over a cup of tea. And it must be your cup of tea.

Chapter 2 Reception

Part 1 Listening

Task 1 Dialogues.

Dialogue 1

A: settle your account

B: By credit card

Dialogue 2

A: passports

Dialogue 3

A: king-size, rate

B: I'll take that

Dialogue 4

A: registration form

Dialogue 5

A: reserved a single room

Task 2 Conversations.

Conversation 1

check in; executive; fully booked; junior; deluxe; available; separate; balcony; high-speed; registration

Conversation 2

R: Good morning, sir. How may I help you

R: May I have your name and room number, please

R: How long would you like to extend your stay, Mr. Smith

R: Would you mind changing to another room on the ninth floor tomorrow

R: Please change your departure date and sign your name here

R: I hope you are enjoying your stay with us

Conversation 3

G: We have made a reservation with your hotel

R: Is there any change

R: Could I see and copy your group visas

R: Sorry to have kept you waiting

R: Please have a check

G: I'll assign the rooms among my members

Part 2 Speaking

Task 1 Work in pairs.

R: Have you made a reservation

R: There is no reservation under your name

G: I feel like taking a bath right now

R: every room is equipped with a bath, a telephone and an air-conditioner

R: Can I see your passport, please

R: Please fill in this registration form

G: Shall I have my key

R: The bellboy will take you to your room

R: Is there anything else I can do for you

G: You have been very considerate

Task 2 Work in pairs.

1. D 2. F 3. A 4. B 5. C 6. E

Task 3 Role-play.

Situation 1

(Reservationist-R Guest-G)

R: Good evening, sir. How may I help you?

G: I'd like to check in.

R: Have you made a reservation, sir?

G: Yes, I have reserved a deluxe single room yesterday.

R: May I have your name, sir?

G: Peter Anderson.

R: Thank you, Mr. Anderson. Wait a moment, please. Let me check the reservation record... Thank you for your waiting. So you've reserved a deluxe single room for the nights from February 14th to 16th. The room rate is 500 yuan per night. Is that correct?

G: Yes.

R: Could you fill out the registration form, please?

G: OK.

R: Thanks. Could I see your passport, please?

G: Yes, here you are.

R: Thank you, Mr. Anderson. Here is your passport. How would you like to pay? In cash, by credit card or with traveler's check?

G: By credit card, please.

R: May I take a print of your card, please?

G: OK. Here you are.

R: Thank you, Mr. Anderson. Your room number is 602 on the sixth floor. Here is your receipt, and these are your key card and room card. Please keep them. The bellman will carry your baggage and show you up to your room. Anything else I can do for you?

G: No more. Thank you.

R: You're welcome. We hope you'll enjoy your stay with us.

Situation 2

(Receptionist-R Guest-G)

R: Good afternoon, lady. How may I help you?

G: I'm Julie Brown. I've made a reservation with you for a group of 20 guests. Here's the confirmation notice.

R: Thank you, Miss Brown. Let me check... Sorry to have kept you waiting. So you've reserved 10 TWBs for two nights and the room rate is 680 yuan. Is that correct?

G: Exactly.

R: May I have your group visas?

G: Yes, here you are.

R: Thank you, Miss Brown. Could you please fill out the registration form with your personal information?

G: OK. I'll take care of it. By the way, since we are in a group, I'd like our rooms on the same floor. Could you arrange that for me?

R: Certainly. I've put your group on the seventh floor from Room 701 to Room 710. Here are your group's room cards and keys. Is there anything else I can do for you?

G: No more, thanks.

R: You're welcome. Please take the elevator there up to the seventh floor. The floor attendants will meet you there and show you to your rooms. You may leave your baggage here and our bellmen will deliver it to your rooms. If you have any problems or requests, please don't hesitate to ask us. I wish you would have a good stay in our hotel.

Part 3 Reading

Task 1 True or false statements.

1. T 2. F 3. F 4. T 5. T 6. T

Task 2 Questions.

1. The receptionist should check in guests with or without reservations, answer any questions from the guests, help guests with any problems, answer telephones, take messages, and handle complaints.
2. When a guest arrives at the Front Desk, the receptionist should greet him/her and asks if he/she has made a reservation or not.
3. After registration, the receptionist should tell the guest his/her room number and the floor it is on, then gives the guest his/her room card and key card.
4. With the formalities concluded, the receptionist will inform the bellman to carry the baggage and show the guest to his/her room.
5. If the visitor is a foreigner, information about his/her passport number, place of issue and date of issue also need to be recorded.

Task 3 Blank filling.

1. reservation 2. honored 3. give in 4. waiting 5. give out 6. completed
7. answering 8. responsible to 9. give up 10. responsible for

Part 4 Translation

Task 1

风筝是中国传统的民间艺术之一。中国的风筝在春秋时期就已出现,迄今已有2000多年的历史了。最初,风筝用作军事用途,如测量距离、测试风向和通信。后来它逐渐与神话故事、花鸟瑞兽、吉祥寓意等结合,从而形成了独具特色的风筝文化。在阳光明媚的春日里,人们常常结伴去放风筝。中国的风筝也受到世界各国人们的喜爱,因为很早以前它就传到了世界各地。

Task 2

When tea was first imported from China, the necessary utensils in which to infuse it and also those from which it was drunk were imported with the tea itself. But later, various firms began to design and make teapots, cups and saucers with the result that British pottery and earthenware industries received a tremendous impetus.

Chapter 3 Concierge

Part 1 Listening

Task 1 Dialogues.

Dialogue 1

B: Could you introduce some scenic spots here in Hangzhou

Dialogue 2

A: Can you possibly help to hire a taxi for me

Dialogue 3

B: Our hotel has tour buses that can carry you wherever you want to go

Dialogue 4

A: Where can I have my hair done

Dialogue 5

A: You've got five pieces of baggage altogether

Task 2 Conversations.

Conversation 1

Bell Captain's Desk; check out; pick up; luggage; packed; come for; suitcases; handbag; valuable; fragile

Conversation 2

B: Let me take care of your suitcases

G: That's very considerate of you

B: we offer Chinese and Western cuisine in the two restaurants on the second floor

B: a beauty salon, a souvenir shop and a business center

G: where could I get a brochure about the hotel

B: I hope you enjoy your stay

Conversation 3

free; recommend; try; business center; copying; faxing; Information Desk; luggage stand

Part 2 Speaking

Task 1 Work in pairs.

B: Is this your first visit to Hangzhou

B: Shall I open the blinds

B: I'll put your suitcase here on the suitcase stand

B: There is a documentation folder on the table

B: Over there is the bed-head console

The one on the left is to control the TV

B: under the minibar which is next to the TV

B: there's a shaver point

Task 2 Work in pairs.

1. F 2. E 3. A 4. C 5. B 6. D

Task 3 Role-play.

Situation 1

(Bellman-B Mr. Lee-Mr.)

B: Good morning, sir. Welcome to City Holiday Hotel.

Mr.: Good morning. Thank you.

B: Do you have any luggage?

Mr.: Yes. It's all in the trunk.

B: So you've got four pieces of luggage altogether?

Mr.: Yes. That's right.

B: Let me get a luggage cart for you. Please wait a second...Sorry to have kept you waiting. This way to the Front Desk, please. I'll show you to your room soon after you finish checking in.

Mr.: Thanks.

B: Mr. Lee, your room is on the 10th floor. This way to the lift, please.

Mr.: Can I ask you a question? Do you have Internet access in the guestroom?

B: Yes. Every room is equipped with broadband Internet. You'll find it very convenient to do business online.

Mr.: Great. By the way, is the Internet service free of charge?

B: Yes, it's free of charge... Here we are. May I have your key card, please? Let me open the door. This is your room, Mr. Lee. Here's your key card. Anything else I can do for you?

Mr.: No more. Thank you very much.

B: You're welcome. Have a good rest.

Situation 2

(Bellman-B Mr. Green-Mr.)

B: Good evening, sir. Welcome to Shangri-La Hotel.

Mr.: Thank you.

B: Do you have any luggage?

Mr.: Yes. It's all in the trunk.

B: So you've got four pieces altogether?

Mr.: Yes. That's correct.

B: Let me carry the luggage cart for you. This way to the Front Desk, please. I'll show you to your room soon after you finish checking in.

Mr.: Thanks.

B: Mr. Green, your room is on the 11th floor. This way to the lift, please.

Mr.: I enjoy swimming. Do you have a swimming pool?

B: Yes. We have an indoor pool and an outdoor one. The outdoor pool is especially good. You can enjoy fresh air there.

Mr.: Sounds interesting. I'll go there. And I hear the Chinese food is delicious. Do you have a good restaurant here?

B: Sure we do. There's a Chinese restaurant on the second floor. There you can try different but delicious food. Here we are. May I have your key card, please? Let me open the door.

B: This is your room, Mr. Green. Here's your key card. Anything else I can do for you?

Mr.: No more. Thank you very much.

B: You're welcome. Have a good rest.

Part 3 Reading

Task 1 True or false statements.

1. F 2. T 3. F 4. F 5. T 6. T

Task 2

C B A D E

Task 3 Blank filling.

1. arrival 2. surrounding 3. attractive 4. arrangements 5. register 6. qualified 7. efficient 8. assistants 9. rental 10. accompany

Part 4 Translation

Task 1

十二生肖是中国用十二种动物组成的纪年方法。我国自古就有“干支纪年法”，而我国西北地区的游牧少数民族则以动物纪年，两种纪年法相互融合，形成了现在的十二生肖，即子鼠、丑牛、寅虎、卯兔、辰龙、巳蛇、午马、未羊、申猴、酉鸡、戌狗、亥猪。属相的基本意义在于使人们圆融通达、和衷共济。

Task 2

Mid-autumn Day is a traditional Chinese festival. It usually comes in September or October. On that day, families stay outside in the open air to eat a big dinner and mooncakes. The most important thing is looking at the moon. On that day, the moon looks brighter and rounder. We call this moon the full moon. On that day, families get together, so we call this day Reunion Festival. This is Mid-autumn Day.

Chapter 4 Business Center

Part 1 Listening

Task 1 Dialogues.

Dialogue 1

A: but can you help me with these documents

B: I will send the copies to your room at noon

Dialogue 2

A: Do you have the fax machine

Dialogue 3

A: I'd like to book two tickets to New York

Dialogue 4

A: Can you type and print them

Dialogue 5

B: Our Business Center provides the professional translating service

Task 2 Conversations.

Conversation 1

have this report copied; How many; What time; urgent; 30 minutes left; binding them up; how much; tariff list; sign the bill; pay in cash

Conversation 2

G: Could you book two tickets for me

C: Are you going there by train or by air

C: It is a non-stop flight

C: Please sign your name here

G: Could you send the tickets to my room as soon as possible

C: It's my pleasure to be at your service

Conversation 3

G: I'd like to have my business card redesigned

G: I want to change my title to

C: How about the font style

G: I will need the business cards tomorrow

G: Can you give me a discount

C: you will enjoy 30% discount

Part 2 Speaking

Task 1 Work in pairs.

G: We are in urgent need of your help

G: Our flight has been delayed

But my laptop computer doesn't work well now

M: I'll ask a technician to fix your laptop

you can send emails to your company.

G: How much do you charge for it

M: Since you are the VIP guest, it is totally free

G: I have to make an international phone call

M: you can make the call in your room

is equipped with an IDD telephone

Task 2 Work in pairs.

1. B 2. E 3. A 4. F 5. C 6. D

Task 3 Role-play.

Situation 1

(Clerk-C Guest-G)

C: Good morning, welcome to Business Center. How may I help you, Mr. Black?

G: Good morning. Could you type the manuscript of the address list and print it out for me?

C: No problem, sir. What font and size do you want it to be?

G: The title should be in 20, and the names and addresses should be in 16.

C: OK. Do you need the address list to be double-sided printed?

G: Yes. It will save 50% papers. Moreover, you should photocopy the list for 20 copies, and staple each copy on the left side. How much should I pay for that?

C: Here is the price tariff. The total is 110 yuan. Since you are our registered guest, you may sign the bill.

G: That's fine. When can I have the copies? The lists should be sent to the committee members' rooms this afternoon, from Room 2001 to Room 2020.

C: I see. I promise to send the lists to each committee member's room by 4:00 p. m..

G: It's very nice of you.

C: It's my pleasure. Goodbye.

Situation 2

(Clerk-C Guest-G)

C: Good morning, welcome to Business Center. How may I help you, Mr. Green?

G: I'm leaving for Xiamen the day after tomorrow. Could you book tickets for me?

C: That's November 22nd, isn't it?

G: That's right.

C: Are you going there by train or by air?

G: By train. How many trains are there to Xiamen in the morning?

C: There are more than five trains from 7:00 to 12:00. I suggest the D58, which leaves at 8:30 a. m. and arrives at Xiamen at 2:02 p. m.. It is the multiple unit train. It's very fast and comfortable.

G: Fine, I'll take it then. I need three tickets for my two children and myself.

C: OK, Mr. Green. If your children are under the height of 1.2 meters, they can buy the child tickets at the half price of the adult ticket.

G: That's great. My daughter is only 4 years old and she is under the 1.2 meters line. But my son is 10. He is taller than that line.

C: All right. Mr. Green, you need two adult tickets and one child ticket. Which kind of seat do you prefer?

G: I would prefer the soft seat, please.

C: OK, Mr. Green. Would you please fill in this form? Please sign your name here.

G: All right. Shall I pay cash now?

C: Yes, please pay 700 yuan in advance.

G: Here you are. When can I get the tickets?

C: You can get them in the evening of November 21st.

G: Thank you. Could you send the tickets to my room as soon as possible?

C: No problem, Mr. Green.

G: It's very nice of you.

C: It's my pleasure to be at your service.

Part 3 Reading

Task 1 True or false statements.

1. T 2. F 3. T 4. T 5. T 6. F

Task 2 Questions.

1. The secretarial services, convention services and tickets services are the main jobs of the Business Center staff.
2. A self-contained Business Center should be equipped with computers, Internet access and machines combining printer, scanner and photocopier, etc.
3. The Business Center staff must know how to operate the photocopier, fax machine, and printer. Besides, they must be equipped with some basic skills of computer.
4. Convention services are always related to all-sized meeting room rental, convention equipment rental (such as laptop computers, projectors, screens, white-boards with mark pens, roving microphones, etc.), and sometimes catering service.
5. Because Business Center staff should help the guests to book airline tickets, train tickets, concert tickets, and show tickets, etc.

Task 3 Blank filling.

1. looking for 2. non-stop 3. rental 4. catch up with 5. valid
6. suggestions 7. put forward 8. taken away 9. arrange 10. looking after

Part 4 Translation

Task 1

桂花是友好和吉祥的象征。战国(公元前 475—前 221 年)时有些国家就以互赠桂花表示友好。在盛产桂花的少数民族地区,青年男女还常以互赠桂花表达爱慕之情。因"桂"谐音"贵",所以桂花又有尊贵的寓意,桂花开放意味着贵客的到来,尤其是远方贵客的到来,主人会以桂花茶或桂花酒来款待他们,这一习俗可追溯到春秋时期(公元前 770—公元前 476 年)。在封建社会,古人又常用它来赞喻秋试及第者,考中称为折桂。

Task 2

Porcelain is one of China's most important handicrafts. Chinese porcelain has a history of more than 3500 years, its most prosperous period being Ming and Qing Dynasties. Porcelain can be used as daily dinnerware and vases, and delicate porcelain is even commonly used for home decoration by people. As symbols of high-end works of art, authentic porcelain is often of extremely high artistic and economic value and therefore they are often regarded as precious collections by many people. Chinese porcelain is popular with people around the world, and they are often used as presents for expressing friendship between Chinese and foreign people.

Chapter 5　Chamber Service

Part 1　Listening

Task 1　Dialogues.

Dialogue 1

H: May I come in

Dialogue 2

H: When would you like me to do your room

Dialogue 3

H: do you need anything for the room

Dialogue 4

G: extra soap and shampoo

H: I'll attend to that immediately

Dialogue 5

G: light bulb

H: report it; send someone to

Task 2　Conversations.

Conversation 1

shower; replace; light bulb; shower; lamp; report; hair dryer; check; missing; enjoy

Conversation 2

H: Just a minute. I need to move the cart first

H: Don't worry, Front Desk can get you a new one

H: I will call Front Desk and tell them that you are coming down

Conversation 3

H: Housekeeping

G: I am just dressing

H: I'm sorry. I didn't mean to disturb you

When is a good time to come back

H: Enjoy your stay here

Part 2　Speaking

Task 1　Work in pairs.

H: May I come in

G: come on in

H: May I do the turndown service for you now

G: I'm having some friends over in about an hour

H: What time would it be convenient for you

H: I'll let the overnight staff know and they will come then

G: Where is the TV remote

H: It should be on the night table

H: How many would you like

H: I will take care of that right away

H: Would you like me to draw the curtains for you

H: Is there anything else you need

H: Please let me know if there is anything else you need

Task 2 Work in pairs.

Scene 2

The right order: 3—4—9—6—1—10—12—13—11—2—8—5—7.

Task 3 Role-play.

Open answer.

Task 4 Dialogue completion.

1. E 2. C 3. B 4. F 5. A 6. D

Part 3 Reading

Task 1 True or false statements.

1. T 2. T 3. F 4. F 5. F

Task 2 Questions.

1. Hand them to the shift leader who records the item in the Lost and Found Book, and hand it immediately to the Housekeeping Office for safe keeping.
2. Check the Lost and Found Book for the record and direct them to the Housekeeping Office. Ask the guest for the description of the items which he claims to be his, to be certain that they are given the right one.

Task 3 Blank filling.

1. duration 2. belongings 3. obtain 4. describe 5. maximum 6. claiming
7. in-house 8. mineral 9. on loan 10. Normally

Part 4 Translation

Task 1

请帮助我们保护环境

亲爱的客人们：

请帮助我们减少使用洗衣化学品，节约宝贵能源。把毛巾放在浴室地板上即表明您希望我们更换干净的日用品。使用过的毛巾若放在架子上，我们将不会更换。

您的行动将让世界大不相同。

Task 2

1. We have two kinds of laundry service. Regular service: you may get your laundry back in 8 hours. Express service: you can get back in 4 hours. Which one do you prefer?

2. I'm sorry to tell you that your medicine bottle was broken by accident. I sincerely apologize for that.
3. The laundry collected between 8:00 a. m. to 6:00 p. m. will be returned before midnight on the same day, while the one collected between 6:00 p. m. to 8:00 a. m. next day will be returned before 2:p. m. on the next day.

Task 3

The Chinese Knot is an ancient art form and the artifacts could date back to 100000 years ago. Chinese people used knots for more than just fastening, wrapping, hunting, and fishing. Knots were also used to record events, and some knots had purely ornamental functions. The Chinese Knot has cultural connotations. Since knot is pronounced as "Jie" in Chinese, similar to the pronunciation of "Ji", which means blessing, good salary, longevity, happiness, fortune, safety and health and is the everlasting pursuit of Chinese people, some Chinese Knots express people's various hopes. For example, the room of newlyweds is usually decorated with a Pan-chang Knot to symbolize eternal love.

Chapter 6 Information Desk

Part 1 Listening

Task 1 Dialogues.

Dialogue 1

the Spa; passage-way; bottom; wooden bridge; Follow the path

Dialogue 2

souvenirs; counter; souvenirs

Dialogue 3

What can I do for you; touring Hangzhou

Dialogue 4

the daily service hours; From 7:00 a. m. to 10:00 p. m.

Dialogue 5

I'm looking for a friend; Could you tell me his room number

Task 2 Conversations.

Conversation 1

accommodate; patrons; fitness; gym; satisfactory; lobby; elevator; extra; free; hours; trainer; present

Conversation 2

S: Just a moment, please. I'll look over the register

S: May I have his full name, please

S: Please wait a minute, let me phone him

S: Mr. Miller said he's waiting for you in his room

S: It's my pleasure

Conversation 3

S: Excuse me, sir, but may I see your Room Identification Slip

S: Could you please sign here for the receipt of your key

S: Could you sign for that, too

Part 2 Speaking

Task 1 Work in pairs

B: What type of tour are you thinking about

B: There are one-day trips or two-day overnight trips, depending on which one you pick

B: All three are guided tours, and meals and transportation are included

A: Do I need to book ahead

B: This company requires that you make a reservation 24 hours ahead

B: I can book that for you

B: Let me know if you have any questions

Task 2 Work in pairs.

1. D 2. H 3. G 4. B 5. E 6. F 7. A 8. C

Task 3 Role-play.

1.

G: Would you please tell me the daily service hours of the dining room?

S: Certainly. From 7:00 a.m. to 10:00 p.m., nearly serving all day long.

G: When will the bar and cafe be open?

S: From 2:00 p.m. till midnight.

G: Does the hotel offer any other service?

S: Oh, we have a barber shop, a laundry, a store, post and telegram services, a newspaper stand, table tennis and so on.

G: Great!

S: You may have your shopping and amusements there.

G: Thank you for your concern. Can I get a tourist map in the hotel?

S: Yes, you may go to the lobby and buy it from the newspaper stand there.

G: Good. And where can I have my laundry done?

S: There's a laundry bag in the bathroom. Just put your laundry in it. It will be picked up by the chamber maid every morning. By the way, the hot water supply in this hotel is from 6:00 a.m. to 12:00 p.m.

G: You give very good service. Thank you for your information.

S: Thank you, sir. I hope you will enjoy staying here.

2. Open answer.

Part 3 Reading

Task 1 True or false statements.

1. T 2. F 3. T 4. F 5. T

Task 2 Questions.

1. To be a qualified hotel information desk clerk, a professional appearance and a pleasant personality are important. A clear speaking voice and fluency in English are also essential. Good spelling and computer literacy are needed. What's more, speaking a foreign language fluently is increasingly helpful. A hotel information desk clerk should also be friendly and customer-service oriented, well groomed, and display the maturity and self-confidence to demonstrate good judgment.
2. Most hotel, motel, and resort desk clerks receive orientation and training on the job, including an explanation of the job duties and information about the establishment. They often receive additional training on interpersonal or customer service skills and on how to use the computerized reservation, room assignment, and billing systems and equipment. Desk clerks typically continue to receive instruction on new procedures and on company policies after their initial training ends.
3. Employment of hotel, motel, and resort desk clerks is expected to grow and job opportunities for hotel and motel desk clerks also will result from a need to replace workers. Opportunities for part-time work should continue to be plentiful. With the increased number of units requiring staff, employment opportunities for desk clerks should be good.

Task 3 Blank filling.

1. supervise 2. assign 3. additional 4. Orientation 5. initiative 6. benefit from
7. resort 8. result from 9. initial 10. Typically

Part 4 Translation

Task 1

亲爱的宾客,欢迎您下榻本酒店。为使您的入住生活愉悦、舒畅,特将本酒店的服务项目和有关事项做如下介绍。

总服务台设在一楼大厅,提供入住登记、离店结账、预订火车票和飞机票、汽车出租等服务项目,并有雨伞、雨鞋、大衣出租。餐厅设在二楼,咖啡厅在一楼,供应各类葡萄酒、烈酒、饮料、点心。酒店还设有特别风味餐厅,位于中院东面,那里有名厨烹制的各种地方名菜。如需预订宴会、接待会、酒会、生日蛋糕等,可直接与餐厅服务台接洽。

Task 2

1. 我们既有团队价,也有散客价,散客是指零散的外国游客。
2. The bar is on this floor. Please go straight along the hall way, turn right at the end and it is on the left.
3. There is a great garden and pond behind the hotel, which is suitable for jogging and walking.

Task 3

A wealth of historical relics, fascinating scenery and interesting local cultures along the Silk Road make this long trip one of the world's most exciting tourist attractions. Many Chinese ethnic minorities scatter along the Chinese portion of the road, all courteous and hospitable to visitors from the rest of the world. The food and crafts in the region are different from those in central China. And the folklore is simply exotic and colorful, just like those fantastic tales in *The Arabian Nights*.

Chapter 7 Cashier

Part 1 Listening

Task 1 Dialogues.

Dialogue 1

altogether; by credit card; cash

Dialogue 2

traveler's cheques; passport

Dialogue 3

That's for

Dialogue 4

Here is your bill; amount

Dialogue 5

receipt; change

Task 2 Conversations.

Conversation 1

settle; Certainly; hotel services; at 500 yuan each; meals; makes a total of; check; amount; charge; long-distance phone call; total; in cash; receipt; change

Conversation 2

G: I'd like to use a safety deposit box

C: Could you fill out this form

C: You would like to use it until July 10th

C: Your box number is 520

Part 2 Speaking

Task 1 Work in pairs.

C: your bill totals 1522 yuan

G: Would you mind letting me have a look at it

C: Not at all, sir

C: That's the extra room service charge

C: there has been an error in your bill
Please wait a minute while I correct it for you

C: It comes to 249 dollars and 12 cents at today's exchange rate

C: Will you be putting this on your credit card

C: Sorry, your credit card has been stopped paying

C: Here is your bill, receipt and change, 88 yuan
Thank you for having chosen our hotel

G: You're welcome to stay with us next time

Task 2 Work in pairs.

1. I 2. F 3. E 4. J 5. D 6. C 7. H 8. L 9. K 10. G 11. A 12. B

Task 3 Role-play.

1.

(8) G (3) C (11) C (1) C (12) G (2) G (5) C (9) C (10) G (4) G (7) C (6) G (13) C

2. Open answer.

Part 3 Reading

Task 1 True or false statements.

1. F 2. T 3. F 4. F 5. T

Task 2 Questions.

1. Yes. A hotel cashier needs to assist Front Desk staff with check-in when required.
2. A high school diploma or equivalent is generally required to be a hotel cashier. He or she must speak, read, write, and understand the primary language used in the workplace, and be with good presentation skills and a good team worker. Completed coursework in hospitality management or customer service is considered a plus for hotel cashier applicants. Previous experience in cash handling, accounting, public relations or customer relations is desirable.

Task 3 Blank filling.

1. variety 2. unified 3. approve 4. equivalent 5. manual 6. assumes 7. fee 8. desirable 9. entails 10. plus

Part 4 Translation

Task 1

中国人喜欢喝绿茶。龙井,或者更确切地说,西湖龙井,是中国最好的绿茶之一。从严格意义上来说,龙井茶只生长在杭州西湖附近。龙井绿茶分为不同等级,最好的是每年第一批采摘并手工炒制的绿茶。

Task 2

1. I'm sorry, but it is not allowed to use credit card to get cash in our hotel according to the hotel regulations. You can get some cash in the bank which is only 400 meters away from here.
2. Sir, I'm sorry but the signature does not match the one that is authorized to open the safe. May I see your passport, for the sake of security?
3. We can only change the foreign currencies listed on the foreign currency board. If you have other currencies you would like to change, please go to the bank.

Task 3

Known as China's national opera, Beijing Opera, which originated in the late 18th century, is a synthesis of music, dance, art and acrobatics. It is the most influential and representative of all operas in China. Beijing Opera is a national treasure with a history of more than 200 years. Owing to its richness of repertoire, and great number of artists of performance and audiences, Beijing Opera has profound influence, which no other opera in China can rival.

Chapter 8 Switchboard

Part 1 Listening

Task 1 Dialogues.

Dialogue 1

O: How may I direct your call

O: Connecting your call

Dialogue2

O: may I put you on hold for a moment while I look up the times
I will be right with you

Dialogue 3

O: Thank you for calling Palace Hotel
How may I assist you

O: Transferring your call with pleasure

Dialogue 4

O: Thank you for calling Lily Hotel

O: Please be on the call while I transfer the call

Dialogue 5

O: allow me to transfer your call to our Reservations Department

Dialogue 6

O: This is the morning call for you

Dialogue 7

apologize; this inconvenience

Task 2 Conversations.

Conversation 1

Operator; outside line; dial tone; place a call; try it

Conversation 2

O: This is the hotel operator

O: May I have your name and room number, please

O: And the time of your wake-up call

G: You wouldn't know how long it takes to drive to Shanghai from here, would you

G: I'll have to be on the road by half past six at the latest

O: you will receive a wake-up call at 5:30 a. m. tomorrow morning

Part 2 Speaking

Task 1 Work in pairs.

O: How do you spell his name, please

O: Just a moment

I'll check it for you and transfer your call to his room

O: Thank you for waiting

Mr. Peter Williams is staying in Room 8202, but I'm afraid there's no one answering the phone

O: I'll connect you

O: Would you like to leave a message

O: Now let me check the message with you to see if it is correct

O: We'll give the message to Mr. Williams as soon as he comes back

Task 2 Work in Pairs.

1. B 2. B 3. A 4. A 5. A 6. A 7. A 8. B 9. B 10. B 11. A 12. B 13. A

6—1—3—10—11—9—7—8—4—12—13—2—5

Task 3 Short telephone scenario cards.

Open answer.

Part 3 Reading

Task 1 True or false statements.

1. F 2. F 3. T 4. F 5. T

Task 2 Questions.

1. Because answering the telephone is an opportunity for telephone operators/Front Desk agents/hotel staff to portray professional image as well as a positive image for the hotel.
2. Be patient with the caller and put the irate caller in contact with another appropriate manager or someone who has the authority to handle the caller's request.

Task 3 Blank filling.

1. endeavor 2. impeding 3. irate 4. regarding 5. permitted 6. hospitality 7. frustrating 8. pick up 9. particularly 10. authority

Part 4 Translation

Task 1

舞龙是中国文化中的一种传统舞蹈与表演形式。它起源于汉朝,并且由信仰并崇拜龙的中国人所开创。人们认为,舞龙一开始是农耕文化的组成部分,起初也是治病和防病的一种方法。舞龙在宋朝就已经成为一项流行的活动。舞龙是中国文化和传统的重要组成部分,已经传遍了中国乃至全世界,而且已经成为中国体育活动中的一种特殊的艺术表演形式。它象征着在来年为世界上所有的人带来好运和兴旺。

Task 2

1. This is the operator. You have an outside line. May I put it through?
2. Good evening, sir. Your friend Mr. White invited you to have dinner in the Chinese restaurant on the second floor at 7 o'clock tonight.
3. The Guest Service Center is to create customer loyalty by offering guests dependable and efficient delivery of service, information and problem resolution. The GSC concept is to

promote the coordinated use of the hotel's resources to increase operational efficiency.

Task 3

August 18th every year by the lunar calendar witnesses a sea of people thronging towards Yanguan in Haining City of Zhejiang to watch the tidal waves of the Qiantang River. The river tide is a remarkable natural phenomenon that has excited many people, Chinese and foreign, ancient and contemporary. It is at its most spectacular day when the combined attraction of the moon and the sun to the sea is the greatest.

Chapter 9 Banqueting & Conferences

Part 1 Listening

Task 1 Dialogues.

Dialogue 1

B: Don't worry, we are quite professional

Dialogue 2

B: Pink carnations! It will create a quite warm atmosphere

Dialogue 3

A: We need the slogan on the LED electronic screen to welcome our honorable guests

Dialogue 4

A: Can you take me to have a look at the International Hall first

Dialogue 5

A: hire a slide projector for tomorrow's conference

Task 2 Conversations.

Conversation 1

arrange a meeting; conference; charge; medium-sized; book

Conversation 2

W: celebrate his birthday

W: Approximately

R: excluding

R: in advance

R: receipt

Conversation 3

R: How may I help you

J: if you could arrange a wedding party

R: When would you like to have the banquet

J: About 200 altogether

R: how much would you like to spend for each table

R: What time would you like the banquet to start, sir

R: Do you have any special requirements

R: we'll get everything ready before the banquet

Part 2 Speaking

Task 1 Work in pairs.

M: How may I help you

V: I am calling to reserve a banquet hall to hold our welcome party to honor Mr. Beckman

V: Do you have any hall available

M: May I know how many people there will be

M: How much would you like to spend for each table

V: Do you have any suggestions

M: We can create special dishes for our guests for special occasion

M: and what drinks would you like

M: what kind of fruits, do you prefer

M: would it be convenient for you to leave your number in case we contact you

Task 2 Work in pairs.

1. D 2. F 3. B 4. C 5. E 6. A

Task 3 Role-play.

Situation 1

(Banquet Service Waitress-W Mr. Zille-Mr.)

W: Good morning. Welcome to Banquet Service. May I help you?

Mr.: Good morning. My grandson is going to be 10 in 2 weeks. I'd like to ask if you could arrange a birthday party for him in your hotel.

W: Of course. When will you hold the party?

Mr.: It will be on Saturday, June 23rd.

W: OK. May I know how many people there will be?

Mr.: 70 guests altogether.

W: Then I will arrange 7 tables for you. Please let me check our bookings... Could I recommend the Prince Hall to you? It's perfect for your grandson's birthday party.

Mr.: Great! We'll take it.

W: Then how would you like the birthday cake and other decorations?

Mr.: I think a three-layer birthday cake is wonderful. As for decorations, I think he would prefer the cartoons.

W: No problem, Mr. Zille. Then how much would you like to spend for each table? Here is the banquet menu.

Mr.: I think the 1000 yuan menu is nice.

W: OK. Mr. Zille, would you please pay 3000 yuan as deposit?

Mr.: Sure. Here you are.

W: Thank you. We'll get it ready for the party.

Mr.: Thank you very much.

Situation 2

(Banquet Reservationist-R Mrs. Bretman-B)

R: Good morning. Welcome to Banquet Service. How may I help you?

B: Good morning. My son will be married next month. I'd like to ask if you could arrange a wedding party for him in your hotel.

R: Congratulations! May I know the date of the wedding?

B: It will be on Sunday, May 12th.

R: OK. May I know how many people there will be?

B: 200 guests altogether.

R: Then I will arrange 20 tables for you. Please let me check our bookings... I'd recommend the Queen's Banquet Hall with splendid decoration, which is perfect for a wedding party.

B: Wonderful! I'll take it.

R: Then how much would you like to spend for each table? Here is the banquet menu.

B: I think the 1500 yuan menu is nice.

R: OK, madam. By the way, we could provide a honeymoon suite to the bride and groom if necessary.

B: Well, I would talk with my son and confirm it later. Thank you!

R: It is my pleasure, madam. We'll get everything ready before the banquet. May you enjoy it!

B: Thank you very much. Bye!

Part 3 Reading

Task 1 True or false statements.

1. F 2. T 3. T 4. F 5. T 6. T

Task 2 Questions.

1. Exclusive dining organized with privacy; food and services being adapted and delivered according to guests' requirements; large organized groups participating in dining, or in events involving exhibitions, auctions or celebration of special occasions.
2. In view of these factors, the successful management and organization of banquet business would require skills in coordinating tasks and personnel, skills in selecting good combinations of food and beverages which are to be served, as well as sound judgment in maximizing profitability through proper pricing and costing of events catered.
3. A banquet manager needs to have a thorough understanding of the business from the perspective of SALES as well as OPERATIONS.
4. The primary function of the Banquet Department is that it is a Food & Beverage outlet within the Food & Beverage Department and provides food and beverages for the event.

   The secondary role of this department is to provide non-food-and-beverage support for the hotel's convention market.

   It is also a specialist for organizing theme parties, weddings, dinner theatres, playhouses, gala dinners and any special events, which are limited only by one's imagination.

This department would very often take on the organization of outside catering functions, providing the food and beverages, set-ups as well as services in any off premises sites.

5. The events organized within or outside the hotel by the Banquet Department would indirectly provide publicity for the hotel through guests' attendance and their recommendations and positive remarks from the hosts of completed functions.

Task 3 Blank filling.

1. perspective 2. coordinate 3. consistently 4. distinct 5. occasion 6. in advance
7. imperative 8. flexibility 9. adapted 10. participate in

Part 4 Translation

Task 1

宴会中的餐桌服务通常都很正式，并且需要遵守由餐饮部经理制定的一些细则规定。这些规定也适用于公共用餐场合的服务。如果宴会中有许多客人，服务人员要接受培训以提供快速而优雅的服务。这样可以确保同时给多位客人上菜，并且让客人感觉他们享受到的是单独服务。

Task 2

SNIEC offers 17 column-free, ground-level exhibition halls, covering indoor space of 200000 square meters and outdoor space of 100000 square meters. Since officially opened in 2001, SNIEC has made a rapid development with annually welcoming more than 4 million guests and around 100 world-class exhibitions. As a multi-functional venue, SNIEC also caters to a diverse range of both social and corporate events.

Chapter 10 Chinese Food

Part 1 Listening

Task 1 Dialogues.

Dialogue 1

B: cuisine

Dialogue 2

B: special

Dialogue 3

A: dishes

Dialogue 4

B: light

Dialogue 5

B: typically

Task 2 Conversations.

Conversation 1

authentic; spicy hot; Cantonese cuisine; light and fresh; Beijing roast duck

Conversation 2

order; tender and tasty; sweet and delicious; recommendations; Chopsticks

Conversation 3

W: Would you like some wine

W: rice wine; white liquor

W: sticky rice; mild liquor; the Chinese yellow wine; it goes well with the crab you ordered

Part 2 Speaking

Task 1 Work in pairs.

W: Have you made a reservation

W: The table has been reserved

Mr.: Can we have the menu, please

W: I'll be back to take your order in a minute

W: May I take your order now

Mr.: would you please give some suggestions

Mr.: It looks nice both in shape and color

W: Dongpo Pork is also our specialty

Mrs.: we also want some soup

W: What would you like to drink

W: Do you want anything else

Task 2 Work in pairs.

1. B 2. F 3. E 4. C 5. A 6. D

Task 3 Role-play.

Situation 1

(Waiter-W Ms. Norris-Ms.)

W: Good evening, madam. May I take your order now?

Ms.: Would you please give us some recommendations? It's our first time to Hangzhou. We are quite unfamiliar with Hangzhou cuisine.

W: No problem, madam. Dishes of Hangzhou are not greasy, have but instead have a fresh, soft flavor with a mellow fragrance. I'd recommend Beggar's Chicken(叫花鸡). It is a local specialty of Hangzhou and also called Hangzhou Roast Chicken. It takes four hours or so to do the roasting, and the chicken roasted is full in taste, delicious and golden-looking. It is worth a try.

Ms.: It sounds amazing. We'll try it.

W: Steamed Hilsa Herring is our chef's recommendation. Fish from the Fuchun River is steamed with ham slices, dried mushrooms, and bamboo shoots. The color and taste are both appealing.

Ms.: Yes, I heard it's one of the local people's favorite dishes. Ah, we also want some soup. What soup do you have?

W: We have Three Fresh Delicacies Soup and West Lake Water Shield Soup. West Lake

Water Shield Soup looks nice. The red ham matches well with the white chicken and the green water shield which grows in the ponds of West Lake's Three Pools Mirroring the Moon. The soup tastes delicious. It smells nice, too. The soup is highly nutritious. Water shield contains a lot of Vitamin C and a trace of iron with high medicinal value.

Ms.: Wonderful! We'll have it!

W: What would you like to drink? We have different alcohol and soft drinks.

Ms.: We'd like some water-melon juice.

W: OK, madam. Let me repeat your order. You've ordered a Beggar's Chicken, a Steamed Hilsa Herring, a West Lake Water Shield Soup and some water-melon juice. Do you want anything else?

Ms.: No more right now. Thank you.

W: It's my pleasure. Your dishes will come soon. May you enjoy your dinner!

Situation 2

(Ms. Norris-Ms. Waiter-W)

Ms.: Bill, please.

W: Yes, madam. Please wait for a moment... Here is your bill. The total is 180 yuan.

Ms.: Can you explain the costs for me?

W: Sure. You've ordered a Beggar's Chicken, a Steamed Hilsa Herring, a West Lake Water Shield Soup and some water-melon juice. And they amount to 180 yuan.

Ms.: But we have changed the water-melon juice to the tomato juice.

W: Oh, I'm sorry. We've made a mistake. I'll get a new bill for you soon... Sorry for keeping you waiting for so long, madam. I do apologize for the inconvenience caused by our mistake.

Ms.: That's all right. Can I pay by credit?

W: Of course. We accept American Express, Master Card and VISA Card.

Ms.: Here is my card.

W: Thank you, madam... Here is your receipt.

Part 3 Reading

Task 1 True or false statements.

1. T 2. T 3. T 4. F 5. F 6. T

Task 2 Questions.

1. The history of Chinese cuisine in China has changed from period to period and in each region according to climate, imperial fashions, and local preferences.
2. Factors such as availability of resources, climate, geography, history, cooking techniques and lifestyle cause the different styles of the cuisines in China.
3. Dim-sum dishes are prepared using traditional cooking methods such as frying, steaming, stewing and baking.
4. With a long history, Shandong Cuisine once formed an important part of the imperial

cuisine and was widely promoted in North China.

5. The unique flavor of pungency and spiciness resulting from liberal use of garlic and chili peppers, as well as the unique flavor of the Sichuan peppercorn and facing heaven pepper.

Task 3 Blank filling.

1. integrate	2. imperial	3. diverse	4. contributed to	5. distinctive
6. favour	7. preference	8. ethnic	9. unparalleled	10. stretch back

Part 4 Translation

Task 1

在19世纪，中国人在旧金山经营高级、豪华的餐厅，光顾的客人主要为中国人。而位于一些小镇上的餐馆则根据客人的需求，经营猪排三明治、苹果派、豆类和鸡蛋等食品。这些小餐馆改良他们的食物以更接近美国人的口味，后来就发展为经营美式中国菜。最初，为了迎合矿工和铁路工人的口味，他们在那些完全不知道中国菜为何物的小镇上开新餐馆，通过改良当地的食材来迎合客人的口味。后来，厨师们改良了诸如炒杂碎之类的南系中国菜，形成了一种中国本土所没有的中餐风格。

Task 2

In terms of Chinese food, it is popularly recognized that Chinese cuisine is world-famous for its perfect combination of "color, aroma, taste and appearance". China's unique culinary art owes itself to the country's long history, vast territory and hospitable tradition. Chinese cuisine gives emphasis to the selection of raw materials, the texture of food, the blending of seasonings, slicing techniques, the perfect timing of cooking and the art of laying out the food on the plate. Among the best-known schools of Chinese culinary tradition are the Cantonese cuisine of the south, the Shandong cuisine of the north, the Huai-Yang cuisine of the east and Sichuan cuisine of the west. These four major varieties of Chinese food have been traditionally noted as "the light flavor of the south, the salty flavor of the north, the sweet flavor of the east and the spicy-hot flavor of the west".

Chapter 11 Western Food

Part 1 Listening

Task 1 Dialogues.

Dialogue 1

B: appetizers

Dialogue 2

A: buffet

Dialogue 3

B: Medium

Dialogue 4

B: Scrambled

Dialogue 5

A: dessert

Task 2　Conversations.

Conversation 1

reservation; available; a table for two; by the window; step this way

Conversation 2

with fried eggs; prefer; strong; black coffee; sign this bill

Conversation 3

A: Can we see the menu

B: I'd recommend crispy and fried duck

A: we'll begin with mushroom soup

B: Would you like any dessert

Part 2　Speaking

Task 1　Work in pairs.

W: Would you like to sit smoking or no-smoking

W: How about this table

W: I'll take your order a moment later

Mr.: What is today's specialty

W: We have a good selection of desserts

W: It is one of our Chef's specialties

W: Would you like some wine to go with your dinner

W: champagne for the fish

Task 2　Work in pairs.

1. D　2. C　3. F　4. A　5. B　6. E

Task 3　Role-play.

Situation 1

(Waitress-W　Mr. Simpson-Mr.)

W: Good evening. Would you like to order now?

Mr.: Yes, I'd like to start with shrimp cocktail, then the veal cutlet. I'll have a vanilla ice-cream for dessert, and some coffee with cream.

W: I'm sorry, the veal cutlet is not being served today, but we have sirloin steak, it's very delicious. Would you like to try it, sir?

Mr.: That sounds like a good idea. I'll have a sirloin steak.

W: How do you like your steak done, sir?

Mr.: Rare, please.

W: OK.

Mr.: Please bring me two slices of bread and butter with the soup.

W: Yes, sir. Can I get you something to drink with your meal?

Mr.: I'll have a gin and tonic with lemon and ice, please.

W: Would you like anything else, sir?

Mr. : No, thanks. I think that's enough.

W: Yes. So one shrimp cocktail, a cup of coffee with cream, a gin and tonic with lemon and ice and two slices of bread and butter. And the main course is a rare sirloin steak.

Mr. : Thank you.

W: You are welcome. Just a moment please, I'll go place your order and get it for you right away.

Situation 2

(Waiter-W Ms. Curtis-Ms.)

W: Good evening, madam. What would you like for your dinner, table d'hote or a la carte?

Ms. : A la carte, please. What is today's specialty?

W: There are two: Brazilian Style Rib Eye Steak and Australian Sirloin Steak.

Ms. : I'll take Brazilian Style Rib Eye Steak.

W: How would you like the steak done, madam?

Ms. : Medium-well, please.

W: Would you like a dessert? We have a good selection of desserts.

Ms. : I like the Parfait with Cream Caramel Flavor.

W: No problem. Would you like some wine to go with your dinner?

Ms. : Would you please make some recommendations?

W: I would suggest Botter Chianti or Wolf Blass White Label Cabernet for the Rib Eye Steak.

Ms. : Perfect! I'll have a glass of Botter Chianti.

W: No problem. So a Brazilian Style Rib Eye Steak, a Parfait with Cream Caramel Flavor, a glass of Botter Chianti, right?

Ms. : Yes.

W: Well, your dinner will be ready soon. I hope you'll enjoy your dinner!

Ms. : Thank you!

Part 3 Reading

Task 1 True or false statements.

1. T 2. T 3. F 4. F 5. F 6. T

Task 2 Questions.

1. If invited to begin before others are served, wait until three or four people have been served before starting to eat.
2. At the table, ask others to pass you dishes that are out of your reach. Good phrases to know are "Please pass the..." or "Could you hand me the..., please?"
3. When eating spaghetti, wind the noodles up on your fork. You may use your spoon to assist in winding the noodles on your fork. The spaghetti on your fork should be eaten in one bite. It is very impolite to eat half your noodles and allow the other half to fall

back on your plate.

4. If you are not sure if it is proper to eat something by picking it up with your fingers, watch what others do before doing so yourself.
5. The best way to learn good manners is to watch others. Observe the way your Western friends eat.

Task 3 Blank filling.

1. observed 2. signaling 3. napkin 4. folded 5. refuse 6. host
7. crisp 8. lean down 9. be sure of 10. winding up

Part 4 Translation

Task 1

<u>汤</u>
玛莎拉牛肉汤
鸡茸蘑菇汤
<u>冷菜</u>
黑森林火腿加黑麦面包
烟熏三文鱼加烤面包片和黄油
<u>主菜</u>
巴西风情肋眼牛排
意式培根卷大虾比萨
西西里风情肉酱满溢千层面
意式罗勒鲜美虾面
意式黄金蛋包海鲜饭
普罗旺斯风情焗鸡腿排饭
<u>甜点</u>
热樱桃浇干邑，配香草冰激凌球
苹果馅卷，配香草酱汁
两个核桃冰激凌配鲜无花果和奶油
巧克力法式芭菲

Task 2

In formal settings, all the silverware, glassware, cups and saucers are placed on the table, so it's often difficult to tell which fork to use or which water glass is yours. Generally speaking, silverware is lined up in the order in which a person will use them, going from the outside to inside. For instance, the fork and knife used for the salad is placed in the outermost of the setting. Dessert silverware is placed at the top of your entrée plate. The glassware, cup and saucer are placed to your right, while the napkin, bread plate and butter spreader to your left.

Chapter 12 Beverage Service

Part 1 Listening

Task 1 Dialogues.

Dialogue 1

B: but not too bitter

Dialogue 2

B: Please have a look at the Drink List

Dialogue 3

B: With water and ice

Dialogue 4

A: I'd like a glass of red wine

Dialogue 5

B: Would you like to say "when" please

Task 2 Conversations.

Conversation 1

cocktails; alcoholic; non-alcoholic; brandy; liqueur

Conversation 2

with your meal; go very well with; house wine; delicate body; allow it to breathe

Conversation 3

B: What tea do you prefer

G: black tea

B: it can help people reduce weight

B: you're slim and green tea is the wisest choice, especially in summer

B: They prefer a strong tasting tea

Part 2 Speaking

Task 1 Work in pairs.

B: Which wine would you like

W: What's the favorite Chinese wine, please

B: especially in the north part of China and the taste of it is not bad

W: I'll try it next time when I go to a Chinese restaurant

B: The most typical one is Shaoxing rice wine, a kind of mild wine, Some people even like to warm it before drinking

W: I seldom drink wine without ice, cheers

Task 2 Work in pairs.

1. C 2. E 3. A 4. F 5. B 6. D

Task 3 Role-play.

Situation 1

(Waitress-W Mr. Gary-G)

W: Excuse me, would you like to have some wine with your dinner?

G: Well, do you have any good recommendations?

W: Er, I think that Sauvignon Blanch or Muscatel would be perfect for your fish.

G: Sounds great. Then we'd take half a bottle of Muscatel.

W: Certainly, sir. Please wait for a moment.

W: Sir, here is your Muscatel. Shall I open the bottle right now?

G: Yes, please.

W: Would you like to have a taste now?

G: Sure.

W: How do you like it?

G: Fabulous! Thank you very much.

W: It's my pleasure. Wish you a nice meal!

G: Thank you.

Situation 2

(Waiter-W Customer-C)

W: Good evening, madam. Would you like to have some wine with your dinner? Here is the wine list.

C: Wow, it really makes me at sea. Would you please give us some suggestions?

W: Well, I think the Domina Schloss Castell goes quite well with your steak. It is tasting and smooth.

C: It sounds a good idea. I'll take a glass first.

W: Certainly, madam. Please wait for a moment.

W: Your Domina, madam. Shall I open it now?

C: Yes, please.

W: Would you like to taste it now?

C: Sure. Thank you.

W: How is it, madam?

C: Fine, thank you.

W: Good, enjoy your dinner!

Part 3 Reading

Task 1 True or false statements.

1. T 2. T 3. F 4. T 5. T 6. F

Task 2 Sentence completion.

1. barley 2. fermenting grape juice 3. grog 4. tea 5. the United States

Task 3 Blank filling.

1. civilization 2. placate 3. colony 4. distills 5. compulsory 6. urge ... to
7. ritual 8. disdain 9. invasion 10. associate with

Part 4 Translation

Task 1

酒,或饮料,是专供人类消费的液体。除满足人类的基本需求外,饮料成为人类社会文化的一部分。虽然大部分的饮料,包括果汁、软饮料和碳酸饮料,本身含水,但水本身通常不归为饮料这一类。"饮料"这个词已经被反复地定义为不包括水。酒精饮料是指一种含有乙醇俗称为酒精的饮料,尽管在化学上酒精的定义包括许多其他化合物。酒精饮料,如葡萄酒、啤酒和烈酒,在过去的8000年里一直是人类文化发展的一部分。非酒精饮料,通常是指含有酒精但酒精含量低于5%的饮料,如啤酒。

Task 2

There are different kinds of places that serve alcoholic beverages. The most common one is the bar, often with a long counter from which drinks are dispensed. Bars and pubs are usually to be found in a residential neighborhood and are often referred to simply as "The Local". A tavern is an old fashioned term for a pub. A cocktail lounge or wine bar usually has a bar, small tables, a relaxed atmosphere, and minimal entertainment. Night clubs offer the additional attractions of dance, music, meals, and entertainment.

Chapter 13 Room Service

Part 1 Listening

Task 1 Dialogues.

Dialogue 1

B: request an early morning call at 6 sharp tomorrow morning

Dialogue 2

A: request some bandages

B: in about five minutes

Dialogue 3

B: Chilled orange juice; toast with butter; coffee or tea

Dialogue 4

B: a minimum tip of 15% of the food bill will be expected

Dialogue 5

A: Which kind of juice would you prefer

Task 2 Conversations.

Conversation 1

turn on and off the lights; lights master controller; inserted into the flat hole; the panel of the door controller; beside the doorframe; automatically turned off

Conversation 2

American and Continental; Peeled oranges, toast with butter; Let me confirm your order; Your order will be ready soon

Conversation 3

daily supplemented; dial the inside line 61555 or 61666; complete the list and sign your name; room account; settled together when checking out (Once unsealed, beverages, wine and food will be added to your account)

Part 2 Speaking

Task 1 Work in pairs.

1. Please go to Front Desk and find the Service Information Booklet in which you can get all useful information.
2. I'm sorry to hear that. I will let...come here at once.
3. Would you mind repeating that? I didn't quite catch on.
4. You can take a taxi or you can go by bus there.
5. Please wait a moment. I will do it right away.
6. OK, I will let... come here at once.

Task 2 Role-play.

Situation 1

(Guest-G Clerk of Room Service-C)

G: Hello, Room Service?

C: Yes, how may we help you?

G: I would like to have breakfast in my room this morning.

C: That will be no problem. What would you like?

G: I'd like to order an English breakfast, please.

C: Alright, sir. What kind of juice would you like?

G: Apple.

C: Would you like bacon, sausage or ham?

G: Ham, please.

C: And how would you like your eggs, sir?

G: Two fried eggs, sunny-side up.

C: Certainly, sir.

G: Could I have croissants with my breakfast?

C: Yes, you can, sir. Tea or coffee, please?

G: I would like to have coffee.

C: Certainly, sir. So that's apple juice, two eggs, sunny-side up, croissants and coffee.

G: That's right.

C: Your room number?

G: Room 931.

C: OK, we'll have that right up to you.

G: Thank you.

Situation 2

(Clerk of Room Service-C Mrs. White-Mrs.)

C: Room Service. May I help you?

Mrs.: Would you please send a dinner for my room?

C: Yes, madam. How many people in your room?

Mrs.: 2.

C: What would you like to have? We have steak, green beans and Brussels sprouts, and so on.

Mrs. : I will take steak for two and green beans.

C: What else do you want to order?

Mrs. : I want to have a salad.

C: OK. May I have you room number?

Mrs. : Room 516.

C: Okay, I'll bring them to your room as soon as possible.

Mrs. : Thank you.

Part 3 Reading

Task 1 Questions.

1. Room service is the service of food or beverages in guests' room in hotel or order from accommodation establishments, such as motels or serviced apartments.
2. Room Service Department must work closely with the Kitchen, Front Office and Housekeeping departments to make sure that the standard of service satisfies, or more than satisfies, guests' expectations.
3. The use of guest's name has the advantage of ensuring that the items requested are delivered to the right guest and charged to the right account as well as making the guest feel known and valued.

Task 2 Translation.

大部分客房服务是通过电话预订的。因此,客房服务人员良好的通话方式可以给客人留下好印象。

正确称呼客人能确保核准服务对象、核实账户及让客人感到被重视。在客房服务的所有阶段都要保证正确称呼客人的名字。

及时将订单派发给客房服务部及其他相关部门,尤其是餐饮部门的相关人员。

Part 4 Translation

Task 1

1. 营业时间是早上 6 点半到 10 点。
2. 我们有不同尺寸的蛋糕,有 7 英寸、9 英寸和 11 英寸,您要哪一种?
3. 早上好,这是您点的欧式早餐。
4. 您的早餐不需要用太长时间准备。
5. 您的午餐需要 20 分钟时间准备。
6. 您要的食品和饮料过几分钟就会送上去。
7. 我马上叫人把您的早餐送上来。
8. 对不起,我们要上午 11 点才开始提供午餐。
9. 您是不是还要点别的?
10. 送餐服务菜单挂在门后。
11. 什么时候把蛋糕送到您房间?
12. 您要几个鸡蛋? 几成熟?

13. 您付现金还是在账单上签字?
14. 请把您的姓名和房号签在账单上。
15. 今天下午有些朋友来看我,能给我一些茶杯吗?

Task 2

1. If you need anything else, just feel free to tell me.
2. What do you want to drink, tea or coffee?
3. Room Service, may I help you?
4. At what time would you like your breakfast?
5. Would you like to have something else besides the Continental breakfast?
6. For how many people, please?
7. In the event that you would like service such as meals in the hotel room, room service can be contacted.
8. I'm always at your service.
9. What kinds of services have to pay extra?
10. If there is minimum charge or service charge, you should explain it clearly in advance.
11. Here is a brochure explaining hotel services.
12. You can make a call from your room.
13. I will bring it up right away.
14. Would you please sign the bill?
15. Thank you, enjoy your breakfast please, goodbye.

Chapter 14 Recreation Center

Part 1 Listening

Task 1 Dialogues.

Dialogue 1: Outdoor Activities.

Dialogue 2: Entertainment.

Dialogue 3: Body Building.

Dialogue 4: Ball Games.

Dialogue 5: Beauty Salon.

Task 2 Conversations.

Conversation 1

Bowling Center; spacious; alleys; registered guests; sizes; warm-up; injury; regulations

Conversation 2

25℃; shallow area; every other day; 9:00 a.m.; 10:00 p.m.

1. T 2. F 3. F 4. T

Conversation 3

amuse ourselves; take a walk; relaxing; recreation center on the ground floor; billiards, table tennis, bridge, go bowling; music teahouse; classical music; modern music

Part 2 Speaking

Task 2 Work in pairs.

(Clerk-C Miss Bellow-M)

C: Good evening, Miss. Welcome to our gym. How may I assist you?

M: I want to lose weight. Could you give me some suggestions?

C: The best way is to do some exercises at the gym every day.

M: Can you show me around?

C: Yes, sure. This way, please. Our gym is well-equipped with all the latest sports apparatus. Here're dumb bells, race apparatus and stationary bikes. They are all for body building.

M: Sounds good. Can you recommend some suitable training classes to me?

C: Yes. We have aerobics and Taijiquan classes every evening.

M: What is Taijiquan?

C: We also call it Chinese Shadow Boxing. It's an important branch of Chinese martial arts. The movements are even and slow. It's used for life enhancement and health building. Many Chinese people are fond of it.

M: I think I prefer fast movements. By the way, do you have a coach here to supervise the exercise?

C: Yes, we have an experienced coach. If you need any help or instructions, just call her.

M: OK. I think I'll get registered in your aerobics training class.

Task 3 Work in pairs.

(Clerk-C Mr. Lee-Mr.)

C: Good evening, sir. Welcome to our Bathing Center. How may I help you?

Mr.: Could you tell me what kind of sauna you have?

C: Our center provides several kinds of sauna baths, such as dry sauna, wet sauna and salt sauna.

Mr.: I want a wet sauna. What's the temperature in the sauna proper?

C: The temperature is about 80 degrees Centigrade. But if you feel uncomfortable, please don't stay inside too long.

Mr.: I see. Thank you. By the way, I've got a pain on my back. Could you do something for it?

C: Sure. I suggest a Chinese massage after you take sauna.

Mr.: What's it?

C: It's a Chinese-style massage with a long history. It can prevent and treat many kinds of diseases by improving the blood circulation.

Mr.: Sounds good. I'll have a try.

C: I'm sure the massage can relax your muscles and ease your pain.

Task 4 Work in pairs.

(Clerk-C Mr. Black-Mr.)

C: Good evening, sir. Welcome to our Bathing Center. How may I assist you?

Mr.: Good evening. What kind of sauna do you have?

C: We have Finnish sauna and Turkish bath. Which one do you prefer?

Mr.: I want a Finnish dry sauna. What's the temperature in the sauna proper?

C: About 176 degrees Fahrenheit.

Mr.: Oh, my God! Will it make me breathless?

C: No, it won't. We have some sauna fragrance to help you breathe easily and the air is good. But if you feel uncomfortable, please don't stay inside too long.

Mr.: I see. Thank you.

C: Please change your shoes here and take a shower before going into it. Then take a towel to the sauna proper.

Mr.: You are most helpful.

(*Some time later, the guest comes out.*)

C: Do you want to cool off under a shower?

Mr.: Good idea.

C: How are you feeling now?

Mr.: Quite good.

C: Here's the robe.

Mr.: I've got a pain in my shoulders. I really feel painful. I hope you can do something for it.

C: Would you like to have a try of our typical Chinese massage? It has a long history and can treat various diseases by improving the blood circulation.

Mr.: Sounds good. How long will it be?

C: About 40 minutes.

Mr.: Can I have it now?

C: Sure. This way to the massage room. I'll call our best masseur for you. Please wait a moment.

Task 5 Role-Play.

(Waitress-W Guest 1-G1 Guest 2-G2)

W: Good evening, welcome to our bar. May I help you?

G1: Yes, could you recommend something to drink?

W: We have soft drink, fresh juice, mineral water, spirit, and coffee. What kind would you like?

G1: Well, coffee, I think.

W: What kind of coffee would you like?

G1: Not strong.

W: Our coffee is not too strong. American style coffee. Black or white?

G1: White coffee. Could you recommend one for me?

W: How about Latte? Would you like to have a try?

G1: Of course, thank you.

W: And you, sir?

G2: I'd like to drink fresh juice, what kind do you have?

W: We have orange, pineapple, grapefruit, mango, peach, and tomato juice.

G2: Give me some mango juice.

W: Yes, wait a moment, please.

G2: Thank you.

W: Sorry to have kept you waiting. Here is your coffee and mango juice. Would you like anything else?

G2: No, thanks.

W: You are welcome. Enjoy your drinks!

Part 3 Reading

Passage 1

equipped; relaxation; surrounded; ease; coach; private; range; revitalizes; sign up; Complimentary

Passage 2

Task 1 Translation.

如今,康乐中心已成为成功酒店不可缺少的组成部分。越来越多的酒店把拥有完备的康乐设施作为其经营的一大特色。

1. 主要包括篮球、羽毛球、网球、高尔夫球、沙弧球、乒乓球、台球、保龄球、体操、射箭等。

2. 主要包括洗浴、桑拿、按摩、水疗、游泳、香熏泡浴等。

3. 理疗

康乐中心员工在提供服务时应牢记以下几点:

介绍主要服务项目及设施并回答客人问询;

Task 2 Choices.

table tennis; singing & dancing; sauna & massage; golf; hairdressing

Task 3 Order.

1. E 2. F 3. B 4. C 5. A 6. D

Task 4 Match.

1—h, 2—f, 3—a, 4—e, 5—b, 6—g, 7—i, 8—c, 9—d

Part 4 Translation

Task 1

1. 卡拉OK 2. 台球室 3. 健身房 4. 舞厅 5. 高尔夫球场
6. 保龄球馆 7. 夜总会 8. 美容院

Task 2

1. B 2. C 3. A 4. D

Task 3

Situation 1

A: the facilities

B: a full range of top-class restaurants and bars; extensive fitness and beauty facilities; full-size swimming pool; how to use the facilities in our room

Situation 2

A: disabled facilities

A: do you have raps as well as stairs

B: no special facilities for disabled guests

Situation 3

A: the Business Center

B: Please take the elevator in the lobby; It is at the end of the corridor

A: Doesn't it provide 24-hour service

B: The Business Center is open until eleven at night

Situation 4

B: Just take the elevator up to the top floor; just follow the signs; Next to the pool, there's also a sauna, one exercise room and changing rooms

B: enjoy your swim

Chapter 15 Shopping

Part 1 Listening

Task 1 Dialogues.

Dialogue 1

B: looking for a very special gift for a very special person

Dialogue 2

B: fashionable

A: latest design

Dialogue 3

B: recommendations

A: Both the design and the color are quite special

Dialogue 4

B: Go straight along this street to the traffic lights; A short way along the right, you'll see it.

Task 2 Conversations.

Conversation 1

gift shop; buy some gifts for my family and friends; anything in mind; typical Chinese gifts for my wife; small gifts for my friends; model cars; silk dresses; silk shirts; silk scarves; ties; lighters; silk scarf; recommendations; Chinese knots; take a two; two cars; silk scarf; Chinese knots

Conversation 2

the souvenir shop; mascots of the Olympic Games and Paralympic Games; the mascots of the 2008 Olympic Games; the mascot of the 2008 Beijing Paralympic Games; crazy; costs a fortune; In that case; take a collection; gift-wrap

Conversation 3

food shop; local food; Do you have anything in mind; Beijing Roast Duck; Beijing preserved fruits; manufacturers; of the same quality; I'll take five boxes of it.

Part 2　Speaking

Task 1　Work in pairs.

1. B　2. G　3. C　4. A　5. E　6. F　7. D

Task 2　Work in pairs.

attended to; latest style; cultured pearls; luster; value; pearl producing area; label; string

Task 3

Situation 1

(Shop Assistant-A　Mrs. Lee-Mrs.)

A: Good afternoon, Madam. Can I be of service to you?

Mrs.: Yes. I'd like to buy a china tea set for my friends.

A: Would you like a tea set for four, six or eight persons?

Mrs.: Mm, a set for six persons will be all right.

A: How about this brown china tea set?

Mrs.: It's really beautiful.

A: It's a traditional Chinese design.

Mrs.: Where does it come from?

A: It's made in Jingdezhen, the porcelain capital of China. This brown china tea set is quite unusual.

Mrs.: I like it very much. (*Looking at the price tag*) But would you give me a discount?

A: I'm afraid not, madam. The price is fixed. Please consider the fine craftsmanship. It's worth the price.

Mrs.: I see. Then I'll take it.

A: You've made a good choice, madam. Shall I wrap it up for you?

Mrs.: Yes, please.

A: Altogether 2000 yuan. Would you please go to the cashier's to pay for it?

Mrs.: Fine.

A: Thank you, madam. They are fragile. Please handle them carefully.

Mrs.: Thanks a lot.

Situation 2

(Shop Assistant-A　Mr. Tony Brown-B)

A: Good afternoon, sir. Are you being attended to?

B: Not yet. I'd like to buy a set of Chinese tableware.

A: How about this set of blue-and-white tableware with the bamboo design?

B: Can you tell me something more about it?

A: Sure. This set of blue-and-white tableware is a typical Chinese style with a long history. It's made in Jingdezhen, the porcelain capital of China.

B: It looks really beautiful.

A: It's the best quality porcelain. You see, the body is decorated with the bamboo. It's of perfect traditional Chinese design.

B: I like it very much. I'll take it.

A: Anything else you want to buy?

B: I want to buy a tablecloth to go with it.

A: I suggest the tablecloth which is hand-embroidered. Many foreign guests give high comments on it.

B: Fantastic! I'll take the two items. How much are they altogether?

A: You have a good taste for art. The total is 4200 yuan.

B: Would you give me a discount?

A: I'm afraid not, sir. Please consider the fine craftsmanship. They are worth the price.

B: I see. Would you please wrap them up separately?

A: OK. Please pay at the cashier's over there.

B: Fine.

A: Thank you, sir. They are fragile. Please handle them with care.

B: Thanks a lot.

Situation 3

(Salesman-S Guest-G)

S: Can I help you, madam?

G: No, thanks. I'm just looking. Well, just out of curiosity. What is that necklace made of?

S: It is made of jewelry.

G: Really? My sister's birthday is tomorrow. She loves jewelry. I just wasn't sure I could afford it.

S: You'll find a lot of our goods are amazingly affordable. It's only 4000 yuan.

G: Well, that's certainly nice to know. I'll take it.

S: It's a good choice. I'm sure she'll love it.

G: I hope so.

S: Cash or charge, madam?

G: Charge, please. Do you accept Master Card?

S: Yes, we do.

G: Great.

S: (*Handing him the charge sheet*) That comes to 4000 yuan. Please sign next to the "X".

G: Here you are.

S: Do you need anything else?

G: Yes, I need to buy some Chinese tea. My father likes Chinese tea.

S：Well，we have both green tea and black tea in the tea counter. It's upstairs.

G：Thank you.

S：You're welcome.

Part 3　Reading

Task 1　Choices.

embroidery；porcelain；arts and crafts；lacquerware；jade carving；cloisonné

Task 2　True or false statements.

1. T　2. F　3. T　4. T

Task 3　Match.

1—d，2—f，3—g，4—a，5—h，6—c，7—e，8—b

Task 4　Translation.

每年数以百万计的外国人来中国出差、观光或进行经济、贸易、体育、科学和文化等领域的交流。

在中国，酒店商场部给外国游客提供了品种繁多的商品。很多外国游客来中国时都抵挡不住这些商品的诱惑。

比如，在国内外都享有盛名的景泰蓝，造型优美雅致，图案华丽，色彩鲜艳；玉雕以其简朴、优雅、精致透明的民族风格而独具一格；漆器，工艺精湛，以其造型典雅、外观精美、色彩鲜亮而闻名；瓷器或许是中国人对世界做出的最重大的贡献，产自"瓷都"景德镇的瓷器以"白如玉，薄如纸，明如镜，声如磬（一种古老的中国乐器）"而著称；丝织品和刺绣，工艺精湛，色彩设计和谐，民族特色鲜明，非常值得在中国购买。

他们要千方百计地让每位顾客感到他们所花的每一分钱都是值得的。

Part 4　Translation

Task 1

1. 瞧，这就是清式三合板木屏风。过去这样的屏风通常是由三至五块木板做成的。它可以折叠，摆放在屋里来挡风或者防止外人看到室内。每个屏风上都绘有不同的图案，看见了吧，有花、鱼、鸟、哺乳动物和古代美女。
2. 大约在公元12世纪，中国风筝传到了西方，此后经过不断发展，逐渐形成各具特色的东西方风筝文化。在风筝的发展过程中，具有悠久历史的中国传统文化与风筝工艺相融合，从而形成了独具地方特色的风筝文化。

Task 2

1. Among the various folk handicrafts，Chiuchow Xiu Hsiang Bao (embroidered perfume sachets) is colorful and unique. It is a kind of handicrafts enriching in the local elegant appearance，and it can be used both for appreciation and decoration. Most of them are exquisite small toys，while some of them are big ornaments and practical handicrafts. These unique articles are popular with people for their exquisite shape，wonderful color and rich agrestic flavor.
2. Tiger-head shoes are a kind of shoes made for toddlers. It is named so because it really looks like tiger heads. The people who live in the Central Plains Area are quite familiar with them. These hand-made shoes do not only bring happiness to the family but also

bring hopes to parents. They are practical articles as well as a traditional good luck symbol. They are endowed with a function of chasing away ghosts and scaring away bad luck.

Chapter 16 Complaints Handling

Part 1 Listening

Task 1 Dialogues.

Dialogue 1

rather cold; turn off; getting a cold; extra blanket; take some medicine

Dialogue 2

complain; overcharged; faxes; confused; apologize for the inconvenience; settle my bill; a plane to catch

Dialogue 3

half an hour; previous occupant; extended his checkout time; making up the room; it's a little bit messy; providing clean and tidy rooms; guarantee; appreciate your insistence; sixteen hours' flight; in the lobby

Dialogue 4

unreasonable; extra charge; case; reserved; check out; extra half day charge; contact

Dialogue 5

No pillow cases are stained; the bathtub is not clean; towels; attend to it; extremely busy; conference; peak season; overlooked; chambermaid; the water closet is clogged; flushed; overflew; mess; get your luggage ready; porter

Task 2 Conversations.

Conversation 1

1503; smelly; air fresher; inconvenience; hesitate

Conversation 2

the baggage elevator made; at the end of the corridor; spare room; in a quiet suite; have a sound sleep

Conversation 3

931; checked in; help you with; there are no towels; send someone up right away with towels; any inconvenience; quite alright

Part 2 Speaking

Task 2

W: Is everything to your satisfaction

W: Oh, sorry to hear that. I will change it for another one

W: I'm sorry, sir. Do you wish to try something else? The compliment food would be on the house, of course

W: How about a delicious dessert then, with our compliments

W: Please sign the bill. I'm sure everything will be right again the next time you come

G: All right. I will come again

W: Thank you very much, sir

Task 3

Situation 1

A: if someone entered the room; it confirmed that she didn't steal your clothes

B: Can I review the tape myself

A: the security manager's office

B: It's really strange; the housekeeper did not leave carrying parcels

A: No matter who is responsible for the theft of your belongings, it is on our part. We will accept the responsibility and compensate you in three days

Situation 2

A: Maintenance Department

B: The air conditioner is not working properly

B: The remote control doesn't work; can't adjust the temperature

A: the batteries should be changed; replace them with two new ones

Task 4 Role-play.

Situation 1

(Duty Manager-DM Guest-G)

DM: Good afternoon, Raymond speaking, how may I help you?

G: I want to complain! Just now your room attendant opened the door without pressing the button or knocking at the door. It is very impolite. I feel the room I am staying in is not private. I want your hotel to pay me back some money because of the rude action made by your employee.

DM: Is that Mr. Lee in Room 9087? I'm very sorry, sir. I will investigate this case and give you feedback as soon as I can.

G: Thank you.

(*Then the Duty Manager checks with the Housekeeping Department and confirms the incident. After discussing with the Housekeeping Manager and the Front Office Manager, they decide to give a dinner coupon to the guest. The Duty Manager calls back to Mr. Lee.*)

DM: Hello, Mr. Lee. I'm the Duty Manager Raymond. I'm sorry for what happened to you because of our room attendant's carelessness. I discussed with our department heads; we will give you our dinner coupon valued at 200 yuan. I hope you will enjoy it in our restaurant. We will guarantee that such things will not happen again. Thank you for your understanding.

G: Sounds good. I also hope such things will not happen again

Situation 2

(Concierge-C Guest-G)

C: Good afternoon, Concierge, Mark speaking, how may I help you?

G: Yes, I have been waiting in my room for almost half an hour. Why hasn't my luggage been sent up yet? Is there a problem?

C: Oh, I'm sorry, sir. May I have your name and room number please?

G: Turner, David Turner, Room 1118.

C: I'm sorry, but you are in the tour group. Your group is big, so we need to send the luggage one by one. Would you please give me some features of your luggage?

G: Sure, I have two bags. One is a big blue suitcase and the other is a medium-sized black suitcase.

C: Is your name tag attached to them?

G: Yes.

C: Mr. Turner, please wait a moment. I will check them for you and call you back in five minutes.

(After Mark checked the luggage area, he called Mr. Turner back.)

C: Hello, Mr. Turner. I am sorry to keep you waiting. I've already checked and your luggage is on the way.

G: Thank you.

C: You are welcome.

Situation 3

(Receptionist-R Duty Manager-DM Guest-G)

R: Excuse me, Mr. White, but have you seen two bath towels from the bath room?

G: Sorry, I can't remember.

R: Our room attendant entered your room, and she couldn't find your towels. I'm sorry to tell you, Mr. White, we need to charge you 100 yuan for the two towels.

G: No way! I didn't take your towels, why do you charge me? Do you think I stole your towels? I can show you my bag!

R: Please calm down, Mr. White. I will call our Duty Manager to handle it.

(Mr. White is angry and will not pay the towel fee. The Duty Manager is called by the reception staff to explain. The Duty Manager approaches Mr. White.)

DM: Good morning, Mr. White. I am the Duty Manager Merry. Nice to meet you.

G: Yeah.

DM: Do you remember where you put the towels or did you bring them to the Health Club when you went to do the exercise?

G: I've already told your staff I didn't take them, and I don't know where I put them.

DM: OK, no problem. We always trust our guests, but it is our job to account for all the items in the room.

G: So how much should I pay for my final bill?

DM: We will print it and show you. Please don't worry, Mr. White. We will not charge you.

G: Of course you will not. Thank you, Merry.

DM: You are welcome.

Situation 4

(Receptionist-R Duty Manager-DM Guest-G)

R: Good evening, sir, how may I help you?

G: Yes, I just received an annoying call asking me if I need a massage. I was already sleeping. Why did your operator put through strange phone calls to my room?

R: I'm sorry, sir. May I have your room number and name please?

G: My name is Matthew Smith, and room number is 1502.

R: I will ask our Duty Manager to check our phone records and give you feedback very soon.

(*After* 10 *minutes. The Duty Manage found out the crank call was from an internal customer. He made several calls to different rooms in the hotel, so the Duty Manager informed the security to investigate. The Duty Manage calls back to the guest.*)

DM: Good evening, Mr. Smith. We have already checked the operator system. The crank call was from another room, and our security people already investigated. I'm sorry for bringing you trouble. From now on you don't need to worry. I hope you have a good sleep. Good night!

G: Thank you, good night.

Part 3 Reading

Passage 1

Task 1 Multiple Choices.

1. D 2. C 3. B 4. C 5. A

Task 2 Translation.

数千年前,盐宫酒店周围是一个大湖,但随着时间的推移,所有的水都消失了。今天,该地区只有两个小湖泊和两个盐沙漠,那个大点的沙漠——乌尤尼盐沙漠有 12000 平方千米。由于有盐,所以,沙漠白天很亮。整个乌尤尼盐沙漠都没有公路,所以必须由当地人带着客人去酒店。

Passage 2

Task 2 Translation.

当然了,每个酒店都有床和浴室(我们希望这样),但是商务酒店并不都一样。在你下次订商务酒店的时候,这些技巧可能会派上用场。

在享受了太多个晚上的客房套餐后,你会发现自己的裤子有点紧了。出差途中,你可以利用酒店的锻炼设施来保持健康。

你如果要做一个规模宏大的演示,或者需要在开会前找个地方开展团队工作,这时会议室就会非常有用了。另外,你如果在开会前需要大量的准备时间,或者有很多样品要演示,你可以让客户到酒店,而不是带着那么多的大物件满城转。

Part 4 Translation

Task 1

1. 请相信我们很理解您此时沮丧的心情,并且会尽力帮助您。
2. 开心点!事情一定是有办法解决的!

3. 没问题,先生。我们会处理的,但是现在没有任何空位,您是否介意……
4. 抱歉我不能为您做那件事,那违反我们的规定。
5. 不要曲解我的意思。我是想说我们双方是否都能保持冷静的态度,尽快达成一个合理的协议来解决问题。
6. 我妻子被运送行李的电梯所发出的嘈杂声弄醒了几次。
7. 非常抱歉,您应该把贵重物品寄存在接待处。
8. 相信服务员并不是有意无礼,他可能没有听懂您的意思。
9. 很抱歉,先生。我想这里面可能有点误会。
10. 很抱歉,但事已至此。请坐一会儿,我尽快为您安排。

Task 2

1. I'm terribly sorry about this, sir. I will contact with that hotel immediately to see how to solve the problem for you. Would you please give me more details?
2. I will ask someone to look into this matter at once to see who is responsible for this mistake.
3. Sorry, we'll take action right away. Don't worry about it, please.
4. If there is a fire alarm, you can escape from the emergency exit and stairways.
5. I'm sorry indeed that this should not have happened. But I assure we will make every effort to reduce your losses to the minimum.
6. We'll manage it, but we don't have any spare room today.
7. I'm afraid you have misunderstood what I said. May I explain?
8. I must refuse to do as you wish, otherwise it will give harm to our hotel's reputation.
9. I'm sorry, it is beyond my power to do this.
10. We feel sorry we cannot be able to do what you ask for.
11. Would you please tell us what has happened in detail?
12. We are terribly sorry and we will look into the matter immediately.
13. Please calm down, and we will try all means to find your luggage.
14. If you need anything else, please tell us at any time.
15. Please wait a moment, and we will send someone up right now to fix it.
16. I'm sorry, and I will get contact with the Food and Beverage Department right now.
17. Thank you for telling us all and we will have a closer check on that as soon as possible.
18. We will inform you once we find the watch.
19. We are so sorry that we get so busy in the kitchen. We will send your food right now.
20. Sorry, we probably misplace your luggage for there are too many guests.

参考文献

[1] 杨静怡. 新职业英语：酒店英语 1[M]. 北京：外语教学与研究出版社，2010.

[2] 杨静怡. 新职业英语：酒店英语 2[M]. 北京：外语教学与研究出版社，2010.

[3] 陈江生. 实用酒店英语[M]. 大连：大连理工大学出版社，2011.

[4] 袁露，阮蓓，等. 酒店英语[M]. 天津：天津大学出版社，2010.

[5] 肖璇，吴建华. 酒店前台实用英语口语教程[M]. 北京：世界图书出版公司，2011.

[6] 匡仲潇. 星级酒店常用英语大全[M]. 北京：化学工业出版社，2013.

[7] http：//edition. cnn. com/2014/03/14/travel/bizarre-hotel-requests/index. html，2014-03-14.

[8] http：//www. canyin168. com/glyy/yg/ygpx/yypx/201204/41370_2. html，2012-04-23.

[9] http：//www. wwenglish. com/en/life/6. htm，2004-10-27.

[10] http：//www. lingtonginfo. com/upload/shfe/201083154738. pdf，2010-08-31.

[11] http：//www. wikipedia. org，2009-06-15.

[12] http：//www. en8848. com. cn/hangye/hotel/.